2282

Editing the News

1,2,6,7,8,9,10,11,12,13

Editing the News

Roy H. Copperud
University of Southern California,
Professor Emeritus

Roy Paul Nelson
University of Oregon

ωcb
Wm. C. Brown Company Publishers
Dubuque, Iowa

Book Team

Louise Waller
Editor

Maxine Kollasch
Production Editor

Lisa Bogle/Jack McCullough
Designers

Mavis M. Oeth
Permissions Editor

wcb group

Wm. C. Brown
Chairman of the Board

Mark C. Falb
Executive Vice President

Wm. C. Brown Company Publishers, College Division

Lawerence E. Cremer
President

David Wm. Smith
Vice President/Marketing

David A. Corona
Assistant Vice President/Production Development and Design

Marcia Stout
Marketing Manager

Janis M. Machala
Director of Marketing Research

William A. Moss
Production Editorial Manager

Marilyn A. Phelps
Manager of Design

Mary M. Heller
Visual Research Editor

Contents

Preface

This text is intended for use in newspaper copy editing courses at the college level. It covers the principles of copy editing, including the writing of headlines, page layout, typography, the law of libel, use of illustrations, and the new printing technology to the extent that copy editors must be conversant with it.

The symbols used in pencil-editing are explained for the benefit of schools that continue to use this method, though young journalists now enter a workaday world in which the use of electronic equipment has almost entirely displaced it. The essence of copy editing is the detection and correction of errors and general improvement of the copy. The skill required to do this has no necessary connection with the mechanical means by which it is accomplished, whether on a video display terminal or by using a pencil on hard copy.

This book, therefore, gives a great deal of attention to grammar, usage, and punctuation, and discourages the objectionable mannerisms, sometimes lumped under the heading of "journalese," for which newswriting is often justly criticized.

Because of the growing trend toward the publication of magazines with the Sunday edition, a chapter on magazine production has been included. The first thirteen chapters deal with copy editing and headlines, including problems in handling language, and the last seven with layout, typography, illustration, and magazine production.

William Hale, Jr., of the *Los Angeles Times* and Frederic C. Coonradt, professor emeritus at the University of Southern California, made valuable contributions to the treatment of copy editing and law of the press, respectively.

Roy H. Copperud
Roy Paul Nelson

Newspaper Organization

1

All newspapers must carry out tasks that fall under three functional headings: editorial, mechanical, and business.

In newspaper terminology, the term *editorial* refers to the primary purpose of the newspaper: publishing the news. The word may be used to designate all nonadvertising content of the newspaper. That content is principally news, to be sure, but it includes other elements, such as comic strips, columns of comment and analysis, and instruction such as recipes and medical advice. All such nonadvertising content is the responsibility of the editorial departments.

The *mechanical* departments have to do with physical production of the paper. This task in turn has two major stages: *composition,* the job of assembling the words and pictures of the whole content of the paper, both advertising and nonadvertising, and converting them into a form that makes *printing,* the second stage, possible. Composition may involve producing raised metal images of the letters and pictures, which are then arranged into page forms. This method, called hot-type composition, is usually intended for letterpress printing; it has been displaced by electronic cold-type composition. Information about composition is given in more detail later. The new technology has brought composition out of the mechanical department and into the editorial department.

The *business* departments have the important task of handling advertising, the means by which a newspaper exists as an economic entity, as well as such duties as handling subscriptions (circulation), carrying on the paper's bookkeeping and billing, preparing its payroll, and handling tax and insurance withholding.

These, then, are the three main subdivisions of a newspaper. Let us now consider how a newspaper is organized to perform these functions. All these functions must be carried out, regardless of the size of the newspaper. The complexity of the organization relates directly to the size of the operation. Some small weeklies are operated by one or two people, perhaps a married couple, who do

Figure 1.1 Every newspaper has its own way of organizing a staff, so a typical organization chart has to be somewhat arbitrary. This chart could work for a medium-size daily. Note the vital role the managing editor plays. On some papers, the church editor and the business editor might report to the city editor rather than to the managing editor.

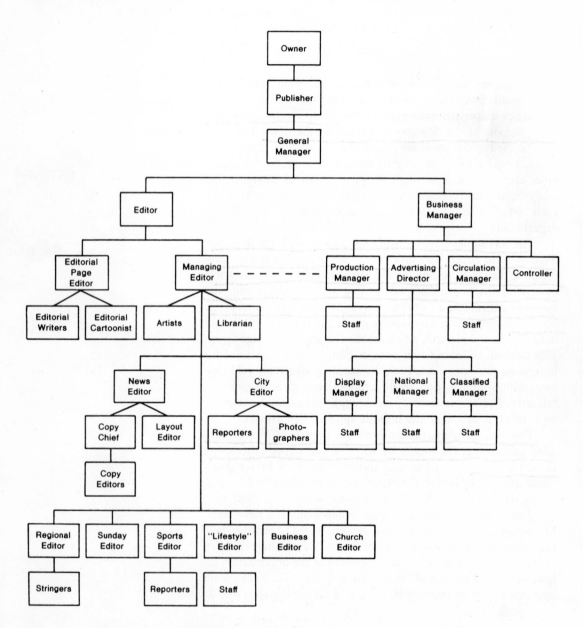

everything: gather and write the news, set the type, sell and set up the ads, lay out the pages, run the press, label the finished copies for mailing, and do anything else that needs doing, such as collecting bills and keeping the accounts. At the other extreme, a large metropolitan daily may have scores of people working in just one subdivision, such as handling subscriptions.

At the top of the organization is the *publisher*. Sometimes the publisher is the owner or part-owner. If the newspaper is owned by a corporation, the publisher may be an executive hired to supervise the publication of the paper. This person may have as lieutenants a general manager, a business manager, or both, to whom some responsibilities are delegated.

Editorial Organization

The chief editorial executive generally has the title of *editor;* sometimes a publisher who is the owner may also carry this title. The editor's chief concerns are usually more with editorial policy and the editorial page than with the day-to-day operations of gathering and publishing the news. The title *editor-in-chief* is sometimes held by this executive, but it now has an old-fashioned ring and is little used.

The chief operating executive of the editorial department is the *managing editor*. Sometimes, if more than one newspaper is published in the same plant (say, one in the morning and another in the evening, an arrangement usually resulting from the consolidation of previously independent papers), each will have its managing editor and they will be supervised by an *executive editor*.

On the next level are the city editor, the news editor, the sports editor, the financial editor, the foreign-news editor, the entertainment editor, and other editorial department heads. The most important of these are the city editor and the news editor.

The City Editor

The *city editor's* responsibility is the coverage of local news, and thus the city editor supervises the work of reporters and rewrite people. The city editor gives reporters their assignments and judges the adequacy of their work.

Reporters fall into two general categories: general-assignment reporters and specialists. A general-assignment reporter is, as the term implies, a generalist who is sufficiently well-informed, theoretically at least, to be assigned to a story on any subject. With the increasing complexity of our society, specialists have proliferated in the last generation: labor writers, science writers, medical writers, political writers, and others. Such reporters usually handle only stories in their special fields, in which they have become highly expert and have cultivated a wide array of news sources. Specialists usually develop from the ranks of general-assignment reporters on the basis of their own interests. Staff members who remain general-assignment reporters may do so because they prefer greater variety in their work than the specialist enjoys.

Academic training is invaluable to the specialist. Science writers, for example, generally have laid a solid foundation for their work through studies in college. A delusion sometimes harbored by academicians and scientists is that the best science writers are developed from scientists who have learned to write for publication. Experience has shown beyond a doubt that the ability to write is the primary qualification. Someone with a talent for writing can acquire the factual background necessary to deal with a specialty, but one who possesses the background but does not write well cannot easily be taught to do so.

Coverage of courts, of the various levels of government, and of police work have always been specialties, but as noted, usually a fund of solid experience as a general-assignment reporter is considered a prerequisite to any specialty. Aspiring journalists who expect to start as critics or columnists are deluding themselves; it is almost unheard-of for such performers to be recruited anywhere but from the ranks of experienced reporters. On very large newspapers, however, where critics are expected to be experts in their fields, there is a tendency to recruit at least some critics from the ranks of free-lance writers or magazine staff members who have always been specialists and have no interest in writing on subjects other than their own.

The term *rewrite man/woman* is something of a misnomer; persons who carry this title do not ordinarily rewrite copy. They are, rather, experienced reporters with a talent for composing stories at high speed, using facts that have been telephoned to them by reporters at the scene of the news. The reason for this arrangement is speed; with a deadline approaching, there may not be time for the reporter to go to the office and write the story. This rewrite arrangement can be displaced by modern technology, however. There is a special kind of typewriter that a reporter may use in a telephone booth. The reporter calls the city desk and lays the receiver in a cradle. As the reporter types out the story, impulses are transmitted over the wires, carrying the words to the office, where another machine produces the typewritten copy.

The News Editor
The *news editor*'s domain is the other of the two most important editorial departments; the first, already described, is that of the city editor, embracing newsgathering and writing. The news editor's responsibilities, which may be shared with assistants, depending on the size of the operation, include supervising the editing of copy, the writing of headlines, and the layout of pages. This is

the work with which courses in news editing are concerned. Implicit in all this, of course, is the evaluation of the importance of the news.

If both local news and wire-service dispatches are handled by a single copydesk, it is known as a *universal desk*. Sometimes two desks are used, one for each kind of copy; this arrangement is known as a *split desk*. On very large newspapers there may be further subdivisions—for example, a national desk, foreign desk, and others. Like reporters, copy editors often develop specialties, such as labor, education, or politics, and they are assigned to edit and headline stories dealing with their field of expertise.

On a large newspaper, the sports department, headed by the sports editor, is a little empire with its own reporters and copy editors. The same is true of the financial, entertainment, and other departments, as well as the Sunday magazine.

The extent of specialization and the complexity of organization depend on the size of the newspaper. On a small daily, the same person may do the jobs of both city editor and news editor, assigning stories to reporters, editing the copy, writing headlines, and laying out pages.

Sources of News

Newspapers obtain the news from two major sources: their own staff members and wire services. Local news is the product of the paper's own reporters, and some newspapers, like the *Milwaukee Journal* and *The Des Moines Register-Tribune,* maintain full- and part-time correspondents over a wide surrounding area that covers most of the state. Part-time correspondents are known as "stringers" and are paid by the inch in accordance with how much of their work is published. Stringers are so called because they paste up and periodically submit for payment the accumulation of their published stories, and the collection is referred to as the string.

The Wire Services

For out-of-town news, most newspapers rely on one of the two principal wire services, the Associated Press and United Press International. (Large newspapers such as the *New York Times* and the *Los Angeles Times,* however, maintain their own correspondents in London, Bonn, Paris, Tel Aviv, Tokyo, Hong Kong, and other places throughout the world.) Both press associations are worldwide in scope, and the principal difference in their operations is that the Associated Press is a nonprofit cooperative, owned by its members, while United Press International is an independent organization to which newspapers subscribe. The rates paid for these services in general are related to the size of the subscribing paper.

The Associated Press describes itself as the oldest and largest news service in the world, with more than 10,000 newspapers, radio stations, and television stations as members. (The news transmitted to broadcasters has been edited with oral delivery rather than printed reproduction in mind.) The AP, as it is familiarly referred to, transmits more than three million words of copy a day, as well as hundreds of news pictures. It spends nearly $75 million a year to provide these services. In the United States alone the AP serves more than 1,260 dailies and about 3,350 broadcasting stations.

United Press, founded in 1907, merged in 1958 with International News Service, a wire service that had been operated by the Hearst interests, to form United Press International. UPI delivers its news, pictures, and other services to more than 6,500 customers in 114 countries, and transmits an estimated 4,500,000 words of copy daily. It has more than 1,145 newspapers and 3,600 broadcasting stations as clients in the United States. Major newspapers subscribe to both AP and UPI, and sometimes combine their dispatches on a given subject (perhaps also with those of lesser, more specialized services) and publish them under a designation such as "Compiled from Press Dispatches."

More specialized, supplemental wire services are operated in the United States by individual newspapers, for example, the Washington Post-Los Angeles Times News Service, the New York Times News Service, and the Copley News Service. None of these, however, attempts to provide the full general coverage of the giants, AP and UPI: they are used for supplementary coverage provided by the owning newspapers' correspondents. Some large American newspapers subscribe to Reuters, a worldwide British service, which, however, does not attempt comprehensive coverage of the United States.

Both the AP and UPI for many years transmitted their news over leased telephone wires to teleprinters (typewriter-like machines operated by impulses coming over the wires) in the news offices of their members and subscribers. But the technological advances affecting newspapers have also affected the wire services. For example, pencil-editing of copy is no longer done at transmission points; the editors use electronic display terminals. And instead of receiving reports on paper that unwinds from a roll, newspapers may have reports fed directly into computer storage, from which they can be called up on editorial display terminals for selection and editing.

Wire services also transmit photographs and other graphics, such as maps and drawings, very quickly over special electronic equipment. The images received resemble photographic prints, and are suitable for conversion into printing plates. Every newspaper subscribing to the photo services receives many more pictures every day than it could consider using.

Syndicates

Numerous syndicates supply newspapers with such special materials as comic strips and columns on every conceivable subject from animal care to astrology, as well as with feature articles. This material is transmitted by mail, and the fees, once again, are based on the circulation of the subscribing paper.

The next subdivision in our list of three newspaper functions is the mechanical. Its job, as noted, is the physical production of the paper, as distinguished from the writing and editing that are the responsibility of the editorial department.

Mechanical Aspects of Newspaper Organization

Composition

Originally, metal type was set by skilled craftsmen known as compositors. Typewritten and edited news stories and headlines were sent to the composing room, usually in pneumatic tubes. So were the "dummies" or plans for layout of the pages. This meant a complete separation between the editorial department and the composing room. The only link between them was the makeup editor, a member of the editorial department, assigned to the composing room to solve editing problems that arose in assembling the heavy metal type and spacing material into pages. Such problems might include rewriting a headline that did not fit, or trimming a story too long for the space allotted to it.

Computer typesetting has changed composition procedures greatly. Such technology has been rapidly adopted because of the great advantages it offers in both cost and speed. Proposals to install cold-type systems have at times resulted in labor troubles when management and unions could not agree on what was to be done with the compositors whose jobs would be eliminated. Such disputes, however, have pretty much become a thing of the past.

On some newspapers, reporters and editors do their work directly on terminals known as *VDTs* (video display terminals) made up, in effect, of a keyboard and a television screen. Whatever is typed into the keyboard appears on the screen and can easily be corrected. A more detailed explanation of the VDT system is to be found in chapter 2. One of the effects of the VDT system has been to bring into the editorial rooms the job of setting the type, formerly the province of the composing room. Proofreading was formerly done in the composing room, but now is accomplished on the screens of VDTs. Copy composed on the VDT can be transmitted directly to a machine that photographically produces columns of type and headlines on strips of paper. The job of cutting out these images and pasting them in place in accordance with instructions on the dummy remains a mechanical function, and in some places hot-metal compositors have been retained to do this work. The pasted-up pages are then photographed, and by one of several methods (see chapter 14) the image of each page is transferred to a metal or plastic plate from which the printing is done.

Printing the Newspaper

Printing, or presswork, is the process of laying down the image on the paper, resulting in the final product. If the traditional letterpress process is used, the raised surfaces of the image are coated with ink and pressed against the paper. In the newer offset method the printing is done from a flat surface, and the image and non-image areas are chemically separated by the fact that the first attracts a film of ink and the second a film of moisture. These processes are also explained in greater detail in chapter 14.

Other printing tasks also come under the heading of the mechanical function. They include *stereotyping* (in the letterpress process, converting the flat page forms into curved metal or plastic plates for use on high-speed rotary presses), *engraving* (converting photographs, drawings, and other graphic representations into metal or plastic plates for printing), and *mailing* (bundling and labeling finished newspapers for distribution by carriers or through the postal system). Note that engraving, however, has also been largely supplanted by newer and simpler processes (see chapter 14).

Business Aspects of Newspaper Organization

The advertising department is the largest of those in the business category. On a large newspaper, operations under this heading are supervised by an advertising director. There are subdivisions, each with its own executive, for retail (that is, local) advertising, national advertising (that placed by agencies on a nationwide basis, for example advertising of liquor or cigarettes), and classified advertising (the so-called want ads).

Other Departments and Functions

From one paper to the next, different names may be applied to given jobs. On large papers there are assistant managing editors, each of whom oversees several large subdivisions, such as sports, financial, and entertainment. The city editors and news editors also have assistants. But in general the pattern is similar from one paper to the next except for its complexity, which, as noted, depends on the paper's size.

Papers of medium to large size have other departments. An example is public relations, which attempts to build goodwill for the newspaper through various means, sometimes including the sponsorship of sports events. There may also be a personnel department, whose functions have to do with the recruitment of employees. For the editorial department, however, the personnel department of a newspaper usually functions only in a preliminary way; final interviews are conducted and decisions on hiring are made by the responsible editors.

Newspaper Organization

Depending on its size, each newspaper involves the work of varying numbers of people. The three major divisions of newspaper organization and operation—editorial, mechanical, and business—are essential in any case. The copy editor today is more involved in mechanical aspects of newspaper operation than ever before. The job of editing, whether it involves wire-service stories or special-assignment reporting, remains primarily language-oriented.

We now take a more detailed look at the copy editor's job.

Conclusion

2 The Copy Editor's Job

This chapter will consider what the copy editor does on a typical newspaper. It will discuss how important the job is, how the new technology fits in, and how copy editing changes are made.

The Copy Editor's Role

Copy editing is the process of correcting and improving the work of the reporter to make it ready to be set in type. It has been well said that the copy editor is the last bulwark between the reporter and the newspaper reader. Viewed ideally, then, the job of copy editing would require omniscience. The perfect copy editor would be capable not only of detecting and correcting mechanical errors, such as those in spelling and grammar, but also would be able to decide whether the information contained in a story is factual.

This, of course, is asking more than any copy editor can be expected to deliver. With intelligence and experience, though, copy editors develop a sixth sense for statements that sound mistaken, and raise questions concerning them. Certainly, the copy editor detects inconsistencies within the story itself. In these instances the person supervising the copydesk is informed so that the story may be referred for correction to whoever is able to do it, preferably the writer.

By and large, however, stories as they reach the copy editor are assumed to be factually correct. Point-by-point verification of their content would require that someone go over the same ground as the reporter did, independently gathering the information. While this might be desirable from the standpoint of ensuring absolute accuracy, it is impractical in producing a daily newspaper. The news magazines and some other periodicals, however, employ platoons of young researchers to do such checking. It is an interesting comment on human fallibility that in spite of such care, the letters columns of these magazines often are obliged to publish corrections.

Honest factual errors are common in newspapers. Reputable papers acknowledge errors freely when they are called to the editor's attention, and publish corrections prominently enough so that the reader is not likely to be left with a mistaken impression. Such

Figure 2.1 A copydesk of the kind that has become extinct, having been driven out during the 1960s by the introduction of electronic editing on video display terminals. The eyeshades (once the badge of this occupation) worn by three of the copy editors were already becoming passe when this picture was taken in the early 1950s in the *Los Angeles Times* newsroom. (Photo courtesy of the *Los Angeles Times.*)

candor was not formerly common, but is becoming more so. Considering the tremendous amount of information that a daily newspaper contains and the conditions of haste and pressure under which the information is gathered and published, the wonder is not that there are so many errors, but that there are not more. Still, some newspapers are put together more carefully than others.

Copy Editors, Reporters, and Readers

Few journalists of college age aspire to be copy editors, and some students are impatient with the discipline and attention to detail that they must learn in copy editing courses. Young journalists generally aspire instead to be reporters. That is where the excitement, the recognition, the freedom, and the creativity are, they feel, though copy editing offers its own opportunities for a special creativity that improves the reporter's work. Nevertheless, the work of copy editing is anonymous. Very often the headlines that were the hardest to write seem inevitable to the reader and attract no attention, unlike an excellent piece of writing. Nor do headlines carry by-lines.

E. B. White, one of the finest stylists among contemporary American writers, once remarked that the reader is in serious trouble most of the time. This is a somewhat startling dictum when first encountered by young writers, because young writers tend to be preoccupied with the idea that it is they themselves who are in trouble. And they are right, of course. The need to take infinite pains applies especially well to writing. Is this the right word? Am

I being clear? Am I showing off my vocabulary and attracting attention at the expense of getting information across as effectively as possible? Such questions steadily badger the conscientious young writer, who is further distracted by learning from precept or experience that too much concern with the manner of expression can impede the free flow of ideas and sap the vitality of the writing.

Bemused by all this, how does the young writer feel when told that the reader must be kept in the forefront of the writer's mind; that the writer must mentally see things from the reader's viewpoint and must judge what is set down as coolly and objectively as possible? The young writer may well feel frustrated.

The idea that the reader must come first is not a new one, of course. Sir Arthur Quiller-Couch, a Cambridge don, stated it long ago in an essay entitled "Interlude: On Jargon": "The more difficulties, then, we authors obtrude on him [the reader] by obscure or careless writing, the more we blunt the edge of his attention. . . ."

If, as White says, readers are generally in trouble most of the time, they are in trouble even more of the time when reading a newspaper. There are various reasons for this. The most important is that newspapers are produced in haste and under pressure. These are the worst possible conditions. Not only must the writer often get information down on paper pell-mell; there is no opportunity to let the heat of compositioin cool and to stand back from the work while revising it. Capable reporters do, of course, read over as carefully as possible what they have written before turning it in to the editor. But even the best of them tend to be blind to their own mistakes.

Although the people who edit copy and compose headlines are almost universally referred to as *copyreaders*, this term has been objected to as not accurately descriptive and as actually misleading, since copyreaders do much more than merely read the copy. It can be argued that *copy editor*, which is recommended instead, is not satisfactory either, because the term *editor* suggests a supervisory and selective function that copy editors do not perform. Nevertheless, for the sake of conferring credit where it is certainly due and avoiding any hint of derogation, the term *copy editor* will be used in this book.

Copy Editors and the Newspaper

The complexity of the copy editing arrangement varies, of course, with the size of the newspaper. On very small newspapers, there may be no copy editors as such. The city editor, who assigns stories to reporters and very likely writes some of them, may also check copy, write headlines, and lay out pages. Doing all this requires very fast work, and there is so much to do that obviously no part of the job can be done very well. Very small papers, where the production of each day's edition is a triumph of sheer, unabated exertion by too few people, are sometimes referred to as "jute mills." They do offer excellent experience to beginning journalists, provided standards of some kind are maintained. For the most part, they are springboards to better jobs.

On a very large paper, the news editor does not directly supervise the copy editors, but instead is concerned with deciding, perhaps in consultation with the managing editor, what stories shall be played on the front page, and with laying out that page. Headline styles and sizes have been assigned to such stories by the time they reach the supervisor of the copy editors. In any event, this supervisor is responsible for the work done by the copy editors. It quickly becomes apparent which copy editors can be relied upon for careful and conscientious work and which ones turn in slapdash performances. The latter are not likely to remain long on the desk, because copy editors must be able to discharge a final responsibility for editing. The supervisor also judges whether headlines meet requirements, and if they do not, turns them back to be rewritten. As noted earlier, copy editors on metropolitan newspapers tend to develop individual fields of expertise.

Learning to Edit Copy

Perhaps the greatest difficulty confronting beginning copy editors, apart from that of fitting the headline into what seems like too little space, is that of scanning the copy slowly and carefully. Anyone doing copy editing is likely to be a facile reader. All of us read as fast as the difficulty of the material permits. What we read for entertainment, we race through. What we read for instruction, for example textbooks, we read with more care and concentration. The copy editor must read even more carefully and must, in fact, note every detail when editing. The copy must be examined word by word for mechanical faults as in spelling and punctuation, and scrutinized for grammatical correctness; at the same time, it must be judged for clarity and sense.

The discipline and the critical faculty that are acquired by learning to edit copy competently make better writers of those who have had such training. Sometimes, young journalists who are aiming at careers in public relations or broadcasting wonder why they should have to learn copy editing, which is among the basic required courses in journalism curricula. But public-relations graduates often find themselves working as writers or editors of press releases or as editors of house organs, duties for which knowledge of copy editing is indispensable. The news written to be broadcast also must be edited, although the requirements here are specialized and the structure of sentences to be spoken often differs from that of sentences intended to be read silently. The rigorous discipline of making certain one understands precisely what is meant by a news story, which is acquired by writing headlines under competent supervision, also improves one's ability to study in any field.

Although fledgling journalists usually begin as reporters, those who have a bent for copy editing and have demonstrated competence at it are sometimes put right on the desk and stay there. For the most part, however, the best copy editor has served a period as a reporter, and has become familiar with the problems a reporter faces. Some newspapers conduct a program under which reporters spend a few months gaining experience on the copydesk to sharpen their critical faculties and give them an appreciation of what the copy editor's problems are. Experience both ways makes for better-rounded journalists.

How Copy Editors Work

Conscientious copy editors generally first skim through a story to get its import, and then go back for detailed editing, examining the story word for word and looking for errors of every kind—spelling, grammar, and the like. They challenge the story's clarity in their own minds and clean up muddy expression. They consider its total effect. They look for "holes"—unanswered questions that may occur to the reader. Only then, usually, do they tackle the job of composing a headline. But different people have different ways of working, and methods of approach are always subject to modification, depending on the pressure under which the story is being handled.

The copy editor must understand everything in the story being handled. The cub reporter, having been given a press release to rewrite, sometimes turns in a product containing a statement that is incomprehensible to the city editor. When the reporter is asked, "What does this mean?" the answer may be, "I don't know, but that's what it said in the release." Such a reporter has abdicated responsibility. If the writer cannot understand what has been put down for publication, how can the reader be expected to do so? The same principle applies to copy editing.

Truly talented copy editors are not numerous even among professionals. The gifted copy editor must possess a combination of scholarliness, versatility, and self-effacement. There is little glory on the desk, and the work is confining. There are deep satisfactions in copy editing, but they are for people of a reflective temperament. Charles Fisher, in his book *The Columnists,* said that reporters sometimes look upon copy editing as the fate that is worse than death. On the other hand, young journalists who are able and willing to edit copy find jobs more easily than do aspiring reporters.

The Copy to Be Edited

Even though copy is more or less carefully scanned by the city editor, there is still revision and correction to be done. The serious and careful second-guessing, as well as the writing of headlines, was formerly done on the copydesk, traditionally a U-shaped structure. Within the curve, in what was called the slot, sat the executive known variously as the news editor, or the telegraph editor (an anachronistic term surviving from the days when news from distant points was transmitted by telegraph) or, more descriptively, the slot-man. Around the outer edge, or rim, sat the copy editors. News stories were delivered to the person supervising the desk, who marked them with the size and style of headline desired and assigned them to the rim for editing and composition of headlines. From the copydesk, after the editors had checked and approved the copy, the story went to the composing room to be set in type.

But all this has changed with the advent of electronic editing, which has displaced the copydesk. Copy editors now work at the consoles of VDTs, often at separate desks. The stories they edit may have been composed by reporters working at their own consoles and transmitted electronically to the screens of the copy editors.

On well-regulated newspapers, the copydesk has final authority over the form and content of a story. It is an authority that is exercised with discretion, but the power of decision resides in the desk, nevertheless. There are newspapers, however, where the authority of the desk is not well established and where the copy editors as a result hesitate to correct anything but misspellings. This is a regrettable state of affairs. It demoralizes copy editors and prevents them from doing their best work. It tends to exist where the news editor is subordinate to the city editor. The city editor and the news editor should be equals and answerable not one to the other but to the managing editor or someone else in a higher echelon.

How Much Copy Should Be Changed?

So much stress is laid on scrupulous care and critical evaluation by the copy editor that some copy editors go too far. They make changes in copy that are not necessary, or without knowing what they are doing, and in this way copy editors sometimes introduce errors or cause a statement to give a misleading impression. The competent copy editor learns to follow the fine line that separates what *must* be changed from what is acceptable as it stands, and to let well enough alone. On the *New York Times,* the impulse to make changes when they are not called for has been named as if it were a disease: it is called "itchy pencil." The sufferers from itchy pencil have the delusion that unless they make changes of some kind they have not done what they were hired to do. But, in fact, copy editors are doing their job simply be deciding whether a piece of writing is acceptable as it stands, and whether changes are necessary.

There is more than one way of writing a story, and a dozen competent reporters sent out on the same assignment will come back with a dozen different stories, except for their factual basis.

The copy editor must get rid of any idea that there is only one way to write a story and that changes should be made accordingly. The copy editor must learn respect for other people's ways of saying things, provided those ways are correct and clear. The copy editor who is obsessed with making changes runs the risks of introducing errors and offending sensitive writers who resent having their work changed for no evident reason. A copy editor should make no change without being certain that it will improve the story.

If a story must be cut—that is, shortened to fit into less space—the job must be done with great care. Cutting is an art. It is all too easy to excise some statement on which understanding of something elsewhere in the story depends. Above all, a story that has been cut must be read through carefully afterwards to ensure that it still hangs together, makes sense, and gives a clear and complete account.

The fact that reporters' work is often changed during editing, whether for good or bad reasons, tends to create a relationship between reporters and copy editors that might be termed an armed truce. It was this that prompted Saul Pett, the talented Associated Press feature writer, to predict that the next war will be between reporters and copy editors. There should be no reason for any such hostility, however, and good reporters and good copy editors do not feel it. Good reporters are grateful for having their grammar and punctuation corrected and for having their statements questioned for factual basis and clarity. The good copy editor, on the other hand, respects the reporter and does not change for the sake of change. The competent copy editor makes no change without being prepared to give a reason for it.

How Copy Editing is Performed

Pencil-Editing and Video Display Terminals

Some of the students reading these words may work for newspapers where pencils are still used to mark copy in editing and where the old U-shaped copydesk is still in use. Copydesks however, are being displaced by editing terminals (VDTs). A VDT is essentially a television screen with a typewriter keyboard projecting from its base. Copy appears on the screen in luminous letters, and by using the keyboard the operator can correct, delete, or insert anything from single letters to whole paragraphs. Such equipment can produce a perforated tape to drive a photocomposition machine that will set the type, or it can feed electric impulses directly into the composition machine, which will set the type. More detailed information about this and other automated equipment, which has revolutionized newspaper production, will be found later in this book. Where VDTs are in use, the copy editors are more likely to work each at a desk with its own VDT. An instruction to edit a story and write a headline is sent to a copy editor's screen. Using the keyboard, the copy editor calls up the specified story from central storage in a computer, causing it to appear on the screen, edits

Figure 2.2 The new system: news copy is now edited on electronic video display terminals that justify the lines and effect insertions and deletions with the press of a key. News stories may be written as well as edited on such machines. (Photo courtesy of Tal-Star Computer Systems, Inc.)

Figure 2.3 The copydesk of the *Eugene* (Ore.) *Register-Guard,* a 60,000-circulation daily. Each copy editor has an editing terminal. (Photo by Joe Matheson.)

the story, and writes the headline ordered for it. Then, after the story is scanned on the news editor's screen for acceptability, it may be sent back into storage so that it can be called up again when the time comes for it to be set in type by photocomposition. Or the story may go directly to composition. All these new procedures work at phenomenal speed.

The Copy Editor's Job **17**

In contrast to the changing electronic aspect of editing, the nature of the editing task remains essentially unchanged. The arrangement of words in writing, the correction of errors, and the composition of headlines emerge from the journalist's mental processes. The final product is not changed in any respect by the method used to get the words from the mind of the writer to the printed page. The process has been vastly speeded up by the new technology, however. The VDT is to the typewriter what the typewriter was to longhand. Some copy editors objected to the new equipment until they got used to it, just as journalists objected to the typewriter when it was new and unfamiliar to them.

Such new, computerized equipment has been installed by most daily newspapers. This development has much more meaning for the copy editor than the fact of learning how to operate the new equipment, which is, in itself, not a difficult task. The important meaning is that complete control over typesetting, which was formerly the domain of printers in the composing room, has been brought into the editorial rooms so that full responsibility for all editorial considerations, including proofreading (correction of material set in type), rests there. This makes the copy editor's job more exacting than before and, at the same time, more satisfying.

What is learned about editing copy with a pencil can easily be put to use when the student becomes employed and is confronted with a VDT on the job. Familiarity with VDT operation before employment is important, and it is a great advantage to the young journalist applying for a job.

Certain symbols were developed for use in pencil-editing, as well as in proofreading. In book publishing, editing symbols differ greatly from proofreading symbols, but in journalism there are only a couple of deviations, which will be pointed out. It should be kept in mind that editing symbols are not sacrosanct; they are merely a convenience intended to save the time and labor of writing out instructions. If a piece of copy becomes cluttered with pencil-editing marks, it is best to retype the cluttered paragraph.

Editing marks should be legible, and they should also be decisive. Faint, quavery marks cause indecision and delay. If the copy editor's handwriting is not legible, insertions should be printed. Numerous rules for editing copy, writing headlines, and laying out pages will be set forth in this book. Still, no rule is infallibly applicable in journalism or, perhaps, anywhere else. Sometimes a better job can be done by disregarding the rules, and the journalist should develop the judgment and self-confidence to realize when this is so. The best rule of all may be: Learn the rules so that you may violate them wisely.

The symbols used in pencil-editing, together with some brief explanations, are given in examples that follow. The symbols should be memorized immediately. Deletions, whether of single words, lines, or whole paragraphs, should be indicated in a manner that is unmistakable and yet does not obliterate the material to be removed.

⌊A chilling easterly wind

almost oblivious to the
cold gusts. ⌊Indeed, they
got hot on less than a
hot day, burying

Paragraphs are always hooked, as the expression goes, with an L-shaped mark at the beginning. This mark may seem superfluous when the paragraph is already indented, but it is used nevertheless. One copy editor explained that the paragraph hooks helped him keep his place if he were interrupted in editing a story. If it is desired to divide a long paragraph into two paragraphs, the hook unquestionably serves a purpose.

This:
report will be favorable. ⌊We have

Not this:
report will be favorable. ¶ We have

The paragraph symbol (¶) is a proofreading mark and should not be used in copy editing.

He examined ~~past~~ records of the company

Deletions are indicated by simply drawing a line through a word. The copy editor should not scrub or obliterate the word; it should still be legible.

This:
Do not ~~not~~ use the delete mark

Not this:
Do not ~~not~~ use the delete mark

The looped delete mark should not be used in copy editing. This symbol is intended only for proofreading, in which marks must be placed in the margin.

For the be̸tter part of the

A single letter is removed in the manner indicated. In the middle of a word (but not at either end), closure marks are used above and below.

---

with the i dea that they weren't

The closure marks are used also to close up an unwanted space. If extra space has been left between *words,* however, it is not necessary to indicate closure, because the compositor will use the normal spacing anyway.

Another provision would require that independent auditors supervise the election to ensure its validity

A paragraph should be deleted in this manner so that it remains legible and so that it can easily be restored if necessary by erasing the pencilled lines. Restoration can also be indicated, however, by writing the word *stet* (Latin for "let it stand") beside the deletion and circling it, as should be done with all instructions to the compositor.

These expedients are ^(also) somewhat artificial.

This is a fa^irly new idea.

Insertions are indicated by a caret *beneath* the line, designating the point at which insertions are to be made, and by writing the insertion itself *above* the line.

This: (among the highlights)
These are ^ of a recently completed study

Not this: ^the
Beginners make mistake

An insert consisting of several words is usually bracketed to prevent confusion as indicated here. Brackets may be particularly important if there is more than one insert in a line. Do not place carets *above* the line.

This:
A major argument ⌐the plan⌐against is that it would not take into

Not this:
It has ⌐eliminated⌐
⌐practically⌐ litter of this type.

Transpositions are indicated in the manner shown. This mark is reversible—that is, it does not matter whether its first half is open at the top or at the bottom. It is considered undesirable, however, to run a transposition symbol from one line to the next.

This:
the building was the roosevelt school

or this:
the building was the roosevelt school

or this:
the building was the roosevelt school

Capitalization is indicated by three short lines under a letter or word. Often, however, the lines are connected for ease in marking copy, or sometimes the symbol is simplified to a single line.

Some Writers use Too Many Capitals

Lowercase is indicated by the mark known variously as the slant, slash, diagonal, virgule, or solidus.

This:

some|air is necessary to open|up

Not this:

Some#air is necessary to open|up#

Separation of words that have been run together is indicated by a vertical line. The crosshatch is a proofreading symbol and it should not be used in copy editing.

Quotation marks, hyphens, and dashes may be inserted in place, or, if there is not enough space, hyphens and dashes may be placed above the line, with a caret beneath it.

The U⊗S⊗ was denounced in the U⊗N⊗ for

The insertion of a period is usually indicated by a small circled *x*.

Commas, however, are simply

Commas however are simply

Commas, however, are simply inserted. If a caret is placed over an inserted comma, care should be taken lest the insertion be misinterpreted as a semicolon.

They took a trip to (Minn.) and stopped en route at Kansas City, (Missouri) (6) days elapsed before the mileage totaled (one) (thousand.)

This:

The (LSAT) will be given Monday.

Not this: (Law School Admission) Test) The ~~LSAT~~ will be given Monday.

(stet)

Circling is done to (a) indicate that an abbreviation should be spelled out, or (b) the reverse—that a word should be abbreviated. It may also be done to indicate that a numeral should be changed to a word, and vice versa. An uncommon or confusing abbreviation should be written in full instead of merely circled; in this way, the compositor will not have to spend time looking up the full version. Circling has one other use: to set off instructions to the compositor and thus prevent any danger that they may be read as part of the text. Examples of such instructions are "run in" (to indicate that a list of names should be set in paragraph form), "stet" ("let it stand") and "follow copy" (to indicate that an exception to style is being made).

Copy editors should always make certain that the end of a story is followed by an end-mark of some kind. The old telegrapher's symbol, *30,* was once widely used for this purpose. A crosshatch will also serve. Likewise, the bottom of any page from which a story is continued to the next page must be marked *more* and the word should be circled.

Conclusion

Thus, as we have seen, the copy editor requires a good command of language, scrupulous attention to detail, and the willingness to do a job that lacks public recognition. Readers neither know nor care who writes the headlines; there are no bylines for headline writers as there are for reporters. Nevertheless, the quality of a publication and the esteem and confidence it enjoys among readers depend heavily on the work of the copy editor. Misspelled words, for example, not only indicate carelessness in themselves but also shake the reader's confidence, if only subconsciously, in the factual content. Copy editors should not attempt to impose their ideas of composition on the work they are editing, and changes should not be made except when necessary. This is a matter of respect for the writer. Although most newspapers have installed electronic equipment to set type photographically, and also to edit stories, some classroom editing is done with pencil in the traditional way, using the traditional symbols. But clarity is more important than the symbols, and if copy becomes cluttered with many corrections, it is advisable to retype the story as corrected.

The Copy Editor's Job

Headlines

3

The purpose of a headline, as every newspaper reader knows, is to summarize the news story above which it appears. A good headline is precise and clear; it makes as complete and satisfying a statement as possible within its usually severe spatial limits. We are talking now about headlines on what are called hard-news stories; that is, stories whose primary purpose is to convey new information, not to entertain, explain, or amuse. Hard-news stories greatly predominate. But feature stories, as will be explained, may carry heads that intrigue or amuse or puzzle the reader and draw the reader into the story. Feature heads need not meet the test of making completely comprehensible statements in themselves.

For various reasons, hard-news headlines often fall short of the desired standards. One reason is carelessness and incompetence on the part of headline writers. Every newspaper reader can remember having read headlines that misrepresented or contradicted the story. On some newspapers, neither high standards nor critical judgment are applied to headlines. And there is often, on even the most carefully edited papers, the handicap of deadline pressure and consequent haste.

A basic test may be used to judge the effectiveness of a headline: it should not be necessary to read the story to understand what the headline means. Some imagination is required to apply this test. With the advantage of just having read the story, the headline writer will have to exert some effort to distinguish between what the headline alone conveys, and what the story sets forth.

Beginners sometimes chafe under the high standards enforced by conscientious news editors. They wonder whether the effort that goes into a well-shaped headline is worthwhile, since the reader has the story for clarification and amplification. They forget that newspaper readers get most of their information about what is going on in the world from headlines alone. The newspaper reader is on the run. Well-written headlines help the reader to proceed with the least possible interference. *Thus the reader is able to cover a remarkable amount of ground in a very short time.* The newspaper is designed for this very purpose, and is in this respect a unique publication.

Figure 3.1 The *New York Times* and *The Wall Street Journal* continue to use multi-deck headlines on some of their stories, with the decks conforming to standard patterns. In the *Times'* version *(left)* the first deck consists of even-width lines that step down against a diagonal: a "dropline" head. The second deck, a one-liner, is a "crossline" that fully fills the column width. The third deck is an "inverted pyramid," with the lines getting shorter as the headline progresses. The example from *The Wall Street Journal (right)* comes with a kicker in boldface type, underlined. The top head is flush left. The first deck is a "hanging indention," with the first line flush left and the remaining lines indented a standard distance. The second deck is a crossline. In both headlines, short rules separate the decks. The *Wall Street Journal* headline does not avoid using unimportant words like *and* and *the.*

BREZHNEV DECLARES PACT MAY COLLAPSE IF SENATE ALTERS IT

HE ISSUES WARNING AT DINNER

Carter Says Two Sides Could Not
Reach 'a Common Approach'
in Talks on Other Topics

Assets Abroad
Many Pension Funds Are Looking Overseas For New Investments

They Seek Diversifications
And Increases in Returns;
Is the Timing All Wrong?

Seeking IBMs of Tomorrow

The reader will read all or nearly all the headlines in the paper, but only a fraction of the text. The reader's progress through the pages is much like that of a jackrabbit—hopping, skipping, leaping. Now and then a headline says as much as possible but still does not satisfy the reader's curiosity. In these instances, the lead paragraph, or the first two or three paragraphs, are often enough to do so, however, and the reader will leave off at that point and go on to other headlines. The reader will only occasionally read a story in its entirety. The inverted pyramid construction of hard-news stories, in which the account is summarized at the beginning, makes it possible for the reader to get the essence of things quickly and to stop as soon as interest is gratified. If the reader must go into a story because the headline is inadequate, progress through the paper is impeded.

The inverted pyramid construction has its shortcomings, of course. It often does not put events in the clearest perspective, and it is somewhat confusing in that it may not clearly indicate the sequence of events. Other techniques, such as the chronological arrangement, are often successfully used for feature and interpretive stories and for accounts in news magazines. But for hard-news stories in newspapers, whose primary purpose is to convey fresh information rather than to entertain, explain, or interpret, the inverted pyramid technique is not likely to be displaced. If it were, one of the great advantages of the newspaper over other media of information would be lost.

Purposes of Headlines

Headlines serve other purposes besides that of summarizing news stories. The size of their type indicates what the news editor judged to be the relative importance of the stories. A good deal of subjectivity enters into such judgments. Comparison of newspapers having access to the same information about national and international events and published on the same day will clearly dem-

Headlines

onstrate this. A story that one editor displays on the front page may appear only on an inside page of another newspaper and not at all in a third. Nevertheless, good judgment as to what interests the largest number of readers is developed by experience. And there is always a consensus on the display of news about events of overriding interest, such as a presidential assassination, a moon shot, or a declaration of war.

Because they break up the seas of gray that result from uninterrupted text type, headlines also serve an important function in layout of the material on the newspaper page, which presents the peculiar problem of very large page size in contrast to very small body type. Headlines, which are regarded as a distinct element in layout, are arranged to achieve balance in the pattern presented by the page. This is particularly true of the front page, or any other that does not contain ads.

Beginners sometimes assume that the function of a headline is to mystify or to somehow inveigle readers into reading stories that hold no particular interest for them. Nothing could be more mistaken. At the same time it must be admitted that this assumption is probably based on numerous headlines that created puzzlement because they did not do their job. Writing hard-news headlines with enticement of this kind in mind would be extremely difficult and would require more time and talent than are generally available on the copydesk. The headline should hit the story squarely on its main point; it should neither fall short of nor go beyond the facts stated. The headline on the typical hard-news story should be based on the two or possibly three lead paragraphs. If the editor must go unusually deep into the story for the facts on which to base the head, one of two things is wrong—either the editor is passing by the summary and basing the headline on subordinate information, or the story has been poorly constructed. In such instances the lead is said to be buried; that is, the writer has not used good judgment in selecting the most important aspect of the story. In this event, the story should be revised to bring the newest development (or "angle," to use the journalistic term) to the top.

Beginners often encounter trouble in editing wire stories, particularly running stories that explain a situation that unfolds from day to day or even from hour to hour. The lead is always based on the newest important development, and the head should be based on it also. Consider a second-day story whose lead is based on the investigation of an airplane crash that occurred the day before. The neophyte may make the mistake of reaching down and basing the headline on the crash itself.

There are exceptions to the principle of basing the headline on the lead. It is not only permissible but recommended that the copy editor fall in with the spirit of a feature story and write a headline for it that is amusing or intriguing; such a headline need not summarize the story, and it may properly arouse curiosity rather than satisfy it. Now and then a clever writer will construct a news story with great ingenuity on the principle of O. Henry's short stories, so that suspense is carefully built up to a surprise ending. Then a muttonheaded copy editor gives the whole thing away in the headline. Copy editors have been murdered by reporters in such circumstances, and juries have acquitted the reporters on the grounds of justifiable homicide.

There are wooden headlines just as there are wooden leads; that is, headlines that make such general or commonplace statements that they cannot be expected to arouse any interest. Sometimes they are referred to as "bushel-basket" heads, because they would fit a number of stories. An example is "Professor to lecture." The headline is inane; it should have given the *subject* of the lecture: "Sex lecture scheduled."

Rules of Headline Writing

A headline may not repeat a word, or even a similar form of a word, that has already been used; for example, *educate* and *educator*. A word and its near relatives are regarded as having been used up for a headline by having been given once. As always, there may be exceptions for overriding considerations. A copy editor once handled a story about a prankster who hid dozens of plastic eggs filled with marijuana on a university campus one Easter. Campus police rounded up the eggs and presumably turned them over to the authorities. The copy editor headed the story "Eggs in grass / grass in eggs," and thereby helped to liven up the news.

The use of the names of people in headlines requires judgment. The rule is that a name may not be used unless most of the readers can be expected to recognize it. This, of course, varies from place to place. Readers in a given community can be expected to recognize the name of the mayor, and thus in that community the mayor's name may be freely used in headlines. But only the names of the mayors of large cities such as New York and Los Angeles become household words nationally, and even this does not always happen. The names of people who spring to nationwide prominence quickly become usable in headlines. Sometimes these people fade from view just as quickly, however, and after a few weeks or months it may become desirable to identify them in a more explanatory way: spy-ship captain, ex-N.Y. mayor.

Students learn about the need for attributing matters of opinion when they study newswriting. Attribution is as essential in headlines as in news stories, lest the reader be given the impression that what is merely opinion is fact, or that the newspaper concurs in a statement of opinion.

Patterns of Headlines

Headlines in use today fall into two patterns, for the most part: stepped (or stepline or dropline) and flush left. Until the 1930s the stepped headline was invariable in American newspapers. It looks like this:

```
XX XXXXX XXXX
   XXX XXXXXX XX
      XXXX XXX XXXX
```

The headline may be two lines deep instead of three. In the stepped headline, the top line is flush left (that is, against the left-hand margin of the column), the middle line is centered, and the bottom line is flush right. With two lines, the top one is flush left and the bottom one is flush right. The lines must be written to the same length, or very nearly so, to achieve the cosmetic stepped appearance. This means that stepped heads are more difficult to write.

The flush-left headline, invented in the 1930s, was quickly taken up by nearly all American newspapers. It looks like this:

```
XX XXXXXXX XXXXXXXX
XXXX XXXXXX XXXXX
```

The lines start against the left-hand margin; some space is left at the right end. This space helps to relieve the solid expanse of type on the page. In recent years, great emphasis has been placed on introducing open space (also referred to as white space or air) into newspaper pages under new concepts of design.

Very few newspapers continue to use the stepped headline. The *New York Times* is a conspicuous exception. Many headlines in the *Times* technically qualify as stepped although they do not appear to be stepped heads. These two- or three-line heads fill all the available space, producing a pattern that might be called flush left *and* right (this is especially common in one-column heads). The fact that the lines are written too full only illustrates the difficulty of composing them.

The lines of a flush-left headline should be approximately the same length so that an excessively ragged appearance is avoided. And although flush-left headlines offer more leeway than stepped heads in the matter of length, they should not fall conspicuously short.

A subordinate headline, that is, one beneath the main headline on a story, is referred to in this book as a *deck*. Subordinate headlines are also sometimes referred to as *banks*. Decks beneath flush-left headlines are usually also flush left, or they are indented uniformly from the left margin.

Sometimes other patterns are used for decks, particularly in newspapers that do not use the flush-left pattern for main headlines. One of these is the inverted pyramid, whose name describes its appearance. It is used by the *New York Times* and it looks like this:

XXXXX XXXX XXXX XX
XXXXX XXXXXXXX
XXXXX XXXX

The *Times* also uses a single line *(crossline);* it is placed between two inverted pyramids and spans the column, as its name implies.

A pattern known as the hanging indentation is used for decks by some newspapers, notably *The Wall Street Journal.* The pattern looks like this:

XXXXXXX XXXX XXXXX XXXXXXXX XX
XXXXX XXXXXXX XXXXXXXX XXXXXX
XXX XXX XXXXXX XXX XXXXX XXXX

The tendency is for newspapers to dispense with decks. In Civil War days, an array of decks extended halfway down the page generally and more than halfway down the page for an important story: These decks summarized most of the story's important points. Illustrations of front pages bearing such displays are sometimes included in history books. The page that is reproduced is often one that carried the news of President Lincoln's assassination. Few newspapers other than the *New York Times* now carry more than one deck beneath a headline.

Multiple decks were dropped probably because they used up much precious space and took much time to write. Journalists argue over whether readers read even a single deck; some journalists believe that the reader goes directly from the main head into the story. Even if the deck is not read, the consensus is that the use of the deck is often justifiable for typographical reasons. It affords an easy gradation from a main headline in very large type to the much smaller type of the text.

A new kind of subordinate headline is the *kicker,* sometimes called the "eyebrow." It is a short, usually flush-left, one-line head placed *above* the main headline, which then usually is indented. The kicker was invented as a means of gaining variety in the appearance of headlines and of adding air, since considerable open space is created to its right. Here is an example:

Farmer startled
**Kangaroo pops out
of Illinois cornfield**

As indicated, the kicker is usually underlined and often set in type that contrasts with the main head—perhaps capitals or italics. Kicker headlines fall into a category of new forms. While kicker headlines are common, the other headlines are seldom used, though they meet a need for typographic variety.

Headlines have been traditionally capitalized on the model of titles of books and articles; that is, every word is given an initial capital, except for very short words (short prepositions such as *in, on, to,* and articles such as *a, an*). Nevertheless, each line of a headline starts uniformly with a capital letter.

In recent years, however, with the development of new concepts of newspaper design that stress horizontal layout, wider columns, larger type, and more white space, what are known as *downstyle* headlines have appeared. The downstyle headline is capitalized like a sentence in text; the first letter of the first word is capitalized, and everything thereafter is lowercase except for proper nouns. The rationale for this is that the typical headline is an abbreviated sentence and thus should follow the form of sentences in text, to which readers are accustomed. Downstyle headlines are somewhat easier to write. Capitals occupy more space than lowercase letters, so the downstyle headline gives the headline writer more room to work.

Words set in all capitals are difficult to read. No typographically knowledgable editor would set a news story in all caps. Some editors avoid all-cap headlines on this principle, but such headlines are occasionally used for typographical variety. It is not likely that any problem of readability is presented by the small number of words in an occasional all-caps headline. (Specimen headlines in this book follow the downstyle pattern of capitalization.)

Commas are used in headlines as they are used in text. They serve an additional purpose in headlines, however—to replace the word *and:*

**Russia, Egypt agree
on Palestine question**

Semicolons are used as they are used in text—to separate independent clauses:

**2 food items
found tainted;
recalls issued**

**High court opens session;
record 992 items on agenda**

Colons, dashes, and quotation marks are used as they are used in text. In addition, however, colons or dashes are often used in attribution: "Will not run again—mayor." The colon could as well have been used here; some newspapers use one, some another. Single rather than double quotes are uniformly used in headlines on the assumption that double quotes are too conspicuous in headline type.

Conclusion

Headlines on most news stories, except for features, are summaries, and they must pass the test of being clearly understandable, without recourse by the reader to the text. Readers get most of their information from headlines alone. Editorial judgment of the importance of stories and the consequent prominence with which they are displayed varies; no uniform rule can be applied except in the case of stories of overwhelming interest. Repetition of a word, or a similar form of a word, in a headline is to be avoided. Names may be used only if the reader can be expected to recognize them. Headlines fall into varying patterns; the so-called flush-left pattern is almost universally used today. Many newspapers now use downstyle capitalization, following the practice used for sentences.

Writing the Headline

4

Headlines, as we have seen, are much more important than students sometimes think. In addition to summarizing news stories, headlines indicate by their size the importance or extent of interest of the story. And, of course, headlines attract the reader's attention to the story in the first place. Writing headlines presents certain basic problems because of the nature of printer's type, as will be explained. In addition, the composition of headlines is governed by a number of rules, most of them aimed at ensuring that headlines read as clearly as possible.

Headlines resemble telegrams in that nonessential words such as articles *(the, a, an)* are commonly omitted to save space. Auxiliary verbs such as *is* and *are* are also omitted:

Style

Demonstration (is) held at city hall

The well-constructed headline expands into a normal, grammatical sentence when these missing elements are supplied, and readers are as accustomed to their absence in headlines as in telegrams. It is sometimes supposed that articles and auxiliaries must be omitted, but they may be included if there is space for them. An article is not ordinarily used as the first word of a headline, however.

Opinion is nearly unanimous that a headline ideally should have a subject and a verb, preferably an active verb:

Cresting floods
peril new areas

Floods is the subject, *peril* is the verb. A species of headline known as the "demand" head (or "verb" head), which lacks a subject, is used by some newspapers but is not in very wide favor:

Save women
from flames

Justly or not, the demand head tends to be associated with sensationalism. The subject in the example presumably is *firemen,* but readers cannot be sure. Advocates of this style of headline say that the subject is not always of overriding importance and that the demand head sometimes enables a more meaningful statement in small space.

Critics of the demand head answer that it looks like a statement in the imperative mood; that is, it appears to tell readers to do something ("Shut the door"). This objection seems footless; readers would not conclude from the earlier example that they were being instructed to save women from flames. Some newspapers permit demand heads only when a singular subject (rather than a plural one) is implied:

**Locks husband
in bathroom**

This avoids the resemblance to the imperative, and the example leaves no doubt as to the subject. The fact remains that few newspapers permit demand heads in any form.

Although it is desirable that a headline contain a verb, so-called "label" heads, which lack verbs, are to be found in well-edited papers:

Trends in criminal justice

Riot over prison killing

Forms of the verb *to be (is, are, to be, will be)* are also commonly dispensed with even when they are the main verbs:

Teachers (are) on 72-hour strike in Guatemala

Glendora girl (is) second in state

Space Availability

The greatest difficulty in writing headlines is fitting them into the space available. Experienced copy editors become adept at this, and are able to quickly summon up suitably short synonyms.

The commonest complaint that is heard from beginners at headline writing concerns space; they occasionally insist that a headline cannot be written in the space available. The fact is, however, that a professional can always write a headline that will fit; headline orders are not changed to facilitate writing a head.

Count

Letters formed on a typewriter and those that appear on a printed page both differ in width; the *i,* for example, is noticeably narrower than the *m.* But the typewriter works in such a way that the same amount of space is provided for every letter, so that if an *i* is printed by mistake, an *m* can easily be substituted. Not so with printer's type; letters occupy space in proportion to their size. This is taken into account in headline writing by using a unit system for counting the letters.

The first thing the copy editor needs to know about the headline to be composed is its *count;* that is, how many units it will allow. In general, every lowercase letter equals 1 unit, except for *f, l, i, t, j* (and sometimes *r,* depending on the style of type), each of which equals ½ unit, and *m* and *w,* each of which equals 1½ units. Capital letters equal 1½ units, except for *I* and *J,* which equal ½ unit, and *M* and *W,* which equal 2 units. Punctuation marks uniformly equal ½ unit, except for the question mark and the dash, which equal 1 unit. Spaces between words equal ½ unit. Figures equal 1 unit, except for *1,* which equals ½ unit. The counts assigned here are generally applicable, but not invariably. In some type faces, the lowercase *r* is so narrow that it is assigned a count of ½, and the figures (other than *1*) are so wide that they must be counted 1½. This information is given to new copy editors, of course. This is how the unit counting system works with the headline "County sells two parcels":

$$1½ \;\; 1 \;\; 1 \;\; 1 \;\; ½ \;\; 1 \;\; ½ \;\; 1 \;\; 1 \;\; ½ \;\; ½ \;\; 1 \;\; = 10½$$
$$C \;\; o \;\; u \;\; n \;\; t \;\; y \;\;\;\; s \;\; e \;\; l \;\; l \;\; s$$

$$½ \;\; 1½ \;\; 1 \;\; ½ \;\; 1 \;\; 1 \;\; 1 \;\; 1 \;\; 1½ \;\; 1 \;\;\;\;\; = 10$$
$$t \;\; w \;\; o \;\;\;\; p \;\; a \;\; r \;\; c \;\; e \;\; l \;\; s$$

Counting headlines may seem difficult and tedious at first, but it quickly becomes second nature. The maximum count allowed for this headline was 12. Each line of a headline must come within the limit designated by the count.

On some newspapers, the count specified for flush-left headlines is an ideal total that leaves some space at the right-hand end but also allows room for 2 or 3 more units in a pinch. In these circumstances, the copy editor must know the absolute maximum and must not exceed it. Headlines that are too long and do not fit cause a great deal of trouble, since they must be rewritten. Some computers are designed to reject lines that are too long. Copy editors who often write long heads are not likely to win any popularity contests with the news editor or the compositor. The lines of flush-left headlines should count within a couple of units of each other to avoid unattractive raggedness. Stepped headlines should be precisely the specified count, or at least no more than a half unit off. Otherwise, the stepped effect is not achieved.

Because they are set in small type, decks two columns wide or wider do not need the careful count that regular headlines get. Each character can count as 1 unit. In the span of 15 or 20 letters, the ½-, 1½- and 2-count letters average out. This applies also to main headlines spanning several columns and having long counts.

Decks

On the assumption that decks are, or may be, read—a debatable proposition, as has been noted—specific rules govern their construction. The deck may not be a repetition in different words of the statement made in the main head; it must take up where the main head leaves off and present additional, yet significant, information about the story. The temptation is to stuff anything into the deck to get it out of the way, but this is not permitted on well-regulated newspapers.

A deck may not repeat a word, or even another form of a word (e.g., *resign, resignation*), that has been used in the main head. On newspapers that forbid split headlines, the ban is generally not applied to decks. (The meaning of "split headline" is explained later in this chapter.) And a deck may lack a subject and start with a verb, taking the form of a demand head, if its understood subject is the one that has been expressed in the main headline. A deck may be an independent, additive statement:

> **School-lunch program**
> **upgraded for neediest**
>
> **Administration raises minimum meal cost**
> **to 45 cents under prodding by Congress**

Or it may be a continuation of the statement made in the main head:

> **Cairo won't give up**
> **land for canal accord**
>
> **But U.S. still sees hope for compromise**
> **despite U.N. stand of Egyptian official**

The deck in such instances, however, must take the form of an independent clause; it cannot be so closely linked to the top head that it would not make sense standing alone:

> **Tough gun policy**
> **urged in schools**
>
> **After killing near campus; 40**
> **incidents in city in 3½ weeks**

Writing the Headline

The phrase *after killing near campus* is too closely linked to the statement in the main head and so spoils the deck. The deck may begin with a verb whose subject is also the subject of the main headline:

**State council assails
diploma-mill abuses**

**Will ask lawmakers
to tighten rules
on school charters**

Kickers

Ideally, a kicker should contain a subject and a verb and should stand as an independent statement, like a deck. But it may lack a subject if its subject is the same as that expressed in the main head. Kickers are sometimes used for special purposes, such as bylines or departmental designations, and sometimes they are centered instead of being set flush left, especially on multicolumn heads.

Since the kicker stands above the main head, there is disagreement and confusion as to which element is read first. It seems reasonable to suppose, however, that the main head is read first, despite its inferior position, because it is in larger type and thus is more conspicuous. This means that the principal statement must be made by the main head and not by the kicker. The main head should make complete sense standing alone. A kicker should not be in the form of a prepositional phrase that reads into or out of the main headline; this makes it a closely connected introduction to, or continuation of, the main head, and consolidates the two elements. An example:

In St. Paul
**Criticism backfires
on college student**

This kicker preferably should have stood independently; for example, ***Dean Acts.***

The kicker in the following example is, in effect, a continuation of the main head. *Lost at sea 120 days* would have been better.

During 120 days at sea
**Nearly starved, say
2 ancient mariners**

Meeting the Task

Most newspapers have a printed headline schedule, which is a set of samples of all the headlines in use. Headlines are sometimes designated by a descriptive system, of which an example might be *2–36 TB*. Here the first figure stands for the width of the headline in columns, the second stands for its size in points, and the letters are an abbreviation for the style of type, in this case Tempo Bold. The headline schedule also gives the count for each headline. Newcomers to copy editing quickly learn the designations and counts of the commonly used headlines, so they seldom need to consult the headline schedule. Sometimes headlines are designated by arbitrary letters or numbers, such as *A, B, C,* or *No. 1, No. 2, No. 3*. The headline schedule shows what they look like.

A beginner struggling with a difficult headline sometimes concludes that the task is impossible. But for a professional, there is no such thing as the impossible headline, and the beginner is abashed, perhaps amazed, to see how quickly more experienced hands solve the problem. Yet even old pros have more difficulty with some headlines than with others, and sometimes, with a very difficult head and a deadline at hand, the job may become a cooperative one.

Some people have a flair for writing headlines; after only a little practice they are able to make the words fall into place effortlessly. Others always find writing headlines a hard job. Anyone of reasonable intelligence and verbal facility can learn to write straightforward, acceptable headlines, but no amount of teaching or experience will impart the facility that is inborn like other talents, for example, an ear for music.

Curiously enough, people who are talented writers are not necessarily good headline writers or good copy editors. The reason seems to be that talented writers tend to be truly engaged only by their own writing, and become bored with the task of attentively correcting someone else's work. The constraints of the headline often exasperate rather than challenge these writers.

Tenses and Things

The greater part of the information in a newspaper concerns events or developments that have already taken place. The *accounts* of these happenings are in the *past* tense, appropriately enough, but the *headlines* are almost invariably in the *present* tense:

Striking teachers in Arizona
***vote* to return to classroom**

Mayor *cancels* European trip

Even casual newspaper readers are so conditioned to this that they would be startled, if they are at all observant, by the more logical past tense: "Striking teachers in Arizona/*voted* to return to classroom"; "Mayor *canceled* European trip."

Present Tense

Strictly speaking, the tense used in most headlines is not the simple present but rather the *historical* present; that is, use of the present tense to describe what took place in the past. This technique is sometimes employed by writers of fiction: "It is midnight, and I am sound asleep in bed. All at once there is a terrific crash, and I leap to my feet and run down the stairs." The reader understands perfectly, without being told, that the event took place in the past; the purpose of the writer in using the historical present is to bring the scene before the reader more vividly.

Similarly, the purpose of writing headlines in the present tense is to achieve immediacy. It is not known how this practice originated, or whether it was adopted deliberately with immediacy in mind. The present tense offers an advantage to the headline writer, since the present tense of most verbs is shorter than the past; for example, *demand(s)* v. *demanded, visit(s)* v. *visited.*

Future Tense

A relatively small proportion of the news deals with planned or expected events, and for such stories the headline writer has the choice of the future tense or the infinitive. The future tense in the first example *(will be)* could be readily replaced by the infinitive, as in the second example:

> **New courtrooms *will be* smaller, more secure**
>
> **New courtrooms *to be* smaller, more secure**

Beginners sometimes have the idea that there is a distinction between these forms, to the extent that the future *(will be)* is more definite than the infinitive *(to be),* which they regard as tentative. There is nothing to this. For headline purposes, the choice between the forms is based on which best fits the space available.

Problems and Exceptions

A common fault among beginners and other inexpert headline writers is use of the present tense for future events. Readers see a headline that says "Senator speaks at convention" and discover from reading the story that the event has not taken place, as they had been led to believe, but is still in the offing. A rigid distinction must be observed in this respect: the headline should have said *to speak*. Headlines often are ambiguous enough without confusing the time element in this manner. There is an exception, however, when the headline contains a future time element: "Senator speaks / here tomorrow." Such a headline is perfectly explicit and allows for the present tense in referring to the future, which is indicated by *tomorrow*.

If a *past* time element is stated in the headline, the past tense is often considered more suitable than the present. This form often occurs in headlines over statistical stories.

**Accidents *killed*
113,000 last year**

**Cost of living
rose in August**

The past time elements in the examples are, of course, *last year* and *August*. Occasionally, stories deal with subjects that are recognizably part of history or have to do with the distant as contrasted with the immediate past, and these, too, logically call for headlines in the past tense:

Churchill's eloquence rallied England

Now and then the present progressive tense is used to describe action that is expected to continue at the time of reading:

**Test center seeking
fast train of future**

This could as well be *is seeking,* but forms of the verb *to be* (is, are) used as auxiliaries are commonly omitted if space is tight. Once again, as with *to be* v. *will be* to indicate the future, the choice of form is governed by the space available.

The active voice (the verb form whose subject is the doer of the action: "Officer scolds driver") is generally considered preferable to the passive in headlines (the form in which the subject is acted on by the verb: "Driver is scolded by officer"). The reason is that the active voice has more vigor.

Nevertheless, passive verbs are common in headlines; the test for their suitability is whether the subject, or agent, is of primary importance. If the subject is unimportant, the passive is suitable. Many headlines can be satisfactorily composed only in the passive:

**Plan is proposed
to cut thievery
in city's parks**

Students sometimes arrive in college journalism classes with the idea that headlines in the passive voice are prohibited. This notion has been planted in their heads by high school journalism teachers who have heard and gone overboard with the principle that the active voice is preferable. Such teachers obviously have never paid much attention to what they actually see in newspapers; there is no newspaper in which headlines using the passive voice do not frequently appear. One study showed that about 20 percent of headlines are in the passive voice.

Fully expressed, the passive voice is formed by the past participle plus an auxiliary: *is done, are seen, is voted.* Commonly, however, the auxiliary *(is, are)* is omitted from headlines for lack of space:

**Punishment in schools
(is) called child-beating**

**Football clinic (is) set
tonight for parents**

These could as well be in the full form *is called, is set;* whether or not the auxiliary is used depends on the space available. When space is lacking, the auxiliary is omitted.

This often leads to the misapprehension on the part of students that such headlines are in the past tense, because the past participle *(called, set)* is identical in form with the past tense. It should be understood, however, that they are in the present tense, passive voice, with the auxiliary *(is, are)* omitted. Passive headlines expressing the future require *will be, to be* with the participle:

**Holiday
will be
observed**

With few exceptions, American newspapers forbid what is known as splitting headlines, or "breaking on sense." This refers to dividing certain grammatical elements between one line and the next. The most glaring examples of splitting come from ending the top line with a preposition whose object is on the next line, and ending the top line with part of a compound verb, the rest of which is on the next line. In these three examples, the top lines end with a preposition whose object is in the next line:

**Panel paving way for
dock strike injunction**

**Accord reached on
Jewish emigration**

**Wiretap without
court order upheld**

In the following examples, parts of phrasal verbs have been separated:

Bill seen to
ban cheap
handguns

Emperor can
advise, but
not order

To ban (an infinitive) and *can advise* (a phrasal verb) are separated. Such separations are almost universally prohibited. Some newspapers will not permit the top line to end with an adjective that modifies a noun in the next line:

Government hits new
plan as 'old theory'

British weigh political
reforms for N. Ireland

The ban on this construction is less common, however. Ending a line on a conjunction (e.g., *and, but, or*) is also often considered an objectionable split:

Montreal firemen on strike and
suburb units have to fight blaze

It may be noted that the emphasis in this discussion has been on splitting between the top line and the second. The rule is usually not applied for the second and third lines of a three-line head. Decks are often exempted from it altogether.

The *Los Angeles Times* is a notable exception to the newspapers that forbid splitting. An experienced copy editor who was a newcomer to the *Times* copydesk was startled to notice that the paper contained numerous split heads, and the copy editor asked the news editor about it. "We pay no attention to split heads," was the reply. "The only person who notices whether a headline is split is a newspaper copy editor who has been taught that it is wrong, and we have very few copy editors among our million subscribers."

Nevertheless, in view of the widespread observance of the no-split rule by American newspapers, it is essential that students learn to write headlines without splitting. Some divisions, for example of the parts of a proper name, are universally forbidden. No well-edited newspaper would permit

Crowds greet San
Francisco's mayor

Common sense, too, must be relied upon to prevent the publication of headlines such as

Judge gets drunk
driving case

Too often on newspapers a pathetic and hopeless reliance is placed on special rules to do a job that can be accomplished only by the continuous application of good judgment.

Abbreviations

Some other rules governing headlines are enforced by newspapers that set high standards. One is that abbreviations may not be fabricated to make a headline fit—for example, *sec'y* for *secretary,* or *gov't* for *government.* In general, abbreviations that would not be used or are not permitted in text are likewise banned from headlines. This usually means that days of the week may not be abbreviated (Mon., Wed.), nor may months be abbreviated when they stand alone (Aug., Sept.). Whether months may be abbreviated when accompanied by a date (Aug. 25) depends on the style rule followed by the newspaper; most newspapers prescribe the abbreviated form. Usually, as an exception to rules governing the style in text, headlines may use either figures or words (6, six), regardless of the size of the number.

Some abbreviations that would not be used in text, particularly geographical designations, are often permitted in headlines, however: N.Y. for New York, S.F. for San Francisco, W. Germany, S. America, and the like.

One test of the acceptability of a headline is whether the statement it makes would be given in the same form in text, allowing for expansion by the addition of normally omitted words. If a headline distorts sentence structure or word order, it is likely to be considered deficient. Another basic test of a headline, mentioned earlier, is that it should make a clear and meaningful statement by itself. A headline is useless if it is necessary to read the story to understand what the headline means. This precept, as noted, applies to headlines on hard-news stories, and not necessarily to those on feature stories.

Padding

The inclusion of unnecessary words in a headline is a fault known as "padding." Perhaps the most obvious examples are the words *here* and *now;* a local story is assumed to concern an event in the place where the paper is published, and a story concerning an event elsewhere is identified by a dateline. Similarly, the news is expected to be new, and thus *now* is usually superfluous. These words are called for only when there is danger of confusion without them, or when a contrast with some other place or time is necessary for clarity. Padding wastes space that might be better used for additional information. In general, any information that is dispensable is regarded as padding in a headline. The governing principle is that the small space available must be used as efficiently as possible.

Conclusion

As we have seen, a unit system is used in writing headlines to ensure that the headlines fit into the available space. And a number of rules apply to the composition of headlines. Some of them are universally, or almost universally, observed and others are peculiar to certain newspapers.

A Chamber of Horrors

5

This chapter will show how *not* to write headlines, by means of examples illustrating how the job was botched and explanations of how it happened. An endless variety of boobytraps awaits the neophyte copy editor, and most of these traps are sidestepped only by application of the judgment that comes from experience. Nevertheless, some shortcomings in headlines are recurrent and should be avoidable by studying examples. But the examples are not all negative; some of them illustrate that rare quality, wit, which surely cannot be taught but can be admired and identified for what it is.

Ambiguity

Because headlines must often express complicated ideas in a very short space, the copy editor faces no greater bugaboo than ambiguity. Sometimes, as in the following example, it merely contributes to public amusement. At other times the consequences may be more serious, such as a suit for libel. At any rate, readers of a New York newspaper were diverted one morning to read

**Soviet virgin
lands short
of goal again**

The story, to the possible disappointment of many, did not turn out to be about a frustrated Soviet virgin, but rather about a program for the development of virgin lands. This example illustrates two dangers: that of using words that can be read as either nouns or verbs (in this case, *lands*) and of omitting the verb (in this case, *fall;* i.e., *lands fall.*) This is not to say that a verb is indispensable; many good headlines are verbless. The critical factor is the ability of the copy editor to draw back and consider the headline from other possible angles. This requires imagination and experience.

Ambiguity is seldom amusing and is more often simply baffling, as in "new circulation plans / part of state magazine overhaul." Is *plans* the verb? No, the verb has been omitted: "New circulation plans *are* part . . ." At one time and in some places there was a superstition that *is* and *are* may not be used in headlines as main verbs. This is nonsense; anything necessary for clarity should be used. The most that can be said is that *is* and *are* (except when used as auxiliaries, as in *is fired* or *are promoted*) are weak linking verbs, and if a stronger one can be used it should be done.

Repetition

Overuse of a word in headlines is often discouraged. Some newspapers will not permit repetition of any expression, for instance, *president, foreign, senate,* on the front page. Some sloppily edited newspapers develop a mania for some word, usually one that eases the task of headline-writing. A California newspaper, for example, was full of *eyed*. This is an acceptable headline word for *considered,* but it appeared on nearly every page of every edition, and thus was worn out:

**Animal control
eyed by council
in Porterville**

**Vike five eyes escape
from cellar vs. Troy**

**Citizens group
eyes school
computer program**

It is difficult to judge from the headlines alone whether the word was used appropriately, but such was the fondness for *eyed* that its meaning was often stretched beyond endurance.

Omission

Many headlines are cast in such forms as "Chief says/ mayor's request/illegal" and "Winter floods said/worst in history." Some newspapers forbid the omission of the verb in the clause following *says.* In the first example, the verb is *is:* "Chief says/mayor's request/(is) illegal." They also forbid *said* for *said to be,* as in the second example.

Most such headlines can be cured by the use of *call* instead of *say:*

Chief calls mayor's request illegal

**Winter floods called
worst in history**

It must be conceded, however, that while *calls* will fit in the space of *says, called* is 1½ units longer than *said.* Still *said* is often used when there is enough room for *called.*

A similar practice that many editors criticize and some forbid is using *seen* where *seen as* would be required in the text: "Fuel shortage seen/world peace threat." Such condensation is surely not good English, and yet, as with many headline practices, it must be considered perfectly understandable to the reader, who sees such headlines often. This is so, if the truth were admitted, of *said* for *said to be.* Here too, *called* (though a unit longer) can often circumvent the difficulty.

With experience, copy editors acquire a stock of very short words that may be substituted in headlines for much longer words, but would not ordinarily, or perhaps ever, be used in text. Here is a ready reference list of such words:

Ties for *connections* or *associations:* "Underworld ties."

Panel for *committee:* "Panel OK's confirmation."

Bias for *discrimination,* usually in the racial sense, but not necessarily: "Sex bias criticized."

Hit for *criticize,* one of the commoner headline shortcuts. Beginners, however, tend to overlook it.

Rap for *criticize:* "Mayor raps council."

Score for *criticize* is also familiar, but often unsuitably used. *Score* is a strong word, and should not be called into play unless the criticism is sharp indeed.

Flay for *criticize. Flay* is such a strong word (whose literal meaning is "strip the skin off") that it should be used rarely. Its frequency reflects either sensation-seeking or a lack of feeling for language.

Stir for *prompt, arouse:* "Rezoning stirs disapproval." *Stir* is probably overused, however, like many headline shortcuts.

Bare for *reveal, disclose;* "Police crime link bared."

Probe for *investigate* or *investigation:* "D.A. probes scandal."

Hail for *praise* or *approve:* "Council hails compromise."

Held for *said to be:* "Fallout held dangerous." *Holds* and *held* are also used, however, to refer to judgments of a court, and should be used with care lest an impression of an official finding be given when none is warranted.

Hike for *increase:* "Tax rate hiked."

Remap for *reapportion (ment).* This is probably preferable as a verb: "Senate remaps six districts."

Attribution

Attribution, as has been explained, is as necessary in a headline that expresses an opinion as it is in a story. But attribution introduces just one more space-consuming element, and copy editors sometimes solve the problem by attributing in this way: "Administration favors treaty/to limit armaments—Reagan." There seems to be a tendency to use this kind of attribution sparingly and to desist from anonymous attributions in this form: "Thief shoots manager, then disappears—officer."

Noun/Adjective Uses and Abuses

One too-often-used escape hatch from the pressure of small space is piling adjectives high on their nouns. Another is indiscriminately using nouns as adjectives, as in "Job-safety law enforcement bar voted by House." Four modifiers have been piled against *bar,* and this makes for difficult reading, whether in headlines or in text. How about

> **House votes bar**
> **on enforcing**
> **job-safety law**

The revised version has the advantages of being more vigorous and more easily understood, because it is in the active voice.

The use of the names of countries as adjectives when it would not be acceptable in text is best avoided in headlines: "Britain budget," "Spain crisis." This can get to be a bad habit, practiced when unnecessary; in the first example, "British budget" would have fit just as well. Consider "Italy mail: it/was faster in/Caesar's time." This, too, is a sad performance, because either *Italy's* or *Italian* would have fit.

Out of the Chamber

Sometimes inspiration strikes the copy editor. Then again, the witty headlines that occasionally brighten newspaper stories are just as often the product of hard work and perspiration.

Once a story came over the wires about a soldier who lost a toe during World War II. The Army doctors repaired the damage by sewing on a toe taken from a Nazi soldier who had just been killed. Some years later, the transplanted toe, after having given good service, unaccountably began to twitch, and the owner speculated that a Nazi toe might have been misplaced on an American and a believer in democracy. It sounds pretty apocryphal, and the whole thing may have been an invention. Nevertheless, a newspaper that received it decided to print it, if only as an antidote to the usual run of bad news. The copy editor who handled it came up with this headline:

> **Transplanted digit**
> **starts to fidget;**
> **toe-talitarian?**

An expository story on the increasing use of bulletproof vests by the police said:

Police vests
**Armor: clothes
you won't get
caught dead in**

This was a good pun; that is, it makes sense both ways and does not merely distort meaning for the sake of a cheap play on words.

Wit or a catchy turn of phrase sets the work of the artist (or perhaps that of the headline writer who simply had the time) apart from that of the journeyman. Here are some examples:

**Disobedience called
wrong way to rights**

The following headline appeared in a newspaper that does not forbid splitting:

**French have words for
it, U.S. borrows them**

**Naturalization is, how you say, difficile
in some instances and easier in others**

It is work like this that makes the ephemeral quality of journalism, and the anonymity of copy editors, regrettable.

Puns

A pun or other attempt at cleverness must come off; if it baffles or misleads, it would be better if it had not been attempted. Over stories having to do with dogs there is a dreary procession of headlines using the stereotypes "a dog's life" or "dog days" or some tiresome variant. As an example of an effort to be cute that misfired, consider this headline on a story about the presentation of a conference table by the president: "Nixon tables gift/for cabinet members." The meaning of *table* as a verb (set aside, defer) is so far off target that the effort to be bright was utterly destroyed. A simple, factual statement would have been preferable:

**Nixon gives table
to cabinet members**

Deadheads

Another bane of the copydesk is what are sometimes called "wooden" or "bushelbasket" heads, or "deadheads." They make such a general statement that they could stand over numerous stories of the same kind, and are hardly calculated to arouse interest. Some examples are "Professor to lecture"; "Research program approved"; and "Experts to gather." The copy editor must learn to seize upon the point that makes the story different from most other stories and get it into the headline. Better versions of these headlines would have been:

Law lecture scheduled

Divorce research approved

Biologists to meet

"Rulings of high court/affect life of millions" ran the headline on a story summarizing the activity of the United States Supreme Court for the preceding year. How prosy can you get? The Court's decisions oftener than not affect millions. Consider the following version, which also gets across the idea of a summary:

**Court ranged in 1973
from toplessness to drugs**

What can be said about headlines that miss the point of a story entirely or even contradict it? No purpose is served by giving examples of such carelessness or stupidity, whichever it may be, but every reader has been confounded by them. To repeat a principle that has been laid down before—copy editors must have read the story with scrupulous care, and if they take any pride in their work, must be certain that the headline reflects the story's import precisely.

Imprecise Heads

Some headlines are not erroneous, but imprecise. "Two killed/in kidnap/gunfight" lacks the detail that would make it more meaningful (Turkey was the scene of the incident):

**2 killed as
Turks rush
dormitory**

The headline writer should neither misuse words nor distort normal word-order. Citing as examples "Early sale impends of Yankee Stadium" and "Disposal is urged of ex-Peron papers,"

Theodore M. Bernstein, the late in-house critic of the *New York Times,* disposed of them succinctly: "This kind is lousy of head."

A frequent fault of headlines is that they are cryptic; that is, they are difficult and perhaps even impossible for the reader to understand. There are many reasons for this; the most excusable one is working under pressure. Headlines, especially narrow ones counting 10 or 12 units and dealing with a complex concept, can be extremely difficult to write. When the job must be done without enough time to wrestle the problem to a successful conclusion, copy editors must do the best they can in the time available.

But there are other, less excusable reasons why headlines are cryptic. These are haste when there is no pressure and inadequate self-criticism. Another difficulty is that headline writers, when confronted with complicated ideas to be fitted into a small space, tend to develop a kind of jargon that grows by inbreeding and finally may leave a headline intelligible only to a copy editor—perhaps only to the one who wrote it, and not even to that one a day or two later.

Here was a headline that appeared as a presidential campaign approached:

Guidance pleas a factor
**Budding campaigns
forced a 'cutback'**

Even allowing that it appeared on a sidebar to a well-played announcement on vice-presidential prospects, this headline was not easy to understand. There was no reason for the quotation marks around *cutback,* incidentally, and the kicker was all but incomprehensible. Something like the following would have been more suitable:

Too many candidates
**Why Democrats thinned
their vice-presidents list**

Another defective headline is "Frown on plans/by arts body/can be costly." To begin with, this was ambiguous enough to throw the reader off stride; frown by arts body, or on plans by arts body, or both? How about

**If arts body
objects, plans
can be costly**

Consider the headline "Medical field/drive aimed/at blacks." This, too, was cryptic; *medical field drive* could refer to anything from health insurance to nurses' schooling. Another, more explicit, possibility is

**Drive aimed
at training
black medics**

Words are sometimes misused in headlines, as in text, but in heads the matter is more serious, partly because an ambiguous statement in the headline might discourage the reader from seeking additional information in the story, and partly because heads are so conspicuous. Further, the context that aids comprehension in text is missing from the headline. Here is an example: "House lifts Social Security pay/but takes no action on Medicare." Nobody speaks of *lifting* pay; why not *raises,* when it would have filled out the line better?

Consider "Test leak traced;/French faces red," which was likely to prompt a number of misapprehensions without giving much of a glimmer of what the story was about (the theft of baccalaureate test questions in France). *Test leak* can easily suggest something to do with technology; *faces* is ambiguous. How about

**French exam leak
traced to employee**

In the next edition, the size of the headline was changed, and in the rewriting its quality was brought up to par:

**French find
sources of
exam theft**

Exam is better than *test* in this context because it is not ambiguous.

When the verb, like hope, is too long deferred, the heart grows sick: "Municipal citizen board on police conduct pressed." How about

**Council considers
citizen board
on police conduct**

"Fleeing GIs fire/machine gun" might have left the impression the soldiers were being chased by an enemy. The fact was that they were off on a drunk in Germany and were being chased by military police. How about

**GIs held after
firing at MPs**

"Probers told of massage parlor/door removal to bar prostitution" left something to be desired in clarity. A better headline would have been

**Massage parlor doors removed
to discourage prostitution**

"Rightist party in election/wins over Bengal Marxists." One of the outs of the headline writer is to say that people are "in" something instead of that they do it—another desperate expedient to save space, sometimes excusable, oftener not. Such headlines do not meet the test of easy expansion into a normal sentence, for it would never be said in text that the party was in an election win. "In election win" is a poor and padded substitute for "win election." This headline, furthermore, ignored an important qualification that was contained in the story:

**Rightist party *claims win*
over Bengal Marxists**

"Britain elections/to test Tories'/popularity." *British* would be better English than *Britain,* but either is redundant because *Tories'* tells us where the elections were taking place. And it was possible to include another significant fact:

***Local* elections
to test Tories'
popularity**

"Somewhere in Italy lurks 'Mr. Half a Billion'." This headline is defensible, perhaps, on the basis of featurish treatment, but it does not convey much. The idea is clearer in

**Lottery winner in Italy
evades $480,000 in taxes**

"Migrants descend upon President's villa." This headline exhibited the common failing of going beyond the story—evidence of careless reading. A more accurate headline is

**Migrants protest
near President's villa**

Conclusion

In this chapter we have seen how easy it is for the headline writer to go astray and mislead the reader. Sometimes these slips result from the fact that the headline writer, having read the story, has a clear idea what the story says but fails to communicate that idea to the reader, who is coming to the headline cold. Once again, headline writers must use imagination to put themselves in the place of the reader, who knows nothing of the story. Headlines must be studied for possible ambiguity, especially since the parts of speech are sometimes used in a way that would not be permissible in the text of the story. Wit and humor, especially in headlines on feature stories, are sufficient excuses for the headline writer to disregard the rules, but attempts at humor that baffle or fall flat are worse than a plain but clear statement.

Style and Stylebooks

6

The term *style,* as applied to writing, has two different meanings. One is what might be called literary style, describing a manner of expression. The other is mechanical style, which will be described. Thus we may speak of a flowery style, an economical style, or an archaic style, in the literary sense. The social critic and linguist H. L. Mencken, for example, employed a style that was so racy and distinctive that the adjective *menckenese,* describing this kind of expression, has been formed on his name.

The great lexicographer, Dr. Samuel Johnson, on the other hand, is famous for a style that is ponderous and polysyllabic, and accordingly the adjective *johnsonese* was coined to characterize it. The way one writes reflects personality, education, and other influences. This is what Georges-Louis Leclerc de Buffon, the French naturalist, had in mind when he made his perceptive comment, *"Le style est l'homme même"* (Style is the man himself).

Style in this sense does not figure very largely in journalistic writing. Considered in general, journalistic writing has some admirable characteristics, such as directness and simplicity, that could well be emulated by bureaucrats, lawyers, scientists, and professors, to name a few of the leading offenders against good expression.

Newswriting also has some bad qualities, which are described by the term *journalese.* Chapter 7 of this book has been given over to some of the faults that mark journalese, and other instances are to be found elsewhere. Careful journalists familiarize themselves with these lapses and attempt to avoid them.

Newswriting, because of the exigencies under which it is done, has become pretty well homogenized. By and large, it has distinctive qualities, as noted, but seldom do journalists develop distinctive styles.

Mechanical Style

The kind of style that reporters and copy editors are primarily concerned with might be referred to as *mechanical* style. It has to do with such matters as selecting appropriate capitalization, abbreviation, spelling, and punctuation where two or more styles are correct. For example, we might regard as inflexible the rule that the first word in a sentence begins with a capital letter. This is not a matter for stylistic determination, because there is no choice in ordinary prose. (For our present purpose we disregard the work of James Joyce, Gertrude Stein, e.e. cummings and other literary artists who departed from standard practice for special effects.) But there is no generally accepted principle dictating that either *Roosevelt school* or *Roosevelt School* is correct. Either form of capitalization is considered acceptable.

Upstyle/Downstyle

For about the first half of this century, American newspapers generally tended to use the first of the two forms: Roosevelt school. This practice, in which the generic, or general, term is lowercase (in the example, *school*), is referred to as "downstyle." For some reason, downstyle (Mississippi river, Market street) was thought to be racier and more appropriate to journalism than the more formal upstyle (Mississippi River, Market Street). But the upstyle is what children generally are encouraged to use in school, and newspapers discovered that the downstyle was to be found nowhere else but in their pages. Consequently, a strong trend toward the upstyle has developed. (The application of the term *downstyle* as applied to headlines and discussed in chapter 2 should not be confused with its application to text. As applied to headlines, downstyle refers to capitalization as sentences are capitalized.)

Abbreviations

The use of abbreviations also offers a choice between equally correct forms. Should it be *Third St.* or *Third Street; Minneapolis, Minn.,* or *Minneapolis, Minnesota?* Both forms are considered correct. Choices like this set the stage for uncertainty, confusion, and inconsistency. To prevent uncertainty and inconsistency and to expedite writing and editing, newspapers and publishers usually use stylebooks prescribing the forms to be used. The preface to a stylebook once said that consistency in such matters is desirable because it gives the reader the impression that the staff knows what it is doing.

Style Variety

There is good reason to believe, however, that readers do not notice stylistic inconsistencies, especially as between different news stories, though the more sophisticated of them might notice such inconsistencies within a single story. Readers are confronted with such a variety of styles in the numerous things they read every day that they pay little or no attention to matters of consistency. Style is useful, then, primarily to facilitate the writing and editing of newspapers by settling as many mechanical questions as possible in advance.

Style and Stylebooks

Until about 1960 it was common for newspapers of medium size and larger to have their own stylebooks, which were formulated on the premises and offered the editor's revelations on what constitutes preferable practice. Each of the wire services also had its own stylebook, and since such guides were regarded as expressions of individuality and pride, there were noticeable differences in the rules they laid down. Thus the copy editors on a newspaper usually found themselves obliged to change press association copy to conform with local style.

In the late 1950s, however, a system of teletypesetting under which newspapers received press association dispatches on punched tape that could be fed directly into a linecasting machine (or, later, into a photocomposition machine) was widely adopted. This meant that press association copy could not be edited to local style without expensive and time-consuming changes on proof, defeating the advantages of speed and convenience afforded by use of the tape. Inevitably, this led to the production of a joint wire services stylebook by United Press International and the Associated Press in 1960, because many papers subscribe to both. In turn, many newspapers adopted the joint wire services stylebook for their own practice, amplifying it as necessary to deal with strictly local problems. In 1978 the wire services published a completely revised, voluminous stylebook in separate editions that are almost identical. They are vast improvements over their predecessors. Most newspapers use them.

The Stylebook

The chief business of a stylebook, then, is to lay down rules governing capitalization and abbreviation, as well as spelling in those instances when there is more than one recognized way to spell a word (cigaret, cigarette; drought, drouth; employee, employe). It may be of interest that just as newspapers affected the downstyle, they also preferred shorter or Anglicized spellings, like *cigaret* and *employe*. But newspapers are rapidly coming back to the predominant versions (cigarette, employee, etc.).

Copy editors (and, for that matter, reporters) are expected to familiarize themselves with the rules governing frequently encountered points of abbreviation, capitalization, spelling, and punctuation, and to look up in the stylebook any point on which uncertainty arises.

Stylebooks do not deal exclusively with matters of choice between correct forms. Often they take up common mistakes in standard practice. The placement of periods and commas inside rather than outside quotation marks, for example, is standard practice in America (as contrasted with Britain); this rule and others are often given. Stylebooks often also contain lists of commonly misspelled, misused, and confused words.

The decision on what should be included in or excluded from a stylebook is a matter of intelligently defining the field. It is well to confine a stylebook to generally applicable principles, with as few exceptions to those principles as possible. This will make conformity to those principles easier. It is well also to allow plenty of blank space for changes and corrections and to organize the book in dictionary form, like that of the *New York Times,* to make for easy reference.

The first duty of copy editors is mastery of the stylebook of the newspaper they work for. Students, however, often learn style rules, as indicated by their performance on tests, without being able to apply them in marking copy. Learning style rules just to be able to repeat them is a useless exercise. On well-regulated papers, and in well-conducted news editing laboratories, errors in style are regarded just as seriously as any other kind of lapse.

Usage

Usage is another matter with which newspaper writers and editors are properly concerned. This is a matter of literary rather than mechanical style, though newspaper stylebooks sometimes deal with certain aspects of literary style. Usage has to do, essentially, with putting the right word in the right place—that is, the choice of language—in accordance with educated practice. Determining what the consensus is on such questions, however, is a tricky business, because usage keeps changing.

Most students recognize instantly that people who use such forms as *we is* or *it do* are lacking in education and in a feeling for what is unanimously considered correct. Usages that are considered undesirable are shunned for fear of leaving a bad impression on the reader. For the most part, unacceptable usages, like the glaring ones cited, do not interfere with meaning or with conveying information; they simply create an impression of ignorance.

No one would disagree that the examples cited are unacceptable. But what about the use of *contact* as a verb, as in "I'll contact him next week"? Twenty years ago, or perhaps even more recently, this usage was regarded by many educated people as unacceptable. Some people still think so. The overwhelming consensus of authorities is that *contact* as a verb is now acceptable. Newspaper offices abound with superstitions about what is right and what is wrong in such instances. Some of the superstitions are based on rules that were once generally observed, like the one concerning *contact.* For example, it is a part of newspaper folklore that *none* must always take a singular verb. In fact, *none* may be considered either singular or plural, depending on which aspect the writer wants to stress, and authorities agree that the plural use is commoner.

What constitutes correct usage is often an arbitrary matter. There are at present about a half-dozen reasonably current manuals of usage presenting judgments on this subject, as well as one dictionary that gives it particular attention. They differ so much that one of the authors of this book, Roy Copperud, wrote yet another, entitled *American Usage and Style: The Consensus* (New York: Van Nostrand Reinhold, 1980), to show where the weight of opinion lies concerning the most commonly disputed points.

There are many misconceptions about style among journalists, as indicated in this chapter. The next few chapters of this book point out further misconceptions and structural defects of newswriting that are objectionable because they mislead the reader, because they are awkward, or for some other reason.

At the end of this book is a list of books that are useful to writers and editors. In the field of usage there is no immutable right and wrong, and no final authority to which an appeal can be made. What was generally considered wrong five or ten years ago might well win an approving consensus today.

Conclusion

7 Journalese

Before 1954, when pressure was successfully brought to bear against the G.&C. Merriam Co. by Sigma Delta Chi, the professional journalistic society, the definition of *journalistic* in the Merriam-Webster dictionaries was more or less equated with that of *journalese;* it was as if the words were *journalese* and *journalese-tic.*

Journalistic Writing: Good and Bad

Journalese is what linguists like to describe as a pejorative; that is, a word that indicates disapproval. It applies to all that is bad in journalistic writing. *Journalistic,* on the other hand, properly means *pertaining to journalism,* and ought not to have any derogatory connotation. Nor does it, ordinarily. The old Webster definition of *journalistic* was "characteristic of journalism or journalists; hence, of style characterized by evidence of haste, superficiality of thought, inaccuracies of detail, colloquialisms, and sensationalism; journalese." In the revised definition, the derogatory aspects were replaced by "appropriate to the immediate present and phrased to stimulate and satisfy the interest and curiosity of a wide reading public—often in distinction from *literary.*" The definition of *journalistic* in the third edition of Webster has been further revised, but the effect is the same and it remains neutral.

The distinction is carefully observed in another new dictionary, the *American Heritage Dictionary of the American Language.* It defines *journalese* as "the slick, superficial style often held to be characteristic of newspapers and magazines" and *journalistic* as "pertaining to or characteristic of journalism or journalists." The thesis of this book is that journalistic writing should be no slicker or more superficial than any other writing, and that the sleazy tricks that often disfigure journalistic writing are to be avoided, not imitated.

Much that is unpretentiously journalism is superb, as for example the kind of writing found in the *New Yorker;* much that aims at being literary is atrocious. This is true also of much academic and scholarly writing, whose obfuscation and pretentiousness have become legendary.

Now and then, *journalese* is mistaken for a neutral, rather than a derogatory, descriptive. An author of a book on English usage ludicrously misapplied it as a term for the cant, or technical terminology, of journalism.

Most inferior writing is cliché-ridden, but newspapering has developed its own clichés. In journalese, a thing is not *kept secret,* but *a lid of secrecy is clamped* on it; rain and snow do not *fall,* but *are dumped;* a river does not *overflow,* but *goes on a rampage;* honors are not *won* or *earned,* but *captured;* army divisions are too often *crack;* a reverse does not *threaten,* but *looms;* a development is not *unprecedented,* but *precedent-shattering;* buildings are not simply *large* or *high,* but *sprawling* or *towering;* and brush fires must inevitably *blacken acres.*

All such expressions have something in common besides extreme fatigue. If you can shake off, for a moment, the anesthesia they produce, you will see that originally they were dramatic. Even if they were too dramatic to suit the occasion—another characteristic of journalese, not necessarily related to clichés—when they were new they piqued the reader's attention. But that was long ago. Since they are such conspicuous stereotypes, why do journalists continue to use them? The obvious explanation is laziness and lack of discrimination.

When reporters are taxed with the stereotyped flavor of newspaper writing, they sometimes offer as an excuse that much of their work must be done in haste to meet a deadline. This does not happen to be a good excuse, however, because it would be easier and faster to use the plain language that the clichés displace.

Plain language—the kind cliché experts use when talking instead of writing—looks surprisingly fresh in print. It will never wear out, as clichés have, because it is the natural and inevitable currency of expression. Faults that are described in this book as journalese are prevalent in news publications, but by no means peculiar to them, because the news media exert tremendous influence on usage in general. Newspaper writing tends to exaggerate, to overdramatize. It also tends to compress by omitting needed or desirable words, so that sometimes it sounds telegraphic.

"Brightening Up"

A news story can often be identified out of context by the supercharged effort that has been exerted to make it sound bright and lively. The rawest cub learns at once—misguidedly—to strive for this effect. To the old hand, it has often become second nature. "Brighten it up" are the words that have accompanied innumerable stories as they were handed back by the city editor for rewriting. In view of this, how is it possible to explain the fact that only the rare news story sounds bright to the reader?

The situation is analogous to that described in the story about the boy who hollered "Wolf!" too often. Many journalists have yet to learn that they cannot brighten a story by using words whose color or vigor are too much for the occasion.

We are on difficult ground here, for the exercise of restraint in writing is one of the things that helps to make it an art. It seems foolish to have any artistic pretensions or aspirations about news-writing, considering the exigent conditions under which it is often done. About the best that can be reasonably expected is straight-forward communication of facts, leavened as far as possible by felicitous touches of description, bits of humor, and pointed insights.

Obviously, it is easier to tell the story in conversational language than to overwrite. Stories in a conversational tone are easier to read, too. The fact is that readers find overwritten prose tiresome, if not absurd. Reporters know, of course, that the situations they describe seldom live up to the overcharged language they too often use to describe them. Thus the frequent state of affairs is that writers have their tongues in their cheeks and readers have their fingers crossed.

Criticism of and by public officials, for example, may range from the mild to the severe. In reporting criticism, however, reporters often fail to take into account its tone. Their stories use words like *attacked, blasted, flayed, lashed out at, lambasted,* or *scored*—all very strong words.

Are readers diverted or stimulated by this overexcited stuff? Not at all. They are more likely to be bored by the incessant effort to startle them with what is not startling, and what interest they do feel will be inspired solely by the factual content. Things are so much the worse when, as is often true, the attempt to enliven is made with clichés—*hurl* for *make* (an accusation), *smash* or *shatter* for *break* (a record), *soar* for *rise* (as in reference to a few degrees' change in temperature). Life is not that exciting most of the time, and when it is, the circumstances will speak for themselves.

In a survey of the American press, the *Times* of London commented:

> It is this fundamental striving to attract the attention of, as well as to inform, the normally indifferent citizen which gives modern American journalism some of its most striking characteristics. Notably, it is the cause of its tendency to oversimplify political and diplomatic situations and developments to the point of distortion; to heighten personalities and the part played; to describe complex events in vivid, breathless, exciting prose so that the regular reader must live with a perpetual state of crisis or develop a deliberate indifference as a protection against it.

Jacques Barzun has taken note of the overexcited tone of much journalism by referring to reporters as "writers whose professional neurosis is to despair of being attended to and in whom, therefore, a kind of solemn ritual clowning is inevitable."

Clichés

Another general characteristic of journalese, in addition to the tendency to overdramatize, is its heavy reliance on clichés, as we have seen. To some extent, this is perhaps unavoidable because of the pressure under which much newswriting is done. But some reporters accumulate a large store of catch-phrases that they drop into place as they proceed from one story to another.

The dictionary definition of *cliché* is "a trite phrase; a hackneyed expression." This leaves wide open the question, Trite or hackneyed to whom? Language is full of stock expressions, many of which are indispensable or at least not replaceable without going the long way around. The expressions that draw scorn as clichés, however, are generally those that attempt a special effect, such as drama or humor.

Whether a given expression is regarded as a cliché depends upon the discrimination of the regarder. A good way to acquire an acute and extensive awareness of clichés is to read Frank Sullivan's reports from his cliché expert, Magnus Arbuthnot, as set down in such books as *A Pearl in Every Oyster, A Rock in Every Snowball,* and *The Night the Old Nostalgia Burned Down.*

What follows is a shameless exercise in putting into Mr. Arbuthnot's mouth the words he might have used if he had been interviewed on the subject of clichés peculiar to journalism:

Q. Why, Mr. Arbuthnot, what are you doing here?

A. I am playing hooky from my mentor, Frank Sullivan, that witty man of letters who made me what I am today. I used to be a journalist myself, you know.

Q. Felt impelled to return to the scene of the crime, eh? Does Mr. Sullivan know about your background as a journalist?

A. He considered it my finest qualification when he hired me as a cliché expert.

Q. Ah, yes. Well, to work. Shall we inaugurate the interview?

A. I'd rather you didn't swipe my stuff. But let's launch it.

Q. Theft is a serious charge, Mr. Arbuthnot. And incidentally, charges, in the press, are always . . .

A. Hurled.

Q. To be sure. I would prefer *made,* but then newspaper readers can seldom be choosers. Now, would you tell me . . .

A. Sorry to interrupt, but as a newsman, I never *told.* Always *advised.*

Q. Thank you. I suppose you claimed your sources were authoritative?

A. *Claimed,* yes. Seldom *asserted.* Often *contended,* though.

Q. Indeed. How has your health been?

A. I'm in the pink of condition now, although I suffered a leg fracture in a mishap a year ago.

Q. You mean your leg was broken in an accident?

A. You heard me. I also sustained some lacerations, contusions, and abrasions, but, as I said, I'm OK now.

Q. Glad to hear it. That you're OK, I mean. What about the time thieves broke into your apartment?

A. The place was a shambles. The marauders made their getaway with upwards of $500.

Q. Too bad. What do you do for amusement?

A. Oh, I witness a ball game now and then. They hiked the admission charge recently, but attendance has been boosted in spite of it.

Q. Do you expect to get a car when the new models are out?

A. I anticipate that I will secure one, yes. I am anxious to see them unveiled.

Q. I'd like to secure—I mean buy—one myself. But I wish the dealers would slash their prices.

A. You're learning. If you keep at it, you'll be able to turn plain English into journalese promptly.

Q. You mean *on time?*

A. No, I mean *promptly*. At once.

Q. About your job as a cliché expert—does it pay?

A. You mean, is it lucrative? Well, it pays, or lucres, pretty well.

Q. What did you do before you were a newspaperman?

A. Well, prior to that time I had no visible means of support, although I was a genial host. After I inked the pact with Mr. Sullivan, I really hit my stride. Although I am famous, I have been described as quiet and unassuming.

Q. Are you easily embarrassed?

A. Well, I am red-faced when I am beaten to the cliché.

Q. It was very good of you to take this time out for us, Mr. Arbuthnot. Clichés must be the lifeblood and, paradoxically, at the same time the *rigor mortis* of newswritting.

A. You can say *that* again.

The castigation of redundancy and clichés in newswriting often seems like a hopeless exercise. Indeed, faint-hearted critics of those faults regularly conclude that attempts to discourage them are wasted effort. And in the large sense, they are probably right. The problem comes down to a matter of taste. Taste can be cultivated, but it seems unlikely that the capacity for discrimination in choice of language can be implanted.

There will always be dull-witted and ill-read reporters who are proud of having picked up and of using expressions that the finer-grained despise. Even on the upper levels of ability, opinions will always differ as to whether a particular expression is overworked. George Orwell once fiercely proposed that writers should rigorously excise from their work every turn of phrase they did not devise themselves. This may be going too far. Writing that contained nothing familiar or at least recognizable in this respect might well leave the reader ill at ease. In any event, no writing exists that does not contain clichés by one standard or another. This state of affairs was once described in verse:

> If you scorn what is trite
> I warn you, go slow
> For one man's cliché
> Is another's *bon mot*.

Among other characteristics of journalese are certain mannerisms of construction, such as misplacing the time element too early in the sentence ("Mayor Jones Tuesday completed the survey"); the use of so-called false titles ("Massachusetts Institute of Technology political scientist Susan Shirk"; "French journalist Pierre Fontanne"; "he told wife Shirley and brother John"); excessive and erroneous use of quotation marks; piled-up modifiers; and others, which present enough of a problem to warrant detailed examination in succeeding chapters.

Wrong Tenses in Time Elements

A standard formula of journalese calls for the misuse and misplacement of time elements. Excessive and pointless caution seems to prompt the use of the past tense in places where it tarnishes the freshly minted news. Some newspapers seem to be fearful lest the situation at the time of writing may change before the account is read.

"A seaplane with 17 persons aboard *was* missing south of Japan, the Navy said today." Conceivably, the plane might have been found before the newspaper reached the reader. But is it really necessary to pussyfoot like this, or may the reader be left to assume that the paper is stating the facts at the time of writing? Saying *is missing* would have been better.

Many news stories deal with conditions that will unquestionably persist until the account is read. Take, for example, an account that began "Connecticut *was* in for a wide-open and exciting election." Why *was,* since the election was a long way off, and there was no indication the situation might change? Having started with the past tense, however, the writer had to stick with it, thus giving a musty flavor to something that could have been kept fresh by the use of the present tense. Greater immediacy is achieved by "Connecticut *is* in for a wide-open and exciting election."

Here's a general principle that will brighten things up: Avoid the past tense except in narrating completed events. Use the present, as far as possible, to describe conditions in effect at the time of writing. Nothing is lost by saying "A seaplane with 17 persons aboard *is* (rather than *was*) missing," and immediacy is gained.

Use the present tense, too, for general statements, and stand clear of such absurdities as "The people who did the most to break the Solid South in the election *were* Democrats and they *intended* to remain Democrats," when in fact they still *are* and still *intend*.

Another illogical phrase is *was a former,* which does not make sense in reference to a living man: "Like Hull and Padrutt, Johnson *was a former* Progressive." Once a former, always a former. *Was a former* (and *was a onetime*) can be properly used only of dead people to describe a condition that ceased to exist before they died. Even then, the meaning is better expressed with different wording: "The late governor was at one time a Farmer-Laborite."

When a sentence contains both a past and a past perfect tense, the reader is entitled to assume that the occasion described by the past perfect came first. "A doctor recently *discovered* the nail in a bronchial tube and had recommended surgery." *Had discovered* and *recommended* would be more logical, but *discovered* and *recommended* are what come naturally, because the sequence of events is self-evident.

Much the same difficulty arises in sentences containing a past time element and a past perfect verb: "He *had been* the youngest member of the College of Cardinals when he was elected in 1946 at the age of 46." This is nonsense, for he could not have been the youngest member until he was elected. Instead of *had been, was* or *became* is required.

Placement of Time Elements

Reporters should follow the example of Grampaw in *Annie Get Your Gun* and just do what comes naturally. They would never say "I today went downtown," but in a news story they write, "The City Council *last night* voted a street-improvement program."

The natural place for the time element is generally after, rather than before, the verb, and often at the very end of a sentence: "I went downtown *today*"; "The City Council voted a street-improvement program *last night*." We don't really need to be told this; everyone feels it instinctively.

There are perhaps two reasons for the misplacement of the time element in newswriting. One is overemphasis on the *W*'s formula—the idea that the lead paragraph should tell when, who, what, where, and why, but above all *when*.

Another reason for the misplacement of the time element is that a moment of thought may be necessary to select the most suitable place for it. Thinking, as has been said, hurts the head, and reporters heedlessly drop the time element in where it breaks the natural flow of the sentence: "The Air Force pressed *tonight* the search for a missing plane." Unnatural as it sounds, this kind of disarrangement is nearly standard practice.

When the time element is indispensable (and often it is not, as we shall see) it should be put in a place where it fits comfortably. Let us look at some examples of sheer clumsiness in this respect (examples of better word order appear in parentheses):

A novelist who has written powerful novels of violence and death was awarded *today* the Nobel Prize for literature. ("A novelist . . . was awarded the Nobel Prize for literature *today*.)

It was his own brother who *last year* spoke out against his political tactics. (It was his own brother who spoke out *last year*. . . .)

Negotiations to end the crippling railway strike reportedly reached *today* their most crucial stage. (Negotiations . . . reached their most crucial stage *today*.)

Care in placement of the time element is advisable not only to prevent clumsiness, as in the examples, but to keep it from modifying the wrong word or phrase. "The Indian prime minister arrived in Saigon after visiting Communist China *today*." *Today* belongs after *Saigon,* because it is intended to fix the time of arrival. As the sentence stands, *today* may be taken as fixing the time of the visit to China.

Shifting the time element or any other part of a sentence away from its natural position lays emphasis on the part shifted. This should only be done intentionally.

Sometimes the time element would be better left out because it misleads or confuses. In the following examples, *today* is obtrusive and ludicrous—it suggests that a long-continuing situation is of only a day's duration:

The Soviet Communist chief is in trouble *today*. He is fighting valiantly to hold together the empire left him by his predecessors.

The competitive athletic program here is on the rocks *today* because of a decision earlier this week to close the school gym.

An 80-year-old nun stood firm *today* (is standing firm) against plans to turn her little nation into a Communist state.

A peculiar effect is often created when the day of the week is named: "John Jones *Thursday* shot his brother-in-law." Some newspapers follow this style instead of saying *yesterday* on the theory that the time is then more exactly specified. Certain captious critics have said, however, that *John Jones Thursday* may leave the impression that *Thursday* is John's last name. At any rate, this construction is still open to the same criticism that applies to misplacement of *today* and *yesterday*—clumsy word order.

Writing in the magazine *Editor & Publisher,* Arden Benthien, managing editor of the *Idaho Free Press,* was taken aback by a defense of journalese mannerisms as making for a bright, modern news style. It called to mind, he said, a conversation he heard while visiting a friend whose nephew worked for a press association.

When the lad came home after his day's stint, his uncle greeted him, and the following conversation ensued:
Where did you eat lunch today?"
"I today ate lunch at Joe's."
"That's nice. Anything exciting in the news?"
"A fire of undetermined origin Friday gutted a downtown warehouse."
That's too bad. Anything else?"
"A 33-year-old Center City man today was killed when his car failed to negotiate a curve."
"Mercy. Who was it?"
"Dead is Rufus S. Hencoop."
"That's terrible. Were there any important statements during the day?"
"The 53-year-old executive secretary of the State Association for the Advancement of Civilization today said the Vietnam War was unfortunate. Digbus X. Mishmash told the audience that the war protesters had been on the right track."
"Just a minute. Who is Digbus X. Mishmash?"
"He's the 53-year-old executive secretary of the—Uncle Albert, sometimes I don't think you are listening to me."
"Oh, I listen, all right. It's just that I—let it go. Dinner will be ready soon."
The young fellow went on, and we sat silent for a moment.
"Nice lad," I volunteered.
"Yes," my friend said, "except for—tell me frankly, did it strike you he talks kind of funny?"
"Oh, no," I assured him.
Anyone who thinks I can't supply samples of this kind of thing from the wire copy that comes across my desk had better not bet the baby's shoes on it.

Conclusion

Many of the objectionable peculiarities of journalese could be cured if reporters and copy editors would follow the model of conversation. That is, they might well ask themselves, "Would I *say* it this way?" and if the answer is no, recast accordingly. Spoken expression is looser, often more ungrammatical than what is written, because the writer is more careful and self-conscious than the talker. But talking is also more idiomatic and less stilted than writing. Many of the faults discussed in this chapter can be cured by putting things conversationally instead of casting them in some of the artificial patterns that have become habitual in much journalism.

Wayward Words

8

This chapter is the first of five in which recurrent faults of newswriting that should be corrected by the copy editor will be examined. Although newswriting should be simple and conversational, it is sometimes pompous. For example, unnecessary alarm is often caused among journalists by words described as colloquialisms. Many journalists seem to think a word so designated is poor usage or is unacceptable for some vague reason.

Webster's *New International Dictionary,* 2nd ed. (1934), has an enlightening comment on the subject of colloquialisms:

Colloquial Writing

"It is unfortunate that with some the term *colloquial* has somewhat fallen into disrepute, the impression having gained ground that a word marked *colloquial* in a dictionary or similar work is thereby condemned as not in the best use. See the definition of *colloquial* in the vocabulary." The definition ran: "Colloquial, adj. Pertaining to, or used in conversation, esp. familiar conversation; hence, informal."

The opposite of informal is formal, and in further discussion Webster said that colloquialisms are appropriate in informal writing, among other places, but not in formal written discourse.

Well, what is formal written discourse, anyway? Proclamations and diplomatic communications, which are turgid and often laughable in their choice of language, surely come under this heading. So do legal documents, about whose pomposity even lawyers are growing uneasy, to judge from indictments of legal lingo that have been published in bar-association journals.

Journalists should not shun the conversational or the informal unless they also want to drive off the reader. Even the academician turns with a sigh of relief from the scholarly journal to something written with the pleasure of the reader in mind.

On the unassailable ground that it is impossible to know whether a word out of context is colloquial or not, the third edition of Webster (1961) abandoned the use of *colloquial* as a status label. Some dictionaries now use *informal* to designate words formerly classified as colloquial.

Contractions

The avoidance of contractions is another aspect of the fear of informal writing. The attitude toward contractions usually ranges from outright prohibition to discouragement "except when appropriate." Discouragement of this kind would be all right except that it is usually interpreted as a general ban. Many of us seemingly often lack confidence in our ability to decide when contractions *are* appropriate.

The fact is that the objectionable use of contractions is rare. Rudolf Flesch, in *The Art of Readable Writing,* came to this conclusion: "If you want to write informal English, the use of contractions is certainly essential."

A little girl who had to walk through a graveyard on her way home was asked, "Aren't you afraid?" After this question had gone through the hands of a copy editor terrified by contractions, however, it came out "Are you not afraid?"

Then there was the headline on a feature story that read "It is official! June was hot!" Well, "It is official" is rather stiff; many a reader must have boggled at it, wondering what reason could be given for sidestepping "It's official."

Technical Terms

Should news stories use technical terms that are not common in preference to thoroughly familiar substitutes? Experts on readability say no. Nevertheless, the use of technical language, or of the cant belonging to a specialized field, is a temptation to writers who think it will make their work sound learned and impressive.

The use of technical terms is hard to avoid in writing that deals with advances in physics, medicine, and the other sciences, and often no satisfactory synonyms are available in plain language. The writer who keeps the audience in mind, however, is careful to follow unfamiliar technical terms with definitions written in language that is as simple as possible.

Science writing, a special case, is usually handled by writers who make it a specialty and who have no need to be warned of such pitfalls. But what about writing that deals with such everyday subjects as automobile accidents? Such accounts often abound with *contusions, abrasions, lacerations, fractures,* and other terms redolent of the hospital. Everybody knows, of course, that a fracture is a break. Lacerations are cuts, although the doctor may mean something more complex by this expression. It is doubtful that *contusions* presents any clear picture to the layperson. What's wrong with *bruises* instead of *contusions, cuts* instead of *lacerations,* and *sewing* or *stitches* instead of *suturing* and *sutures?* This much is certain: although many readers may know what the medical terms mean, many more do not.

Hemorrhage is certainly inexcusable for *bleed* in anything but a medical journal. *Coronary occlusion, carcinoma, thrombosis,* and *first-, second-,* and *third-degree burns* all need to be translated for the layperson. Familiar equivalents, or at least approximations, should be obtained from medical sources.

It is a good principle not to send the reader to the dictionary, but to send the writer or copy editor there instead. Let the reader relax.

In one city, an outbreak of sleeping sickness (encephalitis) was attributed to the *culex tarsalis* mosquito. Newspaper stories on the subject, which caused considerable public alarm, ran for weeks before anyone thought of describing *culex tarsalis* and its habits and giving some idea how common this mosquito was among the dozen or so varieties in the area.

In another instance, the term *low low water line* was used again and again in connection with an important waterfront project. Yet no one but seafarers knew what that line was, and the newspapers failed to give any help to the others.

Conscientious writers avoid wordiness and strive to convey a story in the fewest words possible. Writers who let fly a barrage of words ought to be told that they lose their force in bunches. A few well-chosen words will convey ideas more clearly. In general, the fewer the words the better the writing.

Redundancy

The habit of using several words where one will serve may be illustrated by *a sufficient number of* vs. *enough; at the present time* vs. *now;* and *in the immediate vicinity of* vs. *near.* These woolly expressions occur so often that they pop readily into the mind. Hunting them down is a salutary exercise for the copy editor.

A repulsive pair of expressions has grown onto the word *future: in the near future* and *in the not-too-distant future.* Translated, *in the near future* means *soon,* and *in the not-too-distant future* can mean *before long, eventually, finally, next year, sometime,* or *sooner or later.* The reader, poor wretch, must decide.

The word *case* is the progenitor of a hardy breed of villains that seem impervious to attack: *in case (if), in most cases (usually), if that were the case (if so), not the case (not so), in the case of* (which often may be omitted entirely, and if not, replaced by *concerning*), and *as in the case of (like).*

Here is a little beauty: "It is possible that this material may become mixed with clouds in some cases and induce rain sooner than otherwise would have been the case." Stripping this down to what counts, we get "This material may become mixed with clouds and bring rain sooner than otherwise."

Some redundancies have become classical targets of critics: *at the intersection of Market and Main (at Market and Main); consensus of opinion (consensus); entirely destroyed (destroyed).* Also undeservedly popular: *despite the fact that (although), due to the fact that (because* or *since), during the period from (from), during the course of (during), for the purpose of (for).*

Ignorance of what common words mean, or unwillingness to trust them to do their job unaided, is responsible for some specimens of redundancy. *Experience, records, custom,* and *history* come only from the past; thus there is no occasion for *past experience, past records, past custom,* and *past history. Gifts* and *passes* are by definition *free.* An *innovation* is by its nature *new,* as are a *beginner* and a *tyro,* and an *incumbent* is inescapably of the *present. Plans* are willy-nilly of the future, as must be *prospects* and *developments. Planning* can be nothing but *advance.*

What is *friendship* if it is not *personal?* And what is *business* if not *official? Both agreed* offends the thin-skinned, for *both* is two taken together and *agreement* is a coming together. *Equally as* is a horse of the same color. *On account of* is distasteful for *because of,* and *in excess of* is even worse for *more than* because it is not only redundant but pompous.

"In order to balance the budget" might better be simply *to balance. In back of* is a gaucherie for *behind. Advance reservations* seem to be getting ahead of themselves. *In which* is often superfluous, as in "Candidates will be given fifteen minutes *in which* to express their views." An accident victim is taken to a hospital *for treatment,* inevitably; why labor it?

New construction is Navyese for a ship being assembled; why apply it to buildings, when nothing is more self-evident than the newness of what is under construction?

The reason for avoiding redundancy was best stated by William Strunk, Jr. in *The Elements of Style:* "Vigorous writing is concise. A sentence should contain no unnecessary words, a paragraph no unnecessary sentences, for the same reason that a drawing should have no unnecessary lines and a machine no unnecessary parts."

Repetition

Is it true, as it seems to be, that newswriters do not trust the reader to remember what they have just written? If not, why can't newswriters be content to allow what they have set down to stand, without repeating or restating it in some obvious way? What has been said in the lead paragraph, especially, is likely to stick in the reader's mind, for that is what prompts the decision to read on.

Bald repetition of phrases and sentences seems to imply a lack of confidence that the words have sunk in. This is no tribute to the reader's intelligence, nor does it reflect any credit on the writer's.

"The president, smiling broadly, said today that ever since he was 5 years old his brother has been criticizing him." Good enough. But two paragraphs later we get this warmed-over dish: "Smiling broadly, the chief executive replied that his brother had been criticizing him since he was 5 years old."

"The lumber strike is over, and the president of the union calls it 'a draw.'" Passing by the unnecessary quotes around *a draw,* let us proceed to the second paragraph: "'We neither won nor lost the strike. It was a draw,' said George Willard . . ." All right, it was a draw, as the union president saw it. But after having established this in the lead, why not omit it from the next paragraph?

Repetition of Defining Modifiers

The useless repetition of defining modifiers is another common fault. A person who has been identified as a hotel porter should be referred to as *the porter* rather than *the hotel porter*. The examples that follow illustrate other instances of excessive identification (the descriptives that should be omitted are in parentheses).

> George Jones was found guilty of second-degree murder today. A jury composed of seven men and five women returned the (second-degree) verdict after five hours. The (second-degree) (murder) conviction carries a penalty of five years to life.
>
> A dinner will be held Sunday at 7 p.m. Reservations (for the dinner) may be made by telephone.

It is a mark of an undeveloped style to purposelessly sum up what has just been said. Summaries should be made deliberately, with a view to assisting the reader, and should not betray fuzzy-mindedness in the writer, as in these instances (the improved version follows in parentheses):

> He became pastor of the church when it was completed two years ago. Prior to accepting the pastorate, he was a student. (Before that, he was a student.)
>
> They tried to break a safe out of a 500-pound block of concrete. Failing to free the safe from the concrete, they fled. (Failing, they fled.)

Taste

It should be understood that the copy editor must be on the alert against tastelessness. Tragedy, even misfortune, is no fit subject for humor or levity. Treatment of this kind offends sensitive readers, to say nothing of the subjects of the stories, and reflects adversely on the newspaper. An example of this kind of thing was cited in a letter by Stewart H. Benedict, a copy editor with the *Jersey City Journal*, to the magazine *Editor & Publisher*:

> John Brabasco doesn't have to search for his daughter any longer. Four-year-old Brenda was found Tuesday, dead in a creek. . . .

This probably was not so much an attempt at humor as a thoughtless shift in mood, as Benedict suggested. But the effect was the same as if humor had been attempted and, sad to relate, the example came from a wire story. Benedict sardonically listed a number of hypothetical leads in the same vein:

> Mary Todd Lincoln probably won't be much of a playgoer any more.
>
> Dallas undoubtedly isn't on Jacqueline Kennedy's list of favorite American cities today.
>
> Real estate values in Hiroshima are lower today.

If a news story means misfortune to its subjects, humor, levity or a lighthearted tone are out of place. Such stories should be handled with the utmost seriousness, and of course this applies also to their headlines.

Too Long Leads

Another fault that copy editors should beware of is the overlong or complicated lead paragraph. It is from this paragraph, in addition to the headline, that the reader gets an idea of what the story is about, and if the lead is perplexing, the story may go unread. Consider: "The former girlfriend of a man charged with killing a Middletown bar owner almost four years ago testified Monday that she had never seen another man who claims he killed the victim and that she was with him that night."

This mare's nest is almost impenetrable and utterly confusing. Close study of the story was necessary to determine what the state of affairs was. Matters were not helped by the fact that the whole thing was more or less muddled. The lead could have been simplified to "The assertion by a man that he committed a murder for which another man is on trial was contradicted in court yesterday."

Dull, repetitive leads should also be improved. The lead should arouse the reader's interest, not kill it. "Arthur C. Clarke, science fiction author, discussed the space program and the future of an advanced communications system yesterday in the Civic Auditorium." To begin with, the speech had been publicized in advance, and thus the lead says nothing much that readers might not be expected to know or assume already. In these circumstances, some particularly interesting point made by the speaker should be singled out for the lead: "Critics of the space program were challenged by Arthur C. Clarke . . . " or "Permanent bases on the moon will be established by the end of the century. . . ." Both these possibilities and others were included in the text of the story.

Unanswered Questions

The copy editor should watch for "holes in the story"; that is, questions the story raises in the mind of the reader but fails to answer. One such story, which was played on the front page and ran about 200 words, told how a woman had confessed that she killed her brother-in-law because he would not give her a phonograph record. What kind of record, readers must have wondered, would have provoked such ferocity? Was it rock or classical? Did the woman want it for herself or did she want to smash it because she had heard it too often? The reader could only guess, because the story gave no hint.

A news account told how a member of the Korean parliament had thrown filth on another, thereby bringing on a cabinet crisis. What kind of filth?—after all, filth is only a woolly and general term. Mud? Readers of this paper had to await the arrival of a news magazine to find out: human excrement. Not a pretty story, but precision was essential here. Sometimes, of course, the answers to material questions are not available. But the newspaper should at least have the wit to acknowledge that a story raises an unanswered question and to indicate what effort was made to get the answer.

Ellipsis is the grammarian's word for omission of what is readily understood. It is a useful device that should be encouraged, short of ambiguity or conveying a misleading idea. Let us consider instances in which ellipsis is and is not desirable.

Ellipsis

Usually an element may be profitably omitted from the second of parallel constructions in which it would be repeated in the same position. Often such constructions involve numerical comparisons. In the examples cited, the words in parentheses would be better left out:

McDonald said 189,344 members are on leave and 257,026 (members are) on part-time schedules.

In 1958 there were 21 days of 100-plus readings and in 1953 there were 20 (days of 100-degree or higher weather). Here, afraid to repeat *100-plus readings,* the writer strained to invent a variation; it would have been better to end on *20.*

The plant is capable of handling 650 tons per hour, but is handling only 500 (tons per 60 minutes). The substitution of *60 minutes* as a variant for *hour* may strike some readers as ingenious, but it will strike many others, alas, as stupid. This fault is discussed under the next heading, "Variation."

Jones was cited for driving without due caution, and Smith (was cited) for driving without a license.

Turnover totaled 420,000 shares, well below Monday's 570,000 (share figure).

The college has enrolled 10 percent more full-time students this year than (were registered for classes) at the end of the first week of school last year.

Words that may be omitted may involve a comparison rather than a repetition: "The king is now more firmly on his throne than (he ever had been) since he was crowned."

Sometimes, however, it will not do to fail to repeat verb forms: "On her arrival, she was told the job was filled and *offered* $100 as expense money." This should read *was offered.* As it stands, *offered* is ambiguous, and it may sound as if the applicant were doing the offering.

"The executive said another firm *has* or is about to file for a franchise." This should be *has filed,* for the missing word is not smoothly supplied by the reader.

Another form of ellipsis is recommended in relative clauses, usually those starting with *which, who,* or *that*. The idea has sometimes been stated in this way: Cancel the pronoun *(which, who, that)* plus companion forms of *to be (is, are, was, were)* when they can be dispensed with, which is always self-evident. This is how it works (in each example, omit the words in parentheses):

There is a difference between what they announce as crop yields and the amount (that is) available to the people.

Work is under way on an ice rink (that is) scheduled to open next month.

The bridge would give access to the island, (which is) now served by a ferry.

Members of the Pioneer Methodist Church, (which was) built in 1858, will celebrate next week.

Elman, (who was) an amateur musician before he escaped, now performs professionally.

That or *which* may also be omitted when they are the subjects of verb forms other than *to be*.

Sibelius was stricken with a brain hemorrhage at the villa (which) he built near Helsinki 53 years before.

Local issues were responsible for the clobbering (which) the Republicans took in the Maine election.

Ellipsis of a different kind is employed to shorten quotations for the writer's purpose. In these instances the reader must be placed on notice that a curtailed version is being given: "The speaker said the book was 'ill-conceived, hastily written . . . and obviously the work of an ignoramus.' " Usually a paraphrase is preferable to this form of ellipsis. The use of dots for this purpose is standard, having displaced *x*'s and asterisks.

Variation

Variation merely to avoid repetition of a term is not only worse than repetition, as Fowler said, but may suggest a distinction that does not exist. The problem is often neatly solved by ellipsis: "He *played with* Charlie Barnet's Orchestra and *worked with* Red Norvo's Sextet." The writer was merely straining to avoid repeating the same words to express the same idea. Instead, ". . . played with Charlie Barnet's Orchestra and Red Norvo's Sextet" could have been used.

"Russia's army newspaper *Red Star* claims there are now 33 million Communist Party members in 75 nations. The breakdown gave Indonesia 1 million. France was said to have 5 million Red voters; Italy, 1.8 million card-carriers." Are Communist Party members, Red voters, and card-carriers the same? The writer assumed this to be true, but of course it is not. The changes are rung unnecessarily. Once it has been established that *Communist Party members* is the idea under discussion, the writer might have trusted the reader's memory beyond Indonesia; "France was said to have 5 million; Italy, 1.8 million."

In other common instances, such variation is merely silly: "About 76 percent of Russia's doctors are *women,* while in the United States only 6 percent are *female." Women* would have been better repeated, or "But the proportion in the United States is only 6 percent" could have been used.

"Cigarette smokers *puffed* a record 205 billion cigarettes in the first six months of this year, 4.4 percent more than they *lit up* in the same period last year." Lighting up and puffing are different things, and the variation needs explaining: ". . . 4.4 percent more than in the same period last year."

"In cases where both parents are *obese,* 72 percent of the off-spring also are *fat.* When one parent is *fat,* 41 percent of the children are *overweight.* When neither parent is *obese,* only 4 percent of the offspring are *fat."* This writer danced an ungainly dance between *obese, fat,* and *overweight* on one hand, and between *children* and *offspring* on the other. A better way: "When both parents are fat, 72 percent of the children are. When one parent is fat, 41 percent of the children are. When neither parent is fat, only 4 percent of the children are."

Desirable information about locale or anything else should be offered for its own sake and not made a device to avoid naming the place again. One aspect of what Fowler called elegant variation might be described as the geographical fetish, since it requires that the second reference to a place should take the form of a geographical description. In Southern California, under these ground rules, it is permissible to name San Francisco once, but the second time it is mentioned it must become *the northern city.* Other samples of this aberration are: "The caravan plans a dinner in Podunk and an overnight stop in the Razorback County city" and "A three-day international convention opened today in Nagasaki on the anniversary of the atom bombing of the southern Japanese city."

From map-making, the fashioners of this kind of prose often graduate into zoological classification: "Children who want to enter a frog in the event may pick up an amphibian at the Chamber of Commerce office." Here, pearls of another branch of knowledge are being cast before readers, but they may not appreciate it. What's wrong with *an overnight stop there* instead of *an overnight stop in the Razorback County city,* or *may pick one up* instead of *may pick up an amphibian*?

"A search for a mountain lion was abandoned when no sign of *such a carnivore* was found." *Such a carnivore* is a pompous substitute for *such an animal* or even *one.* Here are some common latter-day examples of elegant variation: *simian* for *monkey, jurist* for *judge, bovine* for *cow, feline* for *cat, quadruped* for any four-legged animal, *equine* for *horse, optic* for *eye, tome* for *book, white stuff* for *snow.*

The printed word is a powerful educative force, but it is questionable whether calling an oyster *a bivalve,* an elephant *a pachyderm,* a dog *a canine,* gold *the yellow metal,* legislators *solons,* or professors *savants* has contributed anything to public uplift.

False Comparison

Careless reporters who carry ellipsis too far stumble into false comparison. They write "Older houses are still selling here, unlike many cities" or "Like many patient folk, Russian violence can be brutal." If they stayed alert, they would see the need for ". . . unlike *those in* many cities" and ". . . like *that of* many patient folk." The fault in such instances is that a relative pronoun (usually *that*) and a preposition have been omitted. In the examples, as a result, *older houses* are unintentionally compared with *many cities,* and *patient folk* with *Russian violence.*

Here are other examples. (The originally omitted, but necessary, words are in parentheses):

> Addiction in California appears to differ from (that in) other states.
>
> Robert Sarnoff, president, admitted that NBC's situation was in some ways tougher than (that of) the other networks.
>
> Five bids were lower than (that of) the American Seating Company.

Sometimes the error is caused by omitting the preposition alone, as in "Receipts from livestock sales were 7 percent less than the corresponding period last year." The receipts were not less than the corresponding period, as reported, but less than *those in* the corresponding period.

"An illusion of reality can be more completely brought to an audience on the screen than (by) any other medium" is another example of the error of false comparison, caused by omitting the preposition.

Parallelism

Parallelism is the name given to following the same pattern with consecutive constructions that naturally fall into it. It makes for ease in reading and, therefore, is to be encouraged. Many offenses against parallelism consist in switching verb forms: "It is a matter of *letting* tavern owners know their rights and *to avoid* confusion" *(of letting* should be matched by *of avoiding).*

> Benson said the only real answer to the dairy-surplus problem seems to be *to push* consumption of butter through regular marketing channels and *encouraging* farmers to get rid of inefficient cows. *(to push:: to encourage)*
>
> The unit will contain air-to-ground voice equipment *for transmitting* traffic-control instructions and *to obtain* position reports from aircraft. *(for transmitting:: for obtaining)*

Vladimir Petrov was reported as *having asked for* and *was granted* asylum in Australia. *(having asked for:: having been granted)*

Parallelism is desirable in other instances than those involving verb forms:

The fight ends when the losing cricket breaks away from *his* conqueror and is promptly removed from the cage by *its* owner. (*Its* should be used consistently.)

One of the officers was suspended *for 10* days, and the other for *a 5-day period*. (It should read *for 10 days,* and . . . *for 5 days.*)

The production models will have *a speed* of 85 miles an hour, *a range* of 150 miles, and *carry* 800 pounds. (For correctness here, use *and a capacity of 800.*)

Euphemisms

Life is a hard business, and we often seek to soften its blows by giving them agreeable names. This device—for example, saying *passed away* instead of *died*—is known technically as *euphemism,* or pleasing talk. Euphemism is not something that can or should be done away with. Often the bluntest names for things are disagreeable in polite society and distasteful in print.

But writers should at least be aware when they are using terms that are not the most explicit versions. Euphemisms are objectionable when they indicate unnecessary squeamishness. The trend of our ordinary expression for many years has been away from the complex, the pretentious, and the flowery, and toward the simple, the unassuming, and the unadorned.

Not so long ago, *social disease* was as close as anyone but a doctor would come to saying *syphilis* or *gonorrhea*—and even the euphemism was used with reluctance. In fact, the medical campaign to curb syphilis was seriously impeded by the refusal, at first, of newspapers even to name the disease.

Let's skip around among some typical euphemisms. A cut or increase in wages or prices is often glossed over, when it seems desirable, as *a downward revision* or *an upward revision* or *adjustment.* In the jargon of business, especially, prices tend not to be raised, but are delicately *revised upward.* This may be all right for the public relations person, whose vocation is to gloss, but certainly such genteelisms should not be adopted with the idea that they possess some desirable elegance.

Realistic is a key euphemism in collective and other kinds of bargaining. *Realistic,* in this connection, is what the speaker's proposals are in contrast to those of the other side, which are invariably *unrealistic.*

Planned withdrawal has become familiar as the military's euphemism for *a retreat*. General Jonathan Wainwright was so outraged by this kind of mush that he described one reverse in these unequivocal terms: "We took a hell of a beating." The name *Woman's Christian Temperance Union* is a misnomer, for its members advocate abstinence, not temperance. *Abstinence* has an unyielding sound, however, and it may be that the temperance union members can stand the shock of solid words no more than they can stand the fumes of hard drink. *Belly,* though perfectly acceptable, is often considered suspect, if not vulgar: genteel people speak only of the *abdomen.*

Dictionaries

A lack of esteem for dictionaries prevails in some quarters on the ground that they are not infallible. This, of course, is true, as it is of all human endeavors. Scorn for dictionaries was encouraged by the testy Ambrose Bierce, who acidly wrote them off as bloated, absurd, and misleading. In their place, presumably, or perhaps to counteract their evil influence, he offered his own revelation, *Write It Right* (1909). This little book, now pretty much a curiosity, contains considerable patches that don't make much sense any more.

If you turn from the dictionary in haughty superiority, what are you going to turn to? Your own notions of usage, meanings, and mechanical practices? They are likely to be only prejudices and not very well founded. Reputable dictionaries, with all their faults, are the work of platoons of lexicographers who assiduously study words, consult experts in special fields, and analyze writing and speech at all levels to determine what accepted practice really is.

About the worst thing that can be said (and substantiated) about dictionaries is that they are likely to be behind the times. This is hardly avoidable, because a major revision takes years. Sometimes a new word may be born, live gloriously, and die in the interim between editions. Scientific terms, especially in these times, are invented and come into fairly wide use between editions, too.

But such changes are comparatively rare. The great body of the language shifts and takes new directions, but does so very slowly. Divergence from the fiats of the dictionary might most constructively take the form of a more liberal attitude toward slang and toward old words that are swimming into new orbits.

Many are misled by the order in which dictionaries list the various senses of a word. The Merriam-Webster dictionaries, for example, explain in a preface that the order of their definitions follows their historical use in English. But many people assume that the first definition is the most widely accepted one, or at least the one that is unexceptionable in modern usage.

The *American College Dictionary* follows the plan of placing central or common meanings first, and the obsolete, archaic, and rare meanings at the end. This practice seems better suited to the needs of the general user of the dictionary, as contrasted with the scholar.

It is well for journalists to understand that any definition that appears in a dictionary indicates standard usage, regardless of whether it appears early or late, unless it is qualified by some such label as *substandard*. And when a dictionary gives more than one spelling for a word, it means only that the word listed first is the commoner, but all are correct. When more than one spelling is given for a common word, like *employe* (employee) or *cigaret* (cigarette), newspapers sometimes specify in their stylebooks which version is to be used.

Conclusion

In this chapter we have begun a discussion of some of the commoner faults of newswriting that should be corrected by the copy editor. The discussion has covered the meaning of the term *colloquial* and has dealt also with the acceptability of contractions, the use of technical terms in news stories, redundancy, unnecessary repetition, taste, long leads, unanswered questions, ellipsis (omission), variation, false comparison, parallelism, euphemisms, and the use of dictionaries.

9 Watch Your Language

Let us continue the examination of faults in newswriting to which the copy editor must be alert.

Clumsy Construction

Sentence Inversion

The inversion of sentences—that is, standing them on their heads—creates a kind of linguistic smog that puts readers to work sorting out the disarranged words, causes their eyes to smart, and perhaps makes them wish they were reading something else. A desperate straining for variety in sentence structure seems to be the cause of inversion.

Here is an example: "Encouraging the United States were Britain and France." The normal way to say this is "Britain and France were encouraging the United States"; or, passively, "The United States was being encouraged by Britain and France."

The usual word order has been varied by moving *encouraging* forward, but the variety may have been gained at too high a price. Americans, unlike Germans and ancient Romans, are not used to holding some element of a sentence in suspension until the other pieces of the jigsaw puzzle come along, and there is no reason why they should get used to it. Inversion, of course, is not wrong; it is just overdone in much newswriting.

Poets have an excuse for this kind of thing when they need to place the word with the desired rhyme at the end of the line. But they at least can plead poetic license.

When a reporter who wrote "Hiring the men will be ranchers in the vicinity" was asked whether he had a license to mangle prose, he only reddened and fell silent. But he amended the sentence to "The men will be hired by ranchers in the vicinity."

Writing such as "Damaged were the cars of two motorists" and "Suffering minor injuries in the crash was his wife, Viola" and "Caught in the school during the explosion were 20 students" is gawky and inexcusable. These examples call to mind the line from Wolcott Gibbs' classic satire on *Time:* "Backward ran sentences until reeled the mind." No word-mincer, Gibbs.

Emphasis is given to a word that is taken out of its normal position. When a sentence is disarranged for no other reason than to gain variety in its structure, the effect may be awkward. The reader gets an impression of emphasis where emphasis makes no sense. Better methods are available for structural variety.

The uprooted word is not always an auxiliary verb; it may be an adjective, as in "Responsible for all cultural questions is a key member of the city administration." There is no good reason for turning the sentence upside down.

Misplaced Modifiers

FOR SALE: *Piano, by a lady going to Europe with carved legs.*

The authors of books on grammar are so fond of quoting examples like this that we might expect such errors to be extinct by now. The cure for this kind of thing is simple: Critically reread what you have written. The following examples and their corrected versions illustrate misplacement of modifiers:

Details are slipping out of plans for the first Soviet-bloc beauty contest. (Details of plans for the first Soviet-bloc beauty contest are slipping out.)

Hospital attendants said the baby had a history since birth of heart disease. (Hospital attendants said the baby had a history of heart disease since birth.)

They held at gunpoint the woman in her home for four hours. (They held the woman at gunpoint . . .)

The group opposed a proposal calling for a written definition of the positions on disarmament of the great powers. (The group opposed a proposal calling for a written definition of the positions of the great powers on disarmament.)

The Israelis were accused of firing on the Egyptian post of Deir el Balat for 10 minutes without causing casualties. (The Israelis were accused of firing . . . for 10 minutes. There were no casualties.)

He said every chance would be given to complete satisfactorily the negotiations. (He said every chance would be given to complete the negotiations satisfactorily.)

An applicant for a federal job should have a chance to explain informally derogatory information. (An applicant . . . should have a chance to explain derogatory information informally.)

Gerund Construction

Clumsy construction comes of putting a gerund between *the* and *of.* In *The Taming of the Shrew* and *The Shooting of Dan McGrew,* however, it accomplishes what is desired; namely, setting *taming* and *shooting* in the forefront.

"Stevens repeated that the responsibility for *the filing of* the charges was his." In this and other examples that will be held up for criticism, it is recommended that *the* and *of* be left out: "Stevens repeated that the responsibility for filing the charges . . ."; "Officials plan to save considerable time in *the* conducting *of* the charity drive." (It should read, ". . . *in conducting the* . . .") As Perrin notes in *Writer's Guide and Index to English,* the omission of *the* and *of* emphasizes the verbal phase of the word and makes for economy and force.

Attribution

Attribution is the term for citing the source of the facts in a news story. It is an extremely important consideration, because it gives the reader an idea how authoritative the information is. Harold Ross, the founding editor of the *New Yorker,* when selecting cartoons for publication, sometimes asked, "Who's talking?" because the artist had not indicated clearly where the words beneath the cartoon were coming from. The same question confronts the newswriter and copy editor: the source must be clearly identified. Sometimes the source cannot be specifically named because the reporter has pledged confidentiality. But some indication of the source, if necessary an anonymous one, must be given; otherwise the story becomes an expression of the writer's or the newspaper's opinion. This, as all who have studied newswriting know, is editorializing, and has no place in a news story.

Usually, the writer merely names the source and does not quote it directly unless the statements by the source are cutting, offensive, or, on the other hand, witty or entertaining. The copy editor must see to it that controversial expressions of opinion are attributed. Sometimes, statements are quoted directly to convey the flavor of the speaker's talk: "I should've stood in bed."

Attribution of a libelous statement does not remove the danger of suit; a newspaper is responsible for whatever it prints, whether the statement is ascribed to someone else or not, or whether the paper agrees with what has been said. Libel is discussed in more detail in chapter 13.

Troubles with attribution probably have their root in police and court stories, where there is danger of libel. The young reporter quickly learns that damaging statements must be ascribed to the authorities or to privileged documents. The danger of harming someone is impressed on the writer so unforgettably that attribution seems like a virtue.

Like other principles, attribution, when slavishly followed, sometimes carries writers overboard, even in police stories. Here is an example: "*Highway patrolmen said* the car skidded 80 feet before striking the truck, which, *they said,* was parked on the shoulder." Can anyone reasonably hold that the first *said* will not alone easily carry the weight of all that follows?

It sounds silly to attribute innocuous bits of general information, but one school of thought seems to insist on attributing *everything* in police stories. Thus, "The lake is about 20 miles from Podunk and about 12 miles in circumference, *the officers reported.*" The net effect of this is to suggest to the reader that the paper has no confidence in any part of the story. Obviously, the italicized words should be omitted. Such great caution might well result in "The sun rose on schedule, *according to the investigator.*"

Stories about crimes in which no arrest has been made hardly need more than one citation of the source, for an unidentified lawbreaker cannot be libeled. Similarly, the fact of an arrest is a matter of public record and needs no qualification.

Misleading Attribution

Attribution has become such a mania that newswriters sometimes end by saying the opposite of what they intended. In this way they unintentionally associate themselves (or their newspapers) with statements they really want to ascribe specifically to the speaker. A number of commonly and carelessly used expressions imply that what is being quoted, directly or indirectly, is fact. *Pointed out* is one of those expressions: "The senator has an ugly record of broken promises, his opponent *pointed out.*" The effect of this is that the writer, or the newspaper, concurs in the accusation. Even if this is so, such acquiescence hardly has a place in the news columns.

Similar impressions are created by *as* ("as she said"), and by *admitted, noted, conceded, explained,* and *cited the fact that.* "A young TV comedian admitted in New York that all funny people are sick and desperately in need of psychoanalysis." The effect here is not so much that the writer agrees, but that the speaker is conceding a generally accepted fact. There was no occasion for *admitted,* because the point of view being expressed was a novel one, at least at the time.

Other bits of heedlessness can unintentionally convict, as in "The couple were indicted as spies by a federal grand jury, but have denied *their* guilt." *Their* assumes the couple are guilty; *denied they were guilty* would be neutral.

There is also such a thing as winking at the reader and saying, by implication, "Take this with a grain of salt." That is what the use of *according to* does. When that expression does not cast a shadow on the credibility of the speaker, it may merely sound non-sensical, as in "The Rev. John Jones will ask the invocation, according to the chairperson." It is usually preferable to have the speaker simply *say, report,* or *announce,* instead of using the *according to* formula. *Said they believe,* in place of either *said* or *believe,* also may erect a small BEWARE sign in that it may imply the source is not necessarily to be trusted.

Disclose and *reveal* are appropriate only in reference to that which has been concealed. It's stupid to write of the time of a dinner as *disclosed,* or the name of a Rotary Club speaker as *revealed. Report* and *announce* are better.

Sometimes attribution, though called for, is doubled. "The secretary and her associates were criticized for what the committee said were 'political and other considerations.' " Either *what the committee said* or the quotation marks should suffice. "Truman told reporters that his memoirs would explain what he said was the part Eisenhower played in the incident." *What he said was* indicates unnecessary caution. In giving the substance of reports and the like, it is superfluous to tack *the report said* or something of the kind onto every sentence, unless the copy is questionable or damaging.

Advise, contend, and *claim* are sadly overworked and at the same time inexactly used in attribution. *Advise,* when it displaces *say, announce,* or *report,* as in "The meeting will be postponed, he advised," is journalese. Some stylebooks say, "Save *advise* for giving advice." *Contend* is suitable only where there is contention or disagreement, and *insist* only where there is insistence. *Claim* may excusably be bent out of shape in headlines in the sense of *say* or *assert,* but in text, where there is no such space problem, it is questionable in that sense: "The informant claimed he did not know the name of his source." *Stress* and *emphasize* are suitable only where there is indeed stress or emphasis.

Much hinges on the choice between *as* and *for* in certain attributive constructions. To say that a person was criticized *for* committing perjury is to imply that the perjury was committed, thus aligning the writer with the critic. To say that a person was criticized *as* committing perjury, on the other hand, places the burden of proof on the critic.

Said and Its Variants

The word *said* and its relations pose a problem for every reporter. Not many years ago it was customary for reporters to use *said* with the first of a series of quotes. Next came *asserted,* then perhaps *averred, declared,* and of course that old standby, *stated.* These and perhaps a few others, such as *opined,* were enough to see the writer through a typical interview. If not, it was considered legal to start over again with *said,* the theory being that readers would not realize by that time that they were getting a warmed-over word.

The whole point was not to use *said* or any of the others twice or twice in succession. The substitutes were dropped in heedlessly, as if they all meant exactly the same thing. No consideration was given to appropriateness.

There is abundant evidence that the *said* problem is with us still. A distinguished editor, citing an example of a poor choice of a substitute that resulted in a misleading and damaging statement, said (or perhaps declared), "There never was a verb better than *said.*" This enthusiasm, while understandable under the circumstances, may have been excessive.

Here are some expressions that can stand duty for *said,* when appropriate: *admitted, affirmed, agreed, vowed, barked, begged, bellowed, called, contended, cried, croaked, declaimed, demanded, disclosed, drawled, emphasized, exclaimed, hinted, implored, insisted, maintained, mumbled, murmured, muttered, pleaded, proclaimed, proposed, rejoined, retorted, roared, scolded, shouted, shrieked, yelled, wailed.* Some of these words, of course, can lead to trouble if used improperly or indiscreetly. Others are unquestionably touchy: *grumbled, insinuated, prated, ranted, spouted, stammered, whined, whimpered.* All are uncomplimentary to the speaker but may be called for in an accurate account.

Even so, there are neutral substitutes for *said* that will make for less stodgy writing: *added, announced, answered, asserted, commented, continued, declared, observed, remarked, replied, reported, responded, returned, stated.* Yet the choice among these, too, must be made with care to suit the context. *Stated* is overworked, and it conveys a tone of formality that is usually unsuitable.

Utterance by Proxy

The purported utterance of words by smiling, frowning, grimacing, laughing, and similarly impossible methods is frequently criticized.

> "Romance seems to be out of fashion these days," he grimaced.
> "I'd rather work from the neck up," the actress smiled.
> "This equipment is not included in the budget," the auditor frowned.

This is regarded by its users as a cute trick, and it may be only a fad that will have its day and cease to be. In a way, it appears to be an extension of what Ruskin deplored as "the pathetic fallacy"—ascribing lifelike acts to inanimate things, as in describing the sun as smiling.

Those who choose to use this device must be prepared to defend themselves against the logical complaint that words cannot be formed by smiling, frowning, and the like. Those who consider it absurd rather than cute will write *he said, grimacing; she said, smiling;* and *he said, frowning.*

Young writers often become addicted to inverted attribution; that is, instead of making it "he said" they write "said he"; instead of "Smith questioned," "questioned Smith." This device has a faintly poetic tinge and, like anything else that attracts attention to itself, quickly becomes tiresome and is to be avoided.

For the first reference to a preacher, either *the Rev. John Jones* or *Rev. John Jones* is acceptable, although *the Rev.* is considered preferable by sticklers. Thereafter, references should be in the form *the Rev. Mr. Jones,* or more simply, *Mr. Jones,* which is easier to remember and equally beyond criticism. Just plain *Jones* is acceptable, too, even to ministers themselves, although we are not likely to be so blunt with our spiritual mentors.

Quotation

The copy editor must have a clear idea of the difference between direct and indirect quotation. Direct quotations are the exact words of the speaker and are enclosed in quotation marks. More often, instead of using direct quotation, reporters will use indirect quotation, paraphrasing in their own words the news source's statements for the sake of brevity, being careful, of course, not to misrepresent what has been said.

Usually, in a continuing direct quotation it is not necessary to include an attribution in every paragraph. The quotation marks tell the reader that the same speaker is continuing. But if the quotation is extremely long, an attribution every three paragraphs or so will serve as a reminder.

The use of punctuation marks generally is minimized in newswriting, but the quotation mark is hopelessly overworked. This probably reflects anxiety lest the writer appear to be taking the responsibility for opinions or other questionable utterances. Often it will not do to take a chance that the reader may think the writer is talking.

Quotation marks, besides indicating the exact words of a speaker (or of a printed source), when placed around a word or phrase convey that they are to be understood in some other than their literal sense.

The reason for the superfluous quotation marks that confuse much newspaper writing is that the authors suffer from the delusion that they are using words in special senses when in fact they are using standard senses. There is a widespread though mistaken notion that every word has only one meaning, or at least only one that is unexceptionable. The definitions of some of the simplest and commonest words run on for columns in unabridged dictionaries. *Check,* for example, has more than 40 senses; *set* has 286. Before clapping quotation marks around words whose suitability they are uncertain of, journalists would be better advised to look them up. They would discover that most of the senses they feel doubtful about are standard and require no quotes. Nor is there anything to the idea that the order in which senses of a word are listed in a dictionary indicates preferential standing. All meanings given are standard unless otherwise noted (e.g., substandard, slang, dialectal).

Quotation marks are often used unnecessarily when only a word or a phrase is quoted in a sentence that already contains an attribution. The quoted words may have been the ones used by the speaker, but since the speaker has already been credited as the source of the information there is usually no reason for placing quotation marks around them. The press associations are especially fond of fragmentary quotations. Some wire stories are so peppered with fragmentary quotations that hardly a word is actually the writer's. Let's look at some examples:

He declined to say what "action" would be taken.

The department said "some" improvement is expected.

The secretary of commerce said the coming year would be one of the "most prosperous" in American history.

That, she said, would "delay" victory.

It is hard to see what is accomplished by any of these quotations. Nothing is gained by quoting minor fragments like these and the quotation marks clutter up the story. They also interfere with readability, for the reader necessarily pauses at a fragmentary quote to decide why the quotation marks are there. If this becomes too confusing, the reader may give up.

Are all fragmentary quotations, then, undesirable? By no means: "He accused the senator of making 'mean, untrue, and dastardly' statements." No objective account would take the responsibility for such hard words, and even though the statement is cast as an indirect quotation to begin with, the words in quotation marks warrant unmistakable attribution.

In general, however, only especially striking or significant matter should be quoted, and then preferably in complete sentences. Using complete sentences minimizes the danger of giving the wrong impression through quoting fragments out of context. The reporters' job is to present the meat of things in their own words, and they should not be excessively timid about it. To determine the usefulness of quotation marks, try leaving them off fragments. Generally, this test will show they add nothing.

Let us look at some instances when the writer mistakenly thought an expression was something other than standard:

The professor is likely to "hedge" in her answers on this subject.

He protested that the Army was "gagging" him.

Gone are the days when the private could "snub" the general off the post by keeping his hands at his sides.

Hedge, gagging, and *snub* are all standard words used in standard senses, and by enclosing them in quotation marks the writer was not only advertising ignorance of the fact, but causing the reader to stumble.

Quoting Slang

If writers use an expression that is in fact slang, they should decide whether it fits their context, and if so, they should use it forthrightly, without the apology that is intended by quotation marks: "They ripped off the store regularly." If the expression does not suit the context, it should not be used.

Sometimes a word may be used ironically and then it may be necessary to put the reader on notice: "For many years, Kansas was a 'dry' state." The context made clear that at a time when Kansas prohibited the sale of liquor, it was in fact dripping wet because of illegal sales. Instances like this are far rarer than one would guess from the profusion of quotation marks in newspaper stories.

Awkward Attribution of Direct Quotation

Quotations should not be broken into awkwardly for the attribution, or what is sometimes called the "speech tag": " 'I,' the producer said, 'will not accept this responsibility'." This not only interrupts at an undesirable place but lays a meaningless stress on *I*. Some writers obtrude speech tags in this way because they consider it clever.

" 'We have never,' the curator of birds said, 'had any previous complaint about pelicans biting people.' " The writer of this fancied, perhaps, that the awkward placement of *the curator of birds said* enhanced the humor of the remark, but this is a questionable assumption. It would have been better to put the speech tag at the end in both the examples cited.

Insertion of speech tags in every paragraph of a continuing quotation is excessive and annoying: " 'The toughest place to cross is the Southwest,' one of the leaders of the expedition said." " 'The towering mountains and the distances between communities pose particular problems,' he said." The second *he said* should be omitted. One attribution in a continuing quotation is usually enough.

If a quotation runs to more than one paragraph, the quotation marks are left off the ends of the paragraphs except the last, but are used at the beginning of each paragraph. The same rule applies to the use of parentheses.

Quotation marks go outside periods and commas, and inside semicolons and colons. When both a single and a double quote fall at the end of a sentence, *both go outside.* This is a matter of American printing practice, and is invariable, even when logic appears to dictate otherwise. British practice is the opposite with respect to commas and periods.

Converting Indirect to Direct Quotation

Copy editors may *never* convert an indirect quotation to a direct quotation by placing quotation marks around it. This is sometimes done with the intention of brightening the writing. The reporter very likely did not use the exact words of the speaker, but paraphrased them. Thus, by adding quotation marks, the copy editor is converting a paraphrase into a direct quotation and thereby is setting the stage for indignation on the part of the speaker being quoted. Only the reporter, who heard what was said, is in a position to judge what may be given as a direct quotation.

In any event, there is nothing to the idea that direct quotation by itself brightens writing. The matter directly quoted must have some special interest, flavor, or significance. Placing quotation marks around commonplace remarks is pointless.

A misuse of another kind: when a word is used in some other than its expected sense, *so-called* is superfluous with the term that has been placed in quotation marks: *the so-called "blacklist."* Either *so-called* or the quotes will suffice. There is no necessity to use quotation marks around a nickname. The wire services enclose nicknames in quotation marks when used with given names: Paul "Bear" Bryant. Thereafter, if the writer chooses to use the nickname, it is better simply *Bear,* not *"Bear."*

Wrong Person in Quotation

Mr. Truman smilingly conceded that he "feels more kindly toward newspapermen, now that one is about to become a member of his family." Obviously the word he used wasn't *feels* unless he said, "Mo'nin y'all. Ah feels more kindly toward newspapermen."

Writing in "Winners & Sinners," Theodore M. Bernstein thus wittily impaled the mishandling of fragmentary quotations so that the speaker appears to be talking about himself. Quotation marks, as we have noted, are supposed to enclose *the exact words* of the speaker. Any change in the form of those words leads to things like the Truman example, and worse.

" 'In point of fact,' the historian remarked, 'he couldn't bear to go—he was too immersed in the production of his fourteenth book.' " This, culled from *Newsweek,* is another example of confused quotation. The historian, of course, was intended to be referring to himself. This reads correctly as, "I couldn't bear to go—I am too immersed in the production of my fourteenth book."

Confused quotation can cause more uncertainty than when the village atheist married the preacher's daughter. "The board acted on the basis of an appeal by Haymes that 'somebody pretty high had made up his mind to get him.' " To get whom? Haymes, who must really have said "to get *me.*"

Some fragmentary quotations are such a mixture of direct and indirect discourse it is a hopeless task to untangle them: "The defendant told the judge he 'didn't allow people to grab his arm,' " and "Stevens said he 'feels in his heart that the responsibility was entirely his.' "

Copy editors should challenge every fragmentary quotation. A great many of these quotations will turn out to be unnecessary, confusing, or both. One critic of the unwarranted fragmentary quotation protested, "Don't put them on the stage unless they can sing and dance."

Occupational Titles

A wanton bestowal of titles, outdoing even the generosity of fraternal orders, is one of the earmarks of journalese. Occupational descriptives, instead of being made appositives, as is customary in less hurried prose, are often placed in front of names, on the model of true titles like *Dr., Mayor, Health Officer,* and *Dean.* This mannerism is known as a "false title." Thus are hatched such characterizations as *Italian soprano Renata Tebaldi, carnival concessionaire Eddie Crews, registered nurse Edith Hampton,* and *Rome tailor Angelo Litrico.*

One problem in the use of such descriptives is, should they be capitalized? Some authorities think so, on the analogy of true titles. The weight of opinion, however, seems to be that capitalization should be reserved for true titles, such as denote offices, and for established designations like *Dr.* Forms like *Italian Soprano Renata Tebaldi* and *Rome Tailor Angelo Litrico,* such as are used by *Time* magazine, seem to connote an official status that does not exist, and to most people the capitals only look silly.

Time magazine appears to have been the inventor of the false-title mannerism. In extenuation, *Time* at least diverted us with inventions like *cinemactress.* But it is better to use full-fledged appositives: *the Italian soprano, Renata Tebaldi;* or, of course, *Renata Tebaldi, the Italian soprano.*

Some writers seem to feel self-conscious about telescoping what they know to be the more readable form. So they compromise. These are typical results: *Italian soprano, Renata Tebaldi; Nacionalista Party candidate, Carlos P. Garcia; art dealer, Joseph Duveen; Civil War hero, Gen. William Tecumseh Sherman.*

Watch Your Language

The followers of this school, like the barefaced false-titlers, cannot agree on capitalization either, as the examples indicate. Compromises are sometimes worse than the evils they would palliate. That is so in this instance, at least.

It is a good idea to shun false titles entirely as one of the inventions that tend to make writing sound like the text of the telegram. By omitting what is desirable for clarity, or by distorting natural forms, these devices demand unnecessary effort from the reader.

Sometimes there is an attempt to have two styles of titles and mixed capitalization in the same sentence: "Art Dealer Joseph Duveen was once trying to sell a painting to millionaire collector, Samuel H. Kress, whose interest was only lukewarm." It is better to make this "Joseph Duveen, the art dealer, was once trying to sell a painting to a millionaire collector, Samuel H. Kress, whose interest was only lukewarm."

False titles have been the object of continual criticism in wire-service and other critiques, but it seems impossible to weed them out.

The AP Log told how a bureau chief who had been taken to task for "glass jar manufacturing heir John A. Kerr's divorce decree" came back with, "All I can say is it's a good thing for Associated Press members that Kerr's old man didn't invent the International Harvester Company's two-row cotton-picking machine."

Speech sets the pattern for idiomatic expression, and false titles are never spoken except by newscasters, who imitate the bad habits of print journalists.

There is reason to believe this kind of thing has generated a certain competitive spirit among reporters, impelling them to see who can put the *most* descriptives in front of a name. The national, and, perhaps the world, record at this writing is held by a newspaper which once came out with "former Assistant Secretary of Commerce for International Affairs and Occidental College graduate H. C. McClellan." Descriptives like this can be set out in a more literate fashion: "H. C. McClellan, a former assistant secretary of commerce for international affairs and a graduate of Occidental College." But this kind of writing appears unacceptable to many newswriters, who learn as cubs to imitate their seniors in this and other disagreeable mannerisms.

Doubled Titles

It is objectionable to double titles. Although it is good practice in Germany *(Herr Dr. Kurt Weiss,* the equivalent of *Mr. Dr. Kurt Weiss)* and in England *(General Sir Hugh Borrow),* it is not good practice in America. Doubling usually occurs in such instances as *Superintendent of Schools Dr. William Johnson; City Librarian Miss Eulalia Wallace;* and *Councilwoman Mrs. Edna Gleason.* If it is desirable to give both designations, clumsiness can be avoided by writing *Dr. William Johnson, superintendent of schools; Miss Eulalia Wallace, city librarian;* otherwise, simply *Superintendent of Schools William Johnson; Librarian Eulalia Wallace.* Doubled titles are doubly objectionable when there is more than one mention of the name; in such cases the office can be specified on first mention. Subsequent references will take care of the *Dr., Mrs., Miss,* or whatever.

Mr., Mrs., and Miss

The use of *Mr.* is a matter that is settled by a newspaper's stylebook. Few newspapers now use *Mr.* except in special instances such as references to the president of the United States, Protestant clergy, and the subjects of obituaries.

Under what was formerly considered correct practice a married woman using the title *Mrs.* was referred to by her husband's given name, i.e., *Mrs. John Doe,* not *Mrs. Mary Doe.* Some publications attempt to make this a rule, but it is almost impossible to enforce because customs have changed. Almost all newspapers now use the form of the title the owner prefers. There is a spreading tendency to refer to women by their last names alone, following the same style as for men.

Unjustifiable offensiveness is sometimes shown in handling the names of women who are in trouble with the law. Subsequent references are given as *the Smith woman.* This is clearly derogatory.

Some Ms.apprehensions

The feminist movement confronted newspapers with the issue of using the designation *Ms.* in order to conceal the designee's marital status. Most newspapers that adopted *Ms.* soon abandoned it for various reasons.

As noted earlier, most newspapers now refer to women by their last names alone *(Smith, Jones,* rather than *Miss/Mrs./Ms. Smith, Jones),* putting them on the same stylistic footing as men. Confusion may result from this practice. In stories about married couples, *Mr.* and *Mrs.,* or first names, are necessary.

As often happens when a new way of doing something appears, there are those who follow it out the window, writing things such as *Mr. and Ms. Arthur Williams* or *Ms. Arthur Williams,* which of course defeat the intended purpose of *Ms.* Some newspapers have found a way out of the *Ms.* quandary by using it only when a woman requests it, and staying with the traditional forms otherwise.

Names of People

Names make not only news, but also enemies, unless care is exercised in publishing them. Few things affront people more keenly than seeing their names misspelled in print. The only safeguard against misspelled names is actual practice of the care that is incessantly enjoined. As Byron put it in *Don Juan,* "Thrice happy is he whose name has been well spelt in the dispatch."

A common impropriety is the use of a single initial with a name on first mention in a story: J. Anderson, R. Thompson. This is objectionable because it invites confused identity and because many people are likely to feel slighted at having their names truncated. Most newspapers have inflexible rules against the use of names with single initials. Names should be given in the form their holders use, and this ordinarily is ascertained by the reporter.

Conclusion

In this chapter we have continued an examination of common faults in newswriting that should be corrected by the copy editor. Some of these faults are inversion of word order, misplaced modifiers, needless or misleading attribution, use of occupational and other descriptives in the form of titles, doubling of titles, the use of *Ms.,* proper handling of the names of people, and problems involving direct quotation.

10 Beset By Demons

Spelling and punctuation may seem to be minor matters, but their correctness contributes greatly to clarity. Misspellings and wrong punctuation can confuse and mislead the reader.

Spelling

Some journalism students arrive in college with the delusion that spelling, because it is a mechanical matter, is of little importance, and perhaps with a vague idea that someone else will correct their mistakes while they concentrate on more creative work. But the novice journalist who cannot spell may never get the chance to be creative. Editors are increasingly impatient with beginners who have not mastered elementary skills, especially since the use of VDTs has shifted the responsibility for errors from the back shop to the newsroom.

Some people are better spellers than others, of course; the essential thing is that journalists should know when they are sure of a spelling and when they are uncertain, so that they can check it. One editor lays down this rule: If it's a word you don't see every day, look it up. Misspelled words create an impression of ignorance, and in printed matter they cause the reader to lose confidence in factual accuracy. Consciously or subconsciously, the reader reasons that if the writers and editors could not be bothered to correct the spelling, how can they be trusted with the facts? A misspelled word in a piece of writing is worse than a false note in a musical performance; it damages the total effect, no matter what other virtues may be present. Thus close attention to spelling is an absolute must for the copy editor.

Here is a list of words that seem to give the most trouble (asterisks indicate forms that are now considered standard by *Webster III* but are nevertheless uncommon in carefully edited material):

Correct spelling	Typical misspelling
accommodate	accomodate
accordion	accordian
all right	alright*
a lot (meaning *many*)	alot
anoint	annoint
definite	definate
exorbitant	exhorbitant
existence	existance
fictitious	ficticious
fluorescent	flourescent
incidentally	incidently*
inoculate	innoculate
liquefy	liquify
marshal	marshall*
memento	momento
nickel	nickle*
objet d'art	object d'art
Philippines	Phillipines
rarefy	rarify
resistance	resistence
restaurateur	restauranteur*
separate	seperate

British Preferences

British preferences in spelling, while hardly incorrect, are conspicuous when used in America, and the writer who favors them may be accused of affectation. The British preference is for *ou* in certain words where American usage calls for *o: ardour, behaviour, clamour (-ous), colour (-ed), dolour (-ous), favour (-ite), honour (-able), labour, mould, moult, odour (-ous), smoulder, splendour (-ous), valour (-ous), vapour (-ous), vigour (-ous)*. Note, however, that *glamour* is preferred to *glamor* in both Britain and America.

Some other British preferences, followed by the American versions: *defence (defense), cheque (check), connexion (connection), plough (plow), practise (practice), grey (gray), pyjamas (pajamas), apologise (apologize), acknowledgement (acknowledgment), centre (center), jeweller (jeweler), skilful (skillful)*. Numerous similar forms show the same differences, and they are easily recognizable. The danger is not so much that British spellings will be used unconsciously as that some writers use them deliberately on the assumption that they are somehow more elegant than the American versions.

Spelling as Humor

In his preface to *A Subtreasury of American Humor,* E. B. White transfixed a foible that he noted particularly, he said, in the humorous writing of 50 to 100 years ago. It is still to be seen in print today, however, particularly in comic strips and syndicated stuff of the folksy or old-home-town persuasion, and sometimes in newspaper feature stories. White wrote:

> It occurred to me that a certain basic confusion often exists in the use of tricky or quaint or illiterate spelling to achieve a humorous effect. For instance, here are some spellings from the works of Petroleum V. Nasby: he spells "would" *wood,* "of" *uv,* "you" *yoo,* "hence" *hentz,* "office *offis.* Now, it happens that I pronounce "office" *offis.* And I pronounce "hence" *hentz,* and I even pronounce "of" *uv* . . . the queer spelling is unnecessary, since the pronunciation is impossible to distinguish from the natural or ordinary pronounciation. . . .

Making Numbers Count

Large Numbers

Big numbers seem here to stay. Everything is out of sight—government budgets, the explosive force of bombs, almost any figure dealing with the atom and its possibilities, and, as always, distances in the heavens, which, like other technical considerations, are appearing increasingly in newspapers. The least we can do is give the bedeviled, number-stunned reader some consideration and present these large totals as understandably as possible.

Large round numbers can easily be simplified. The zeros in 22,000,000 are forbidding enough, but in 22,000,000,000 they have to be counted. What an imposition on the reader! As a matter of fact, readers usually refuse to be imposed on in this way and they let the tails of such numerical comets swoosh past unheeded. How much easier it is to write, as well as to read, 22 million, 22 billion, or billion-dollar industry, rather than $1,000,000,000 industry. Most stylebooks now specify these more readable forms.

The notion that an expression like $8.6 million is likely to be read *eight and six-tenths dollars million* rather than *eight and six-tenths million dollars* does not stand up. We do not read $8 *dollars eight.*

The fact that an expression like *$8 million* may break at the end of a line, momentarily giving the reader the impression of *$8,* is considered objectionable in some quarters. This objection seems hardly more valid than complaints against the misleading sense that may occur at any line break. Some publications forestall this real or imagined difficulty by linking the elments with a hyphen: *$8-million.*

Rounding off is advisable for large figures in most contexts, unless there is some overriding reason against it; *$18,500,000* is preferable to *$18,478,369*, and *18½ million dollars* (or *$18.5 million*) is preferable to either.

Many reporters not only know how to count, but are unduly proud of it. Perhaps they are only trying to be helpful when they include meaningless totals in their stories. What can it be about little numbers that holds such fascination? The following will be recognized at once as standard procedure:

> They were joined by their *three* children, John, Ruth, and Mary.
> He was referring to Egypt and Saudi Arabia, *two* nations that control much of the strategic Red Sea coast line.
> This facility and the one in Baltimore are *two* of the finest in the country.
> Sports and music are his *two* hobbies.

The love of little numbers also appears in references like *the two, the three, the duo, the trio, the quartet,* and *the quintet,* as used in avoidance of *they.* This quirk is discussed under "Problems of Reference" in chapter 11. Words like *duo, trio,* and *quartet* suggest an organization, as of performers; when they are used simply as variants for *two, three,* and *four,* they reflect adversely on the writer.

Sometimes the adding machine gets jammed, probably from overwork. Then we get "Four examination dates have been approved for the positions of fire captain, senior clerk, keypunch operator, and construction supervisor." Four dates each, or one? Omission of *four* would have made for clarity.

"Christmas Day will be observed with two festival services at 9:30 and 11 a.m." Four services or two? A comma after *services* would help, but why not just leave out *two?*

There are other ways to insult the intelligence of readers than by forcing grammar-school arithmetic on their attention. One is to labor the obvious with something like "The river reached a peak of 30.7 feet, a little below the predicted crest of 31 feet"; or "Sales for 1982 hit $10.5 million, exceeding the previous year's total of $10 million." More judicious wording would be "The river reached a peak of 30.7 feet, as compared with . . ." and "Sales for 1982 hit $10.5 million, a half-million more than the total for 1981."

It is easy to give an ambiguous impression in constructions like "The measure would lower the rate from 3 to 2 percent." The reader must decide whether 3 and 2 percent are the present and proposed rates or the proportion by which the rate would go down. The intended meaning would have been unmistakably expressed by "The measure would lower the rate from 3 percent to 2 percent." Constructions like this are very common in newswriting, and the meaning should be conveyed unmistakably.

Figures vs. Words

Newspapers are much less conservative in their use of figures as against their verbal forms (e.g., *16* vs. *sixteen*) than books and magazines. This, of course, is a matter of style that is prescribed individually by newspapers, or, more likely these days, by the joint stylebook of the principal wire services. In general, newspapers use figures for the numbers 10 and larger, and spell smaller ones out, with numerous (and generally logical) exceptions, such as house numbers, ages, and vote totals.

Figure at Beginning of Sentence

The rule against starting a sentence with a figure seems defensible enough because a number coming first *does* look strange. The usual means of avoiding it are to write the number out or to recast the sentence so that something else comes first. The brewers of that intoxicating potion, style, however, have been known to recommend another way out: placing the word *exactly* in front of the figure.

Thus, "Six thousand, five hundred people attended the concert" would become "Exactly 6,500 people . . ." The objection to this ought to be apparent, because a round number like *6,500* obviously is an approximation. In such cases *about* is preferable to *exactly*. But even with figures that are, or are intended to be, precise, as in "Exactly 6,519 persons passed through the turnstile", the intrusion of *exactly* places an emphasis on the accuracy of the figure, which sounds strange when there is no apparent reason for such emphasis. A better way to say this is, "A total of 6,519 . . ."

The figures 100 and 1,000 are read *one hundred* and *one thousand*, not simply *hundred* and *thousand*. Those who have never taken note of this write "It was a journey of *a* 100 miles" and "He bought *a* 1,000 tankloads of oil."

Some and *-Odd*

Some and *-odd*, with numbers, indicate an approximation. They are inept, therefore, with anything but a *round* number: "Some 69 horses" and "Waco is 94-odd miles south of Dallas" sound foolish. Naive writers are fond of *some* with numbers.

It is unsuitable as a device to avoid starting a sentence with a figure. "The sailors unloaded some 92 cases from the ship" sounded to one critic as if some but not all of the cases were unloaded. When any other indication of inexactness is given, as by *about, approximately, estimated,* and the like, either *some* or *-odd* is superfluous.

Hyphens in Compound Modifiers

The text for the day comes from the gospel according to John Benbow, in *Manuscript and Proof,* the stylebook of the Oxford University Press: "If you take the hyphen seriously, you will surely go mad."

The first thing to remember about the hyphen is that it is a joiner. Two uses of the hyphen seem to give the most trouble. One is linking compound modifiers before a noun. In this instance, the hyphen weds two ordinarily separate words that are used in such a way that they form a single idea. There is some leeway here, for many such combinations are perfectly understandable in the intended sense without the hyphen.

Strong navy agitation, which conveys "strong agitation by the navy" is altogether different from *strong-navy agitation,* or "agitation for a strong navy." Consider also *an old time clock* (an old-time clock or an old time-clock?); a *single tax organization* (a single organization concerned with taxes or one concerned with the single tax?); and *a small animal hospital* (a small hospital for animals or a hospital for small animals?). Use the hyphen when it is needed for clarity.

Hyphens with Numbers

The hyphen is often carelessly omitted part way through compound modifiers, especially those containing numbers: *a 25-mile an hour speed* is properly *a 25-mile-an-hour speed.* Likewise, *a 500-foot long relief map* should be *500-foot-long,* and a *12-foot thick concrete wall* should be *12-foot-thick.* On the other hand, numbers preceding nouns as simple modifiers are sometimes mistakenly followed by hyphens: "sentenced to *180-days* in jail" should be *180 days.* Similarly, "*400 million dollars'* worth of business" should not be *400-million-dollars' worth.*

It should be kept in mind that compound modifiers other than those containing numbers may have more than two parts, all of which should be linked. "Contributors of the *most sought-after* items" was intended to be "contributors of the *most-sought-after* items." The versions have different meanings.

Hyphens with Phrasal Verbs

Hyphens often find their way into combinations of verb and adverb that really are new verbs, such as *cash in, hole up,* and *pay off.* Confusion arises because such expressions can be used as modifiers, and then the hyphen is required. Thus, "The Communists *stepped up* infiltration" (a verb in two parts, no hyphen); and "A *stepped-up* campaign" (compound adjective modifying *campaign,* hyphen required).

When used to join two figures, the hyphen means *through* and serves as a handy, word-saving device. "The convention will be held February 16-20" means the convention will start on the 16th and continue through the 20th.

To prevent misinterpretation, use of the hyphen must be based on good judgment. "Actually, he has had nine million dollar albums." Without the hyphen (million-dollar) this must be read twice to get the sense clearly.

Hyphens are often wrongly inserted between adverbs and the adjectives they modify: an easily-grasped concept, a beautifully-performed concert. Such hyphens are superfluous because the adverbs can modify nothing but the adjectives. Although not all adverbs end in *-ly,* most of them do, so it is a useful rule of thumb not to use the hyphen after such words.

Hyphens in Word Division

It seems hardly necessary to note that the commonest use of the hyphen is to divide words that are broken at the ends of lines. This problem more and more becomes one for the computer, except when its programming is not equal to some unusual division. The basic rule is that words are properly divided only on syllables. The way to resolve questions about this, and they are many, is to consult a dictionary.

Words are often divided in typewritten copy, but this is generally discouraged, especially in material intended to be set in type. Hyphens at the ends of lines in manuscript can raise unnecessary questions for the compositor. The lines as set in type are unlikely to correspond to the way they break in the manuscript, and thus the compositor cannot always be sure whether the hyphen that happens to fall at the end of the line in the copy is intended if the word occurs elsewhere in the typeset version, as in *breakthrough,* for example (correctly, *breakthrough*).

Single-syllable words, no matter how long, cannot be divided: *through, though, would, smooth.* Divisions on one letter, as *around,* are improper. *English for Printers,* the instruction manual of the International Typographical Union, says, "Singular nouns of one syllable, pronounced as if they were words of two syllables when pluralized, cannot be divided: as, 'horse,' *horses;* 'inch,' *inches;* 'fox,' *foxes;* 'dish,' *dishes.*"

Divisions of figures and of names of people are to be discouraged. These are unavoidable, however, in printing set in narrow measure (much newspaper text, for example) although many newspapers have gone to fewer and wider columns in recent years.

Hyphens with Prefixes and Suffixes

Hyphens have a strong tendency to fade away. In certain common uses, they are called on for a time to link ordinarily separate elements. After a while we seem to get used to seeing those elements together, and the engagement, so to speak, is followed by a wedding; the elements are joined and the hyphen is forgotten. This is particularly true of prefixes and suffixes, such as *pre-, bi-, anti-, co-, -down, -goer.* Thus *mid-summer* became *midsummer,* and *prewar* became *prewar.* Yet many writers not only hang onto the hyphen in instances like these, but also wedge it into words like *react, intercede, excommunicate, retroactive, semicolon,* and others where it has never belonged.

Dictionary-makers are often thought of as stick-in-the-muds who don't catch up with accepted usage until 30 years too late. But they are way ahead of many of us when it comes to dropping hyphens that have served their purpose. It seems like a good idea to get rid of hyphens when usage has sanctioned it to the extent that the dictionaries agree.

For ready reference, here is a list of prefixes usually set solid: a, ante, anti, bi, by, co, counter, dis, down, electro, extra, hydro, hyper, hypo, in, infra, mal, micro, mid, multi, non, on, out, over, pan, post, pre, re, semi, sesqui, sub, super, supra, trans, tri, ultra, up. These prefixes are usually hyphenated: all-, ex-, no-, self-, vice-, wide- *(wide-angle,* but *widespread).*

These suffixes are usually set solid: down, fold, goer, less, like, over, wise. These suffixes are usually hyphenated: -designate, -elect, -odd, -off, -on, -to, -up, -wide. Nevertheless, *headon, leanto, close-up, nationwide* are not merely on the way, but already here.

As exceptions, hyphens are often used to keep from doubling vowels (re-elect) and always to keep from tripling consonants (bill-like). Although some stylebooks take up such matters, the most practical recourse in doubtful cases is the dictionary.

Ex-

May *ex-* properly be attached only to its noun, and not to the noun's modifier? This niggling question was resolved by the *New York Times* critique, "Winners & Sinners." For example, should it be *Waldorf ex-headwaiter?* The answer is that *ex-Waldorf headwaiter* is beyond criticism. The subject was, of course, a former headwaiter at the Waldorf, and the way to express this smoothly is to put the *ex-* in front of *Waldorf.* Another possibility is *ex-headwaiter at the Waldorf.*

It is not possible to keep *ex-* attached only to nouns and not to their modifiers; witness *bathing ex-beauty*. "Winners & Sinners" said anything like that would be the work of a copy ex-editor. It may be argued that ambiguity may arise from the likes of *ex-Democratic attorney general* (that is, *ex-Democrat, ex-attorney general*, or both?), but only the wrongheaded will see a problem here, for *ex-* obviously modifies all three words as a unit.

Before exiting on *ex-*, let's have a look at *ex-felon*, a puzzling creation that pops up frequently in the news. It evolved probably on the model of *ex-convict*, and in a strict sense both expressions may be open to the same objection. *Convict*, however, has come to mean almost exclusively "one serving a sentence," and thus *ex-convict* fills a distinct need. But *felon* is not associated with imprisonment; it means simply "one who has committed a felony." Therefore *ex-felon* is impossible; once a felon, always a felon.

Careless writers use superfluous hyphens. Is there any hope for those who write *radio-active* for *radioactive, over-turn* for *overturn, thorough-going* for *thoroughgoing, re-admit* for *readmit, one-time* (single occasion) for *onetime* (sometime)? Not unless they can be persuaded to stop, look, and look up before striking the hyphen key.

Let us close with a wistful comment from Fowler in *The King's English:* "Hyphens are regrettable necessities, to be done without whenever they reasonably may."

Dash and Hyphen

The functions and even the forms of the dash and the hyphen are often confused. The clearest description of the difference between these marks is that the hyphen joins, the dash separates. We have seen how the hyphen is used to connect two or more modifiers to make a unit and to indicate a connection where words are broken at the ends of lines.

Confusion and errors often result because the dash is improperly formed on the typewriter. The dash, as it appears in printed matter, is at least twice as wide as the hyphen, but a hyphen is often mistakenly used in place of the dash in typescript. (Some typewriters have a separate character for the dash, but most of them do not.) The dash is formed on the typewriter, then, by striking the hyphen twice (--) or, as some editors prescribe, three times (---). Dashes are often intended by hyphens with a space at each side - like this, but such indications are likely to be misunderstood by the typesetter. In typed copy, there should be no space at the sides of either a dash or a hyphen.

Very often the dash displaces commas when a sharper break is desired: "That year—my second at the university—I was living alone." This might as easily have been "That year, my second at the university, I was living alone," but that version would not have set the modifying phrase off as sharply.

When dashes are used to set off a phrase for emphasis, care should be taken to put them in the right place. "The minister is giving too big—and too profitable a role—to private industry." The second dash belongs after *profitable,* not after *role; too big* and *too profitable* both modify *role:* "The minister is giving too big—and too profitable—a role to private industry."

A dash cannot properly be used to separate a subordinate and an independent clause: "Although Scranton is still a depressed area because of the continuing decline in anthracite coal mining—such projects have provided more than 10,000 new jobs." The comma is called for here: correctly, "coal mining, such projects . . ."

Either the dash or the comma is required at *both* ends of an element that is set off, not a dash at one end and a comma at the other: "Then—with her appeal matured by further experience, she will be ready for the national prize." Either "Then, with . . . experience, she . . ." or "Then—with . . . experience—she. . . ."

Superfluous Commas

The usual bald admonition, "Use the comma sparingly," is about as good advice by itself as "Use the letter *s* sparingly," which might lead to *succes, misive,* and *imposible.* Pick a classic off the shelf or turn the discolored pages of a very old magazine and you will quickly find what look like superfluous commas to today's eyes. Some of them precede *that.* Others set off adverbs, which we seem to find easier to swallow than our forebears did.

Here are a couple of examples from Fowler's *The King's English:*

"Yet there, too, we find, that character has its problems to solve."—Meredith
"We know, that, in the individual man, consciousness grows."—Huxley

Some people would probably be inclined to remove all the commas from both these sentences. An examination of current writing shows that commas are more often omitted when required than used when unnecessary.

Consider a couple of instances in which commas *are* used unnecessarily. One is in mistaking ordinary adverbs, which do not need to be set off, for parenthetical elements, which do. Here are some examples: "The farm laborer could not start his car but, apparently, a car thief could" and "Yesterday, she drove to the city." Writers who use such commas, which now represent old-fashioned practice, are probably misled by the accepted (but not mandatory) practice of setting off such interruptives as *of course, therefore,* and *however.*

Commas and Adjectives

Another superfluous use of commas appears in separation of adjectives that apply cumulatively rather than separately; for example, "After a hard, second look. . . ." This was not a look that was second and, as a separate idea, also hard, but rather a second look that was hard. The mistaken comma after *hard* makes the word apply to *look* alone and not to *second.* The same reasoning fits *balky, old sultan* and *two, short, gloomy acts* (correct: *balky old sultan; two short, gloomy acts*).

A little thought—but not much—is required to differentiate these constructions from *a hot, dusty road* (a road that is hot and also dusty) and *a short, exciting chase* (a chase that is short and also exciting). But how can we tell for certain, especially in doubtful cases, whether to use the comma to separate adjectives? The comma should be easily interchangeable with the word *and.* If not, it is out of place. Compare *hard and second look,* which is impossible, with *hot and dusty road,* which reads smoothly, indicating that the comma is called for.

Yet the comma may be omitted from any series of adjectives preceding a noun without causing any damage, and this practice seems to be gaining popularity: a hot dusty road, a short exciting chase. At any rate, commas are better left out of such constructions than used where they don't belong.

One-Legged Commas

Some of us, when confronted with the question of setting an element off, often seem to want to have it both ways. To be set off, of course, the element must have a comma at both ends—like the parenthetical *of course* in this sentence. (Or, with one comma, the element must be at the beginning or end of the sentence, which amounts to the same thing.)

Some reporters solve the problem by placing the comma at one end of the clause or phrase and leaving it off the other. This brings about the grammatical infirmity that has been called the "one-legged comma."

The simplest and most numerous example of the one-legged comma occurs with the prepositional identifying phrase: "Judge George Buck of Erskine County, signed the restraining order." This should be either "Judge George Buck, of Erskine County, signed . . ." or "Judge George Buck of Erskine County signed. . . ." The use of commas in this construction is an old-fashioned practice, and generally the no-comma version is considered preferable. The same principle applies to such phrases as "Richard R. Roe of the Foreign Affairs Committee" and "J. David Nelson of the *New York Times.*"

But the commaless version does not sound quite as satisfactory in first-name listings of survivors in an obituary: "Mr. Smith leaves three brothers, Frank of Ossining, George of New York, and Gerald of Los Angeles." Sometimes it's "a sister, Mary of Italy." Somehow, this usage puts one incongruously in mind of such grandiose designations as "William of Normandy" and "Lawrence of Arabia." A better form for the list of survivors might be "Frank, Ossining; George, New York; and Gerald, Los Angeles." If the *of* must be kept, it had better be preceded by a comma. And as for "Mary of Italy," she should become "Mary, *in* Italy."

Some cases of one-leggedness require two commas or none. The place where another comma belongs is indicated in each example by parentheses. Either a comma should be placed there or the existing one should be omitted, as the writer prefers.

Severe storms ( ) accompanied by hailstones up to three-quarters of an inch in diameter, pounded western Texas.

A 47-year-old man ( ) who had just been released from jail after serving a term for drunkenness, was found burned to death beside a fire.

This, obviously ( ) was a planned diversionary movement.

"Committee members ( ) who had feared White House suppression of the report, were jubilant." This one is not as freely a matter of choice between two commas and none; the decision depends on whether the clause is restrictive or nonrestrictive. With commas (nonrestrictive), the sentence would say all the committee members had feared suppression; without (restrictive), that only those who had feared suppression were jubilant. Probably the nonrestrictive sense was meant. The difference between restrictive and nonrestrictive clauses is explained later in this chapter.

Now for examples in which two commas, and no less, are necessary: "All New Orleans schools were closed as a precaution but the storm, bringing winds of 64 miles per hour ( ) passed the city without causing much damage." A comma is necessary, of course, to mark the other end of the participial modifier. A comma before *but,* to separate coordinate clauses, would do no harm but is not essential. "Dr. Manlio Brosio, Italian ambassador to Britain ( ) flew to Rome yesterday." A comma should mark off the other end of the appositive phrase. The same is true of "Joseph Anderson, a carpenter ( ) of 1843 Weyburn Place."

Sometimes it is best to use no comma at all: "A corporation, which is unique in the rubber industry has been formed." Placing a comma after *corporation* suggests a nonrestrictive clause, which would mean that corporations hitherto have been unknown in the rubber industry. This writer meant that the corporation being written about was unique within the industry, and this would have been better expressed by leaving out *which is* as well as the comma: "A corporation unique in the rubber industry has been formed."

"A gray-haired man in a brown hunting shirt, jumped onto the barricade." Presumably the comma sets off, or half sets off, the phrase *in a brown hunting shirt,* but such prepositional modifiers do not take commas.

"A few lawgivers, themselves, call it the biggest boondoggle in Washington history." Commas around reflexive pronouns (those ending in *self* or *selves*) are superfluous.

To call attention to a word as a word, use italics or quotation marks, not commas. "Magnuson suggested that he had used the word, bottle, a little perversely." The writer of this used commas a little perversely. This sentence should read " . . . the word *bottle* a little perversely" or " . . . the word 'bottle' a little perversely."

False Linkage

The tendency to spare the comma may well spoil the sentence. Another manifestation of this is what might be called "false linkage." By omission of the comma, elements that should be separated are unintentionally joined.

"No rain is expected for tonight and tomorrow the high temperature is expected to be between 70 and 75 degrees." Readers must retrace their steps in the middle of the sentence because at first the prediction of no rain seems to cover tomorrow as well as tonight. The omission of the comma might be defended on the ground that a comma is unnecessary between coordinate clauses. But this principle does not hold unless the sentence is clearly understandable without it. Smooth reading requires "No rain is predicted for tonight, and tomorrow. . . ."

Generally, the comma should be used between coordinate clauses unless they are very short. Even then, clarity of sense should govern. "Rain will fall and wind will blow" gets along all right without one, but "He was a man of action (   ) and deeds interested him more than words" does not. Here are some commaless culls:

> The Democrats are counting on regaining rural votes that went to the Republicans (   ) and the committee is working to that end.
>
> She said military aid should not be given countries able to provide for their own defense (   ) and economic aid in the guise of military assistance should be ruled out.
>
> The weather in Asia was unusually favorable for production (   ) and growing conditions in India and Pakistan were the best in many years.

False linkage and confused meaning can also result from failure to set off a clause that interrupts: "The guards and prisoners who refused to join in the break were tied and left in the fields."

No, there were no guards who *consented* to join in the break. What was meant is this: "The guards, and prisoners who refused to join in the break, were tied. . . ."

Appositives

Rare appositives are technically restrictive and do not take commas: *my son Ralph* (distinguished from my other son, John). An only son would be *my son, Ralph.* Others are *Ivan the Terrible, William the Conqueror,* and the like. Omission of commas from other appositives usually occurs in writing that shows other signs of carelessness.

The intrusion of commas and the articles *a* and *an* within certain appositive constructions, however, can raise doubt as to whether one or two persons are being referred to. "The publication will be edited by Dr. Edward Finegan, executive secretary of the conference, and a member of the faculty" is an example of this. Dr. Finegan is both secretary and faculty member, but the sentence may leave the impression that the faculty member is someone else. Omit the comma after *conference* and the *a* before *member.*

Restrictive and Nonrestrictive Clauses

The difference between restrictive and nonrestrictive clauses, sometimes known as defining and nondefining or limiting and nonlimiting clauses, directly affects meaning. Thus the difference is important to every writer and copy editor.

The problem arises with relative clauses. You can always recognize a relative clause as one starting with *that* or *which, where* or *when,* or *who, whose,* or *whom.* And the question is whether or not such clauses should be set off by commas. Consider a sentence like "I waved at the girl who was standing on the corner."

Do we want a comma in front of *who?* It depends on what we mean. As the sentence stands, the speaker waved to a girl who is identified by the fact that she was standing on the corner. Let us put a comma in front of *who.* Now the fact that the girl was standing on the corner becomes merely incidental information. The *who* clause no longer identifies her. In this construction she would have been previously mentioned. While the clause was originally restrictive, or defining, it now has become nonrestrictive, or nondefining, and could be dropped without changing the meaning of the sentence.

The important point to settle is whether the clause is essential to the meaning. If the clause is essential, the comma should not be used; if it is not essential, the comma is required to set it off. If you doubt whether the clause is essential, try leaving it out. Obviously, you cannot leave out the *who* clause in the commaless version of our example without changing the intended sense.

"No woman, whose attire makes her conspicuous, is well dressed." This is preposterous, of course, with the commas. For if we leave out the *whose* clause, as the commas indicate we may, we get "No woman is well dressed."

"Every high school district in the county, which called for a bond issue this year, has won voter support." This was intended to mean that bond issues carried in every district where they were proposed, and not, as the example indicates, that every district in the county proposed bond issues and won approval of them. You cannot leave out the *which* clause without changing the intended sense; thus the commas are erroneous.

"The rule exempts commercial lots where there is no restriction on all-night parking." The writer wanted to indicate that commercial lots are unaffected because they do not restrict all-night parking, but what was said by leaving out the comma before *where* was that the rule affects some commercial lots and not others. A period could have been placed after *lots;* the rest is merely explanatory.

That vs. Which

The question of nonrestrictive vs. restrictive elements inescapably involves the question of *that* vs. *which*.

This much is certain—elegance has nothing to do with the choice between them. As a general rule, *that* may refer either to persons or things, but *which* refers only to things. Popular usage and grammarians alike seem to be pretty well agreed that *that* (in the sense being considered here) should be used to introduce only restrictive clauses. Nonrestrictive clauses, as we have seen, are set off by commas; restrictive ones are not. Save *that* to introduce restrictive clauses. *Which* is all right with either kind, but is preferred with nonrestrictive clauses.

A rule of thumb may be useful here. If *that* will fit comfortably, it is correct, and furthermore, the clause is restrictive. *That* introducing a nonrestrictive clause is a blunder: "The sun, that had a murky orange color, soon burned off the fog." The writer's ear should indicate that *which* is required here. In "It was easy to find the house which was on fire," *that* can easily be substituted for *which,* and in accordance with our rule of thumb it is preferable. A corollary to this is that a clause starting with *which* should be set off by commas; one starting with *that* should not.

Serial Comma

Although traditional grammar calls for a comma before the last element in a series, newspaper writing generally dispenses with it. An example: "A press is a maze of gears, shafts, cams (,) and levers."

Most of the trouble with serial elements grows out of the confusion of one series with another, or, to put it another way, the failure to recognize where one series ends and another begins.

"Voters will go to the polls Tuesday to elect four city councilmen, three school board members, to decide on eight charter amendments and three special propositions." We have here two different groups, and they would be more readably presented as ". . . to elect four city councilmen and three school board members, and to decide on. . . ."

When apparently mixed constructions like this are not unconscious, they are probably imitations of the telegraphic style affected by some publications in sentences like "New construction techniques added strength, durability, sharply reduced costs." Neither this nor the example preceding is either unintelligible or misleading. But a preferable version would be "New construction techniques added strength and durability, and sharply reduced costs."

Comma After Conjunctions

Some of the same writers who neglect the comma when it is needed slip it in after conjunctions, especially *and, but, so,* and *or.* For example, in "They have found it pays, and, we have too"; and "Money may not make you happy, but, it will enable you to be miserable in comfort," the commas after *and* and *but* are wrong.

Don't be confused by sentences in which a comma legitimately falls after the conjunction because it is setting off a parenthetical element, as in "They have found it pays, and, *I must admit,* we have too." Don't be misled, either, by sentences that start with *and* or *but.* This construction is common in informal writing and is perfectly correct. Omit the commas in "And, I took him up on it" or "But, the cork wouldn't come out of the bottle."

Commas and Colons

"Members of the committee are: Jane Doe, Oscar Zilch, Perry Moore, and Lucinda Knight." Why the colon after *are,* any more than in "I am: Oscar Zilch," since the constructions are identical? It seems likely that the use of the colon in sentences like the first example has grown out of the rule, often loosely understood, that a colon is used to introduce a series—but *not* if the series immediately follows the verb, as in the example. A series, to take a colon, should form an appositive: "Members of the committee are all students: Jane Doe, Oscar Zilch, Perry Moore, and Lucinda Knight." The colon balances off (a) *students,* and (b) the names.

A dash or comma would be possible in place of the colon. One of them surely is necessary to make the sentence understandable. The colon may be removed without loss, on the other hand, from the first example. The simplest rule to cover this situation will cover many another as well: Don't put in anything you can do without.

Abbreviations

When Not to Abbreviate

Some little improprieties occur in the use of abbreviations. It is considered poor style, for example, to abbreviate the month without the date (*He left last Dec.,* as against *He left last December,* or *last Dec. 21*); nor is it proper to abbreviate the state without the city (*The factory is in Ala.,* as against *The factory is in Alabama,* or *in Mobile, Ala.*).

Nor should proper names be abbreviated by anyone except their owners: *Wm.* for *William, Robt.* for *Robert,* and the like. When a clipped form of a proper name is used, however, it is not regarded as an abbreviation, and does not take a period: *Ed.* is properly *Ed* for *Edward, Edmund,* and *Edwin.*

Alphabet Soup

Some newswriters make a habit of reducing the name of an unfamiliar organization or agency to initials after its first appearance. The press associations and their imitators do it routinely, but to readers it is often confusing. It probably began after the upsurge of alphabetical agencies in New Deal days. Some of them (AAA, NRA, FHA, CCC) became so familiar that writers took to using the abbreviations without spelling out the names even once. Then perhaps some thoughtful editor, to jog the memories of readers, directed that the names of such agencies be given in full on first occurrence in a story and followed by the abbreviation: Federal Housing Administration (FHA).

Use of the abbreviation alone thereafter is fine, for agencies as well known as the FHA. But the thing has gone full speed into reverse. Instead of helping the reader to learn the full names of organizations whose abbreviations are relatively familiar, reporters use the device to manufacture new and baffling abbreviations for organizations that are unknown to the typical reader.

A security board has found doubt of the loyalty of an official of the International Monetary Fund (IMF). The finding was made after a hearing by the International Organizations Employees Loyalty Board (IOELB). Because the IMF is an international body, the IOELB worked in cooperation with foreign agencies.

It's bad enough when only one such abbreviation figures in a story, but when there are more, we have confusion compounded. Every now and then, readers then have to thread their way back to the beginning for the key.

It is better to use a descriptive instead of alphabetical abbreviations. In the example cited, the International Monetary Fund might have been referred to, after having been named once, as *the fund*. The International Organizations Employees Loyalty Board could have become *the loyalty board,* or even just *the board.*

The practitioners of alphabetism know no shame. They will start out with the translated version of a foreign name, for example General Confederation of Labor, and in going on with the story will use an abbreviation based on the original (*CGT* for *Confédération Générale du Travail*).

There is a place, of course, for FHA, FBI, CIA, and other abbreviations that are widely known. Every town has its own handful that everyone recognizes, and they are both convenient and unobjectionable. But judgment must be employed in their use.

This chapter, continuing the discussion of common faults in newswriting, has taken up problems of spelling, use of numbers, *some* and *-odd,* hyphens and dashes, word division, placement of *ex-,* use of commas, restrictive and nonrestrictive clauses, *that* vs. *which,* and alphabetical abbreviations.

Conclusion

11 Department of Corrections

This chapter continues the examination of faults in newswriting to which the copy editor must be alert.

Being "Too Concise"

The urge to be concise, while generally commendable, is to blame for some effects that place an unnecessary burden on the reader, as in the following examples (the modifiers are in parentheses):

> "He was arrested on (conspiracy and concealing stolen property) charges.
>
> Next on the docket were two (disturbing the peace) suspects.
>
> (A 15 percent per $100 assessed valuation road tax) increase was proposed.

What price terseness? Howard B. Taylor, when he was managing editor of the *San Diego Union,* said it neatly in a memo to his staff:

> Mouth-filling strings of compound adjectives force the reader to go back and retrace the meaning of a sentence: "The strikers presented a *20-cent-an-hour wage-increase demand.*" The compound adjective is too big to swallow. Let's make it "The strikers asked an increase of 20 cents an hour." A wire story recently read, "The strikers are seeking *a 25-cent-an-hour* wage hike, contending that *a 10-cent-an-hour* jump, which gave them *a $2.10 hourly pay* scale, is insufficient." That's really making life tough on the reader.
>
> A string of titles preceding a name likewise is difficult to digest: "Signers included *former Salt Lake City mayor* Albert Sprague." Let's make it "Signers included Albert Sprague, former mayor of Salt Lake City."

Another variation of this quirk gives us "a 9 a.m. February 26 meeting" instead of "a meeting at 9 a.m., February 26," and "the 1939 erection of the Oakdale School" instead of "the erection of the Oakdale School in 1939."

Limiting Adjectives

Limiting adjectives often create ambiguity.

"His labor turnover is nominal, and he is proud of the loyalty of his nonunion workers." This sounds as if the speaker might have referred to two kinds of employees, union and nonunion, and as if only the nonunion ones were loyal. In this instance, however, all the employees were nonunion, so the writer should have said, "He is proud of the loyalty of his workers, who are nonunion."

"The reception was held in Mrs. Cramer's San Francisco home." Does Mrs. Cramer have homes elsewhere, as this seems to suggest? If not, it would better be " . . . in Mrs. Cramer's home, in San Francisco."

It is undesirable, for the same reason, to write "Burglars invaded the 424 W. Oak home of Albert Fresco last night." Since this was Fresco's only home, it would have been better to say " . . . the home of Albert Fresco, 424 W. Oak, last night."

Unnatural placement of modifiers also appears in other contexts: "Receipts were 25 percent ahead of those for the same 1979 month." This is disagreeably unidiomatic: better, " . . . those for the same month in 1979."

"The speaker cited Professor A. M. Low, Britain's inventive version of Thomas A. Edison." Here the adjective *inventive* is intended to give the basis for the comparison, but the effect is to imply that Edison was not inventive. Why not just " . . . Britain's version of Thomas A. Edison" since Edison's claim to fame hardly needs explanation?

Dangling Participles

> Dear Sir:
>
> We enclose herewith a statement of your account. Desiring to clear our books, will you kindly send us a check in settlement?

The reply ran:

> Sirs:
>
> You have been misinformed. I have no wish to clear your books.

This little exchange, adapted from an example in Fowler, neatly exemplifies the dangling participle.

A participle is a verb form usually ending in *-ing* or *-ed,* like *desiring* or *settled,* and used as a modifier. The past participle, of which *settled* is an example, is sometimes formed irregularly, as in *born* or *seen.* Participles may also take auxiliaries (accompanying verb forms): *having settled, being seen, having been born.*

Writers are sometimes sent astray by a participial phrase at the beginning of a sentence. Such phrases usually modify the subject of the clause that follows. The trick in handling them correctly is to be sure that this subject *is* the element intended to be modified: *"Taking* the cue, *he* left immediately"; *"Taken* by surprise, *she* burst into laughter."

Dangling participles rarely confuse meaning. At the least, they cause readers a moment of hesitation while they pair up the modifier with the modified. At the worst, dangling participles create an absurd effect.

"In applying the brakes, the car skidded off the road." The car did not apply its own brakes. It should read "In applying the brakes, *the driver* made the car skid off the road."

"Born of a poor but proud Catholic family, few would have predicted greatness for young Konrad." But it was Konrad who was born, not *few,* as this sentence reads. It should read "Born of a poor but proud Catholic family, Konrad did not seem a good prospect for greatness."

What is the cure for dangling? There is none, perhaps, except close attentiveness to what one is writing, which of course is more of a panacea than a specific.

Bob Considine once quoted D. C. Claypoole, the newspaperman to whom George Washington confided his plans not to run again, as having written, "He received me kindly and after paying my respects to him desired me to take a seat near him." Did Washington pay Claypoole's respects to himself, and if so, how was it managed? The dangling participle is not new to American prose.

Participles and Time Sequence

Modifying phrases containing present participles often go awry in the hands of inexpert writers. No interval is permissible between the time of such a phrase and that of the main part of the sentence. Either a connected sequence or simultaneous occurrence is necessary:

> Going to the door, he inserted the key. (connected sequence)
> Laughing gaily, she turned to go. (simultaneous occurrence)

If there is an interval between what happens in the participial phrase and what happens in the main part of the sentence, a past participle should be used, or some other change should be made. "Joseph Doakes is a graduate of Columbia, *receiving* his degree in 1960." This should be ". . . *having received* his degree in 1960." The linkage here is not close enough to justify the present participle. Recasting to ". . . who received his degree in 1960" is another possible correction.

> The mother said her daughter fell out of the car, apparently *opening* the door when no one was looking. (Here, similarly, *having opened* is required.)

Eriksson has been a resident of the city for 15 years, *coming* here during the war as a naval architect. (*having come*)

He has been in the service since 1967, *starting* as a clerk. (*having started*)

Often a participial phrase inappropriately subordinates an idea that is of equal rank with the main part of the sentence. "The Van Gilders were married on Christmas Day, 1907, in Anabel, Mo., *moving* to the West Coast shortly afterwards." This would be improved by substituting ". . . *and moved* to the West Coast. . . ." A phrase containing a present participle cannot be used to convey a time *after* that of the main clause.

By 1918 he was president, *moving* up to the chairmanship in 1940. (*and he moved*)

Miss Jones began her studies at the college in September 1970, *receiving* her degree three years later." (*and received*)

This is one of the most sensational revelations *coming* from behind the Iron Curtain in several years. (*that have come*)

Misrelated Appositives

Grammarians have been so preoccupied with the dangling participle they have taken little notice of another kind of misplaced modifier. This error grows out of a common appositive construction. If it needs a name, perhaps *misrelated* or *dangling appositive* would be appropriate. "Until recently a resident of San Carlos, *Peaches' real name* is Mrs. Ralph Wilson." It was Peaches herself, and not her real name, that was a resident of San Carlos. The basic fault here may be the attempt to jam unrelated material into one sentence. Still, it can be done grammatically: "Until recently a resident of San Carlos, Peaches is known formally as Mrs. Ralph Wilson." "A devout, old-fashioned Moslem, *his concubines* are numbered by the hundreds." The fault is evident: a possible cure is "A devout, old-fashioned Moslem, he has hundreds of concubines."

Consider one that looks right, at first glance, but isn't: "Now 68, *he and his second wife* live in a Colonial-style house." The writer was led astray by a compound subject—not *he* alone, but *he and his second wife*. Husband and wife could have been the same age, but were not, and the descriptive was intended to apply only to the husband. The correction can be made by recasting the sentence in such form as "Murgatroyd, now 68, and his second wife live. . . ." "Now a widow, *she and her husband* moved to New York in 1956." The way this sentence stands, both the woman and her husband are characterized as *a widow*.

Tricky -ics

Is there a difference between a *dramatic* instructor and a *dramatics* instructor? It seems apparent that an instructor who used acting techniques in putting lessons across would be *a dramatic instructor,* but that a *dramatics* instructor could only be one who teaches dramatics.

This distinction between *athletic* and *athletics,* used as adjectives, is technically the same, but is less observed. On the sports pages, most athletics directors have long since become athletic directors. The difference between an *athletic* director and an *athletics* director is, grammatically, the same as that between a *musical* critic and a *music* critic.

We often read of *electronic* engineers, who, strictly speaking, would be robots, but this is not the meaning intended or even the one the reader assumes. The writer had in mind *electronics* engineers; that is, engineers trained in electronics.

Narcotics, cosmetics, and *economics* sometimes cause the same kind of trouble as *athletics* and *dramatics.* Narcotics agents, who deal with drug-law violations, often see themselves referred to as *narcotic agents.* This designation, which describes them as "tending to stupefy," would better fit some after-dinner speakers.

False Possessives

Many modifiers of the general kind we have been considering end in *s.* If these modifiers are proper names, some writers feel compelled to regard them as possessives and clap apostrophes on them. Note these examples:

> He accepted a *General Motors'* scholarship.
> The applicant was a *United States'* citizen.
> The scene did not pass muster with the *Hays' Office.*

There is really no idea of possession here, so the apostrophes are uncalled for. *General Motors, United States,* and *Hays* are being used simply as adjectives, like *roads* in *roads appropriations* and *athletics* in *athletics director.*

This brings us to a shadowy realm inhabited by names perhaps once regarded as possessive forms, but now often written without the apostrophe: Odd Fellows(') Lodge, Lions(') Club, Taxpayers(') Association, master(')s degree, in 10 years(') time, and Hell(')s Canyon (from which the federal government removed the apostrophe by a specific order). More and more, such words are being considered primarily as describing, and not as indicating possession. In the case of proper names, the form used by the organization itself governs.

Nouns as Adjectives and Verbs

One part of speech easily assumes the role of another; this is one of the most distinctive and useful characteristics of English. Sometimes, however, a disagreeable effect is created when nouns are forced into the role of adjectives, as in these examples:

> The general was retired for *health* reasons.
>
> The architect warned that the situation soon may reach *disaster* proportions.
>
> The service will be discontinued for *economy* reasons.

It is noticeable that two of these examples have *reasons* as the objectionably modified noun. Expressions of this kind are recognizable as journalese. Better: *for reasons of* (or *for his*) *health; disastrous proportions; for economy.*

The copy editor should also be alert to instances in which nouns are forced into the role of verbs: "We are *efforting* to get the money for the project"; "The Wolfpack *defensed* the Tar Heels successfully." Sometimes adjectives are used as verbs: "They had not *precised* it out."

Lost Articles

Somehow the notion has got around that the opening sentences in newspaper stories would be better if they did not start with *the, a,* or *an.* The idea, as sometimes explained, is that the articles convey little or nothing and only stand in the way of the reader, who is panting to get at the meatier words.

Fortunately, this dictum appears to be falling from favor. But like the lie that runs twice around the earth while the truth is lacing its shoes, it persists, and prejudice against—or neglect of—articles is still to be found.

It is not true, of course, that articles convey nothing. If this were so, they would be dropped from conversation, especially at the least literate level, which hews to essentials. *The* particularizes what it precedes; *a* and *an* designate one of a class. Meaning of a sort can be put across without these subtleties. But not the sort of meaning that is the most lucid.

Sentences beginning with *purpose* are often disfigured in this way: "Purpose of the legislation is to ensure fair treatment." It is more natural to say "The purpose. . . ."

Does it really speed readers on their ways to leave an article off the beginning of a sentence? Surely not, if they find themselves obliged to choose between possible shades of meaning. The writer's job has been foisted on the reader, who has every right to feel irked.

An example of this fault: "Crux of the situation is belief expressed by board members that legislation should govern the use of the reservoir by the public." If the aim is to be telegraphic, why not go all the way: "Crux of situation is belief expressed by board members that legislation should govern use of reservoir by public "?

As another sidelight, let us consider the expression *in future* as against "in *the* future". Omission of the article is British practice, like *in hospital*. Such expressions sound affected in America.

It is difficult to generalize about where *the* is or is not normally required. The matter is governed by idiom, which does not yield to rules. We all know when we are leaving out a desirable *the;* it is never done by accident. "Remember what the Bible says: 'If I forget *the,* O Jerusalem, let my right hand forget her cunning,' " Theodore M. Bernstein recommended in *Watch Your Language.*

Careless use of *the* may imply a distinction that is either inaccurate, unintended, or both. Referring to John Jones as "*the* vice-president of the Smith Corporation" implies that the corporation has only one vice-president. "Laurence Olivier, *the* actor" is acceptable on the assumption that he is well enough known so that his name will be recognized. On the other hand, referring to movie starlet Hazel Gooch, lately of Broken Bottle, Iowa, as "*the* actress" (rather than *an* actress) leaves readers with a feeling that they have not recognized a name they should know.

A vs. *An* Before *H*

The use of *an* before words whose initial *h* is sounded *(an hotel, an humble, an historic event)* is now an affectation. This is not true of words beginning with a silent *h: hour, honor, heir.*

Expressions like *an habitual* tend to indicate to the American reader that the *h* is not to be sounded. Instead of achieving the elegance aimed at, such affectations impart a kind of Cockney flavor.

The use of *an* before words beginning with *u* or *eu,* for example *an utopia* or *an eulogy,* is a related peculiarity. These words in fact begin with a consonant sound, *y,* and should be preceded by *a.* It is hard to pronounce *an eulogy* and it is faintly irksome to read.

A is mistakenly used instead of *an* before figures, initials, and even words that begin with vowel sounds, for instance, *a $800 salary, a RCA contract, a Amazonian feat.*

Possessive Forms

Pronunciation can be relied on for a rule of thumb in forming the possessives of both singular and plural forms. If you add an *s*-sound in speaking the word in its possessive form, add apostrophe-*s;* if the pronunciation is unchanged, add just the apostrophe. This gives us, by way of examples, *the boy, the boy's bike; the boys, the boys' bikes; Louis, Louis's pencil; Dickens, Dickens' novels; Moses, Moses' tablets* (you would not say *Moseses,* which is how *Moses's* would sound); *the boss, the boss's order; the bosses, the bosses' orders.* The rule of letting the pronunciation govern is not only easy to follow most of the time, but also conforms to the predominant trend of usage.

It is also considered correct to form the possessive by adding only the apostrophe to words that end in *s* sounds, though not in the letter *s* itself: *Dr. Schultz' office, Mr. Chance' car, Cortez' discovery, innocence' evidence.* Carefully edited writing seems to be consistent, however, in using apostrophe-*s* rather than the apostrophe alone in such instances.

It is generally considered objectionable to make possessives of the names of inanimate things, as in *the water's temperature* and *the sky's color. The temperature of the water* and *the color of the sky* are preferable.

Persons vs. *People*

The superstition persists that *people* cannot be used as the plural of *person* and that *people* correctly denotes only a nation or a large and indefinite group, as in *the British people* or *We, the people.* According to this rule, which is mistaken, one may not speak of *16 people,* or any other definite number, but must say instead *16 persons.*

Bergen and Cornelia Evans comment perceptively that most people now prefer such forms as *three people* to *three persons,* adding that *persons* in many contexts sounds pedantic or bookish. Foolish rules have a way of running amuck, leading to such absurdities as "The job of the comedian is to make persons laugh." The wire services stylebooks permit either *persons* or *people* for small numbers; this leaves examples like the foregoing to the judgment of the writer.

None

About the first thing cub reporters once were told was that the word *none* is singular and consequently always takes a singular verb. They must never write *none are, none were,* but always *none is, none was.* If they questioned the invariable singularity of *none,* some kindly but condescending veteran would explain, "It's a basic rule of grammar. *None* comes from *not one,* and what else can *not one* be but singular?"

The theory is right, but its application is wrong. Authorities on usage agree that *none* may take either a singular or a plural verb, depending on the writer's intention and the context, but the plural is by far the more commonly used. Some examples from Webster: "None of them were intellectually absorbing"; "None of our creeds are entirely free from guesswork." The plurals *them* and *creeds* give a plural feeling to these examples.

Collectives

There are those who insist that words like *couple, group,* and *team* must always be singular. This leads to such sentences as "The *couple* is considered the best *performers* of Shakespeare on the New York stage"; "The *group has been* discussing the problem among *themselves*"; and "The *team* that *wins* the game will have *their* names engraved on the cup."

Words like *couple, group, team,* and other collectives, including *crowd, committee, class, jury, herd,* and *number,* are either singular or plural according to the way they are used. *Number,* perhaps the most frequently used, has its own rule of thumb: preceded by *a,* it is plural; preceded by *the,* it is singular.

The handful of faithful *were* well rewarded.

A score *were* injured in the wreck.

The crowd *was* dispersed.

The crowd *were* waving their programs.

The number of rooms *was* too small.

A number of us *are* going on a picnic.

The words *couple* and *pair* deserve additional mention. In reference to a man and a woman, *couple* should always take a plural verb. Sentences like "The couple will spend *its* honeymoon in the Bahamas" are preposterous.

Adolescent *They*

The misuse of *they, their, them* where *it* or *its* is required is prevalent. This error might well be called the "adolescent *they,*" because it is commonest in the work of immature writers. It occurs frequently, however, in the work of those who are experienced enough to know better. Examples follow.

"The team is proud of their season." Correctly, *its* goes with *is*. "The team *are* proud of *their* season" is another possibility, but the use of the plural with a collective like *team* tends to be British usage and would be unlikely in America. Sentences like "The team is proud of their season" prompted Theodore M. Bernstein, as the in-house critic of the *New York Times,* to ask, "They is?"

"The street will be blocked at night to prevent anyone from parking and leaving their cars after 8 o'clock." The singular construction is required to correspond with *anyone*: This should read ". . . from parking and leaving *a car . . .*" An alternative is, ". . . to prevent drivers from parking and leaving their cars . . ."

"At the request of the star, MGM has changed the advertising copy on their current national newspaper campaign." *Its* should replace *their.*

"The judge said that because the administration finances the project, they have assumed that they are free to suspend it." *It has* should replace *they have,* and *it is* should replace *they are.*

"The church welcomes all students to participate in the varied programs they offer." Here, as in the preceding example, *it* is unavoidable for *they* because *church* has already been established as singular by *welcomes.*

A sentence like "The geography-urban studies major was approved by the Curriculum Committee at their last meeting" is defensible, however, on the ground that *committee* was regarded by the writer as plural. (Regrettably, the committee was referred to in the next sentence as *it*.)

As indicated, in some instances of the adolescent *they* the sentence is grammatically disjointed because a singular verb *(finances, welcomes)* has been used in reference to the antecedent of *they*. In others, an invariably singular collective *(company, church)* is referred to as *they* instead of *it.*

Plural Oddities

Idiom requires that the singular—rather than the plural, which would be logical—be used in expressions like *a 10-year-old boy, a six-mile race, a three-month investigation* (not *10-years-old, six-miles, three-months*). Likewise, it is a 10-foot pole that is used for not touching things. Idiom calls for the plural, however, when the modifying phrase follows rather than precedes the noun. Some erroneous examples are *a man 6 foot tall* and *a ditch 9 foot wide* (correctly: *feet*).

The plurals of compounds like *court-martial* and *right-of-way* formerly were required to be formed on the root words: *courts-martial, rights-of-way.* But *court-martials* and *right-of-ways* are now also considered correct. The possessives of such expressions may also be formed on the last element: *court-martial's finding.*

Names of people that end with *s* (Jones, Dithers, Adams) call for the addition of *es* to form their plurals. Thus, the Jones family are the *Joneses;* not, as we too often see, the *Jones,* the *Jones',* or even the *Jone's.*

Conservative usage still calls for the apostrophe in plurals of letters, figures, signs (the *B's,* the *1940's*) and the like, although there is a strong trend away from it. Forms like *Bs* and *1940s* are perhaps now commoner. Judgment must be exercised in omitting the apostrophe, however; the plural of *A* cannot very well be *As* if confusion is to be avoided.

Even when the apostrophe is dropped in plurals like *GIs,* it is needed to indicate possession *(the GI's uniform)* and seems desirable in verb forms like *OK's* and *OK'd.*

Another curiosity has to do with using plurals when there seems no reason to, and when, in fact, the singular would be more exact. Consider these examples:

Church *services* were held at 11.

Charges of vagrancy were lodged against the transient.

The dedication *ceremonies* were canceled.

In the foregoing, the reference is to a single service, a single charge, and a single ceremony. The plural usage seems fairly prevalent and probably does no harm except, perhaps, when the mistaken impression may be given that more than one charge is lodged.

Editorial (and Royal) *We*

The editorial *we* is customary and justifiable in editorials. But under a byline, the use of *we* can only suggest a split personality in the writer. Few things sound more absurd than *we ourself.*

The use of *I* has been denounced, of course, as immodest. Some writers, then, when they have occasion to mention themselves, masquerade as *this writer, the present writer,* or *the present reporter.* The fact is that such expressions are more obtrusive than *I* and thus really less modest. Rudolf Flesch, among others, has shown how the creation of a personal link between the writer and the audience promotes readability. So, when the circumstances call for it, let the writer have the forthrightness to come out with *I.*

Conclusion

This chapter has dealt with piled-up adjectives, limiting adjectives, dangling participles, participles and time sequence, misrelated appositives, modifiers ending in *-ic* and *-ics,* false possessives, nouns as adjectives and verbs, use of articles, choice of articles with words beginning with *h,* formation of possessives, singular and plural forms, the adolescent *they,* plural oddities, and the editorial *we.*

Writing It Right

This chapter concludes the survey of recurrent faults in newswriting that should be corrected by the copy editor. The survey began with chapter 7.

Like vs. *As*

Conjunction

Don't use *like* as a conjunction. This is the traditional rule, but it is not much observed these days, despite all the indignation generated by that advertising slogan, "Winstons taste good, like a cigarette should." To apply this rule, it is necessary to know a conjunction when you see one. What disturbs the purists is the use of *like* in sentences like "He said the movies are not going to stand still, *like* they have for 25 years"; "She walked to the altar *like* she said she would."

Note in the examples that the groups of words introduced by *like* have subjects and verbs; that is, they are clauses. *Like,* under strict application of the rule, is correctly used only to introduce words or phrases: "He ate *like* a beast" and "She trembled *like* a leaf." The same principle applies to *like* for *as if:* "The Kremlin has been making noises *like* (strictly, *as if*) it wants such a meeting."

A useful rule of thumb was propounded by Frank O. Colby to help those who fear to depart from strict usage: "If *as, as if, as though* make sense in a sentence, *like* is incorrect. If they do not make sense, *like* is the right word."

This rule is easy to use, as will be found by making some trial substitutions, and will keep you in the good graces of the purists even if you don't know what a conjunction or a subordinate clause is. Colby, no purist himself, said he had given up as a lost cause the fight against *like* as a conjunction. So have other authorities.

Some writers have been so terrified by the criticisms of *like* that they won't use it even when it's right. First, we have the *as with* aficionados, who write, "The helicopter, *as with* the horseless carriage of an earlier day, is here to stay." There is a place for *as with,* but the one belonging to *like* is not it.

Then there are those who unnecessarily go the long way around to evade *like:* "The unique plane stands on the ground *in a manner similar to* a camera tripod." It is better to write: " . . . *like* a camera tripod."

Consider the sentence, "Editors, *as* inventors, are creative people." It is not only wrong but misleading. The writer was not speaking of editors in some supposed role as inventors, but intended a comparison, as the context showed: "Editors, *like* inventors, are creative people."

An anchorman on a television news program was also intimidated by *like.* Describing an explosion, he said, "It sounded *as* an atomic bomb." Theodore M. Bernstein observed that such misuses "sound as hell."

Grammarians would agree that the ad slogan writers are well within the pale of informal usage. Shakespeare, John Dos Passos, the *New York Times,* and H. L. Mencken are among those approvingly cited by Rudolf Flesch in *The Art of Readable Writing* as *like*-likers.

Porter G. Perrin, the author of *Writer's Guide and Index to English,* pretty well summed up the views of the grammarians when he said *like* as a conjunction "is obviously on its way to becoming generally accepted and is a good instance of a change in usage, one that we can observe as it takes place."

As vs. Since

As in the sense of *since* or *because* is avoided in careful writing. The reason is that it may be ambiguous.

"As the door was locked, she turned and walked away" is ambiguous, for *as* here may be understood as meaning either *during the time that* or *because.* Even when there is no real ambiguity, *as* for *because* is objectionable because it creates a momentary uncertainty for the reader.

"Porter's design is called the Revised Springfield, as he made it while living in Springfield, Mass." is improved by exchanging *as* for *because*—and improved perhaps even more by removing the comma.

While

While is best reserved to mean *at the same time* and is less happily used in the senses *and, but,* or *although.* "One brother was born June 9, 1893, at Oakland, while the other one was born July 19, 1898, at San Jose" unnecessarily makes readers hesitate, and may make them smile.

"The cannon will be based on Okinawa while the rockets are being sent to Japan" is ambiguous, because what the writer intended was ". . . *but* the rockets are being sent to Japan." "While architecture flourished in Rome, sculpture was less cultivated" would have been understandable as it was meant if the sentence had said, "*Although* architecture flourished. . . ." For some reason, the avoidance of *and, but,* and *although* in favor of the misleading *while* is common in newswriting.

As . . . as, Not so . . . as

The pairs *as . . . as* and *not so . . . as* sometimes present difficulty. "He likes to be known as a philosopher as much as a theologian" lacks an essential *as*. With the construction filled out, it would be "He likes to be known *as a* philosopher *as* much *as as a* theologian." The third *as* is required to complete the comparison, and the fourth one is a preposition that is needed with *theologian* just as much as the first one is needed with *philosopher*. As revised, of course, this sentence is impossible. The cure here is recasting: "He likes to be known equally as a philosopher and as a theologian."

"The critic said the play was as good or better than last season's hits." Another omitted *as,* but this one can be slipped in without difficulty: ". . . as good *as* or better than. . . ."

The idea that *so,* rather than *as,* is required with *not* ("The moon is not *so* large as it was last night") has no grammatical basis. The sentence as quoted is correct, but so is ". . . not *as* large as . . ."; indeed, this is the usual way to say it. *Not only* must be followed by *but also,* not just *but:* "He was not only rich *but also* handsome."

That

The admonition to leave out *that* as a conjunction ("He said *that* he was starving"), when possible, is good advice.

Often, however, we encounter instances when essential *that*s have been omitted.

The question where *that* is called for and where it is not yields only to the capricious law of idiom, and idiom is something that must be sensed. *That* should be retained, in any event, to mark the beginning of a subordinate clause when a part of the clause otherwise may be wrongly associated with some part of the main clause. Often a time element will cause confusion if *that* is left out.

"Metzman said on Jan. 1 the fleet stood at 1,776,000 cars." The speaker was citing the size of the fleet on Jan. 1; therefore, *said that* should be used so the reader does not wonder whether Jan. 1 was the date when he made the statement.

"The speaker said last November the outlook improved." This is another example of the same problem. *That* is needed after either *said* or *November,* depending on the intended meaning. It may be argued that the context is likely to supply the answer to this question, but the reader deserves to be spared even momentary doubt.

Sometimes the omission of *that* sends the reader off on the wrong scent as to the force of the verb: "He added the proposed freeway could follow the existing route." "He added *that* . . ." would read unequivocally, but the first version may appear, for the moment, to make *freeway* alone the object of *added,* as in "He added the proposed freeway to the list of essential projects."

At least one *that,* and preferably a pair of them, should be used with coordinate clauses: "The deputy foreign minister said last night that Panama does not receive its fair share of canal revenues, and sentiment for a 50 percent increase is likely to grow." It is impossible to tell whether the words about growing sentiment for a 50 percent increase were a part of the deputy foreign minister's statement or an observation by the writer. The sentence should have read " . . . and *that* sentiment. . . ."

Before a complete direct quotation, as distinguished from a fragment, *that* is clearly excess baggage: "The relief director in Iran reported *that* 'More than half the population of the village have been killed under the falling walls of their homes.' " This usage was formerly stylistically acceptable but now sounds quaint.

But that sometimes sticks in the craw of the critical, particularly in such sentences as "I do not doubt *but that* society feels threatened by homosexuality." Technically, *but* is excessive here, yet some good writers use this construction.

Prepositions

Prepositions at the Ends of Sentences

The notion that it is wrong or undesirable to end a sentence with a preposition has been refuted by Fowler and many another authority on language. One telling blow was struck by Sir Winston Churchill, who, when accused of ending a sentence with a preposition, is said to have replied, "This is the type of arrant pedantry up with which I shall not put."

You can show that sentences with the preposition at the end are more forceful than those that have been recast to avoid it. You can cite masters of English prose from Chaucer to Churchill who employ end-prepositions freely and consciously. And you can prove that such usage is established literary English, but superstition-ridden writers will still wince at it.

The avoidance of the end preposition is most evident, perhaps, in structural detours that start with a preposition followed by *which.* Few care about making the world a better place *to live in,* but nearly everyone wants to make it a better place *in which to live.* "The car she was riding in" regrettably becomes "The car in which she was riding."

The use of circumlocution to find another place than the end for the preposition not only weakens the sentence but gives it a stilted sound. "What are we coming to?"; "There was nothing to talk about"; "It was something he had always dreamed of"; and "The situation was too much to contend with" are perfectly good English in any context. But they are often distorted to "To what are we coming?"; "There was nothing about which to talk"; "It was something of which he had always dreamed"; and "The situation was too much with which to contend."

The superstition forbidding the preposition at the end of a sentence originated in applying rules of Latin grammar to English. In Latin it is impossible to detach a prepositon from its object. Linguists now, however, have decided that the rules of one language cannot be imposed on another.

Choice of Prepositions

Idiom is often flouted, these careless days, in the choice of prepositions. Let us start with *between* and *among*. No one would use *among* with only two objects (*among you and me*), but there is a a prevalent though misguided idea that *between* cannot be correctly used with *more* than two objects: "Agreements were reached *between* six nations." The proper use of *between* does not depend on the number of objects, but on whether they are being considered in pairs. Even this is open to question as a limiting rule.

Pointless efforts are sometimes made to prescribe *in* or *at,* depending on the prescriber's prejudice, as the correct preposition to use with a place, such as a city, building, or street. Either *in* or *at San Francisco,* or *the Municipal Auditorium,* is correct. Some insist that a house stands *in* a street and, as a corollary, that people live *in* a street. Whatever justification may be advanced for this peculiar usage, popular acceptance is not it. In unaffected parlance, people live *on* a street, not *in* it, and that is where a house stands, too.

"He turned into the Fourth Precinct Police Station" sounds like a feat of magic. We have here a phrasal verb, *turn in,* and the *in* has unfortunately been fused with the preposition *to.* It should have been ". . . turned in to." *Turn into* has its own uses, as in "We turned into a side street."

People used to die *of* things rather than *from* them, and in spite of the widespread use of *from* in this connection, it is still not the best usage. Nor should *of* be used with *off:* write "He jumped off the bridge," not *off of.*

Some writers have people accused *with* crimes rather than *of* them, as they should be. Sometimes they *confess to* the misdeeds, rather than simply confessing them. Do not write "He was accused with the theft, and soon confessed to the crime," but "He was accused *of* . . . and soon confessed the crime."

Confess to appears to have encouraged, by analogy, *admit to:* "Green frankly admits to a youthful membership in the party"; "She admits to having been a brat as a child"; "He admits to a gourmet's interest in food." Fowler said *confess to* is idiomatic and *admit to* is not. Nevertheless, it is observable that *to* is unnecessary with either *confess* or *admit*.

When the defendant is exonerated, it is often written that "the charge was dismissed against Jones." This is a sad arrangement of words, since it tends to link *dismissed* with *against*, and thus to suggest nonsense. Surely it would be preferable to say "The charge against Jones was dismissed." Sometimes we have suspects being exonerated *from* a charge, but here the right preposition is *of*. Likewise, they correctly plead (guilty, not guilty) *to*, not *of*, charges.

Some harbor the delusion that it is wrong to say a man was hit *over* the head, unless the blows missed him. This is a standard sense of the word ("down upon from above"), however, and instantly clear except to those who wilfully misunderstand.

Over often is called into play illogically, as in "Considerable reductions over single-performance prices are again being offered." The reductions, it seems plain, are *from*, not *over*, which suggests an increase.

As as a preposition is unnecessary after such words as *named, appointed, termed, elected*: "He was appointed as vicar" should be "He was appointed vicar."

On

Standardization, by making mechanical parts interchangeable, gave the industrial age a big push. This process is also at work in language, and has been for centuries. The specialists in that field call it not standardization but leveling. That is, diverse forms that do the same or similar jobs tend to merge, or to drive one another out. One evidence of this is the disappearance of *thee, thou, ye,* and the like from all but archaic or specialized usage. *You* has displaced them all.

The losing fight being made by *whom* against *who* is an example of leveling that is under way in our own time. It seems predictable that *whom* will disappear, in spite of the fact that people who are trying too hard to be correct sometimes make it displace *who*. The *New Yorker* calls attention to this from time to time under the heading, "The Omnipotent Whom." (And Ring Lardner wrote, " 'Whom are you?' he asked, for he had been to night school.")

The prize contender for omnipotence is neither *who* nor *whom*, but rather the preposition *on*. An observer of such matters began some time ago to note evidence of *on*'s increasing popularity, especially in the press. *On* was nosing out *about, at, for, from, in, into, of, to,* and *toward*. It may easily press forward and knock all other prepositions out of the language.

Would this be a good thing? Some linguists regard as the most advanced those languages in which leveling has gone the farthest. Certainly it makes communicating simpler. In this instance, the effort now spent on choosing among prepositions would be saved. But *on*, despite its popularity in the press, is not being accepted as an all-purpose preposition elsewhere.

Let us see how *on* has gone berserk (the correct, or more appropriate, words appear in parens):

His worried fans can be reassured *on* one thing, however. *(about, of)*

The officer questioned the woman *on* her wounds. *(about, concerning)*

The mayor was dismayed *on* the permit denial. *(at, by)*

"Don't wait *on* me." This remark was addressed not to a waiter but to a friend by a person who did not want to be waited *for*. This is a Far-Western barbarism, common in conversation. From there it oozes into the newspapers.

The trustees must wait *on* approval by the State Allocations Board. *(await, wait for)*

Complaints *on* dogs running loose are increasing. *(about)*

The man has an elephantlike memory *on* abuse he has taken. *(of)*

Support will be sought *on* the proposal. *(for)*

The wraps may be lifted soon *on* dramatic defense developments. *(from)*

Developments *on* Middle East problems dominated the session. *(in)*

Complaints *on* violations of waterway rules have been received. *(of)*

Science is finding clues *on* possible causes. *(to)*

Little progress has been made *on* racial integration. *(toward, in)*

"The aim is to educate the populace *on* the proper use of English." Let's start now, if it's not too late.

With

"Only citizens of the United States will be eligible for permits with all of them to be issued on a competitive basis"; "Smith was struck in the chest and right hip with the third shot going wild"; "The United States ranks ninth in infant mortality with Sweden having the best record." These uses of *with* are objectionable because the word is used to tack clauses together with no clear indication of their relationship. Usually, the *with*-clauses should be separate sentences or *with* should be replaced by *and*, a stronger conjunction, or a semicolon.

With-phrases can be legitimate, and in any event they must be set off by commas. Here is an example of an unobjectionable *with*-phrase, which unmistakably modifies the main part of the sentence, as it should: "The bandit raced through the corridor, with the police gaining slowly."

But many *with*-phrases are clumsy substitutes for clearer construction. On close inspection, *with* is seen to be introducing elements that ought to be clauses. *With*-phrases are used sparingly by good writers, because they seldom fit happily. Let us see whether a little revision will not improve the examples given earlier:

> Only citizens of the United States will be eligible for permits, all of which will be issued on a competitive basis.
>
> Smith was struck in the chest and right hip, but the third shot went wild.
>
> The United States ranks ninth in infant mortality. Sweden has the best record.

In a usage note, the *American Heritage Dictionary* comments, "Inexperienced writers often use *with* loosely as a means of attaching to a sentence an additional thought that would be treated more clearly and grammatically as an independent clause either following a semicolon or introduced by *and*: *English and history are his major subjects with economics as his first elective* (preferably, *English and history are his major subjects; economics is his first elective*)."

Piled-up Prepositions

It must be an uncontrollable passion for exactness that causes us to pile up prepositions or, in some instances, to use them when they could be better omitted altogether. Doubled prepositions often occur when a range is specified: "Its control spreads *into between* 25 and 30 percent of the economy." Such constructions are clumsy. This reads more smoothly as ". . . into 25 or 30 percent." "The airlift is expected to speed the delivery of mail *by from* 24 to 48 hours" would be smoother with *from* left out. "Investments *of from* two to four million dollars were reported." Here too, *from* is superfluous.

"The weatherman predicted a low temperature *of between* 75 and 80 degrees." In this instance, *of* is expendable. Newspaper weather stories seem especially hospitable to intrusive prepositions. The italicized words would never be missed in "A low temperature *of* near 45 degrees is expected" and "The Sierra received *from* 2 to 4 inches of slushy snow." *At about* may be trimmed to *about*: "About 9 last night."

Sequence of Tenses

Many an absurdity is committed in the name of the widely mis-applied rule of grammar governing sequence of tenses. The general idea is that the tense of the verb in the main clause of a sentence governs the tense in a subordinate clause. Sometimes this is called "attracted sequence"; that is, the tense of the verb in the main clause attracts the verb in the following clause. Let's look at an example: "He *said* he *was* tired of everything." The verb in the main clause, *said*, is in the past tense, so the following verb, *was*, naturally falls into the same tense. Most of the time, this rule is followed instinctively.

Here are some other examples of normal sequence of tenses:

The man *wore* a pained expression as the officer *forced* his car to the curb.

The motorist *explained* that he *tried* to buy a replacement for his defective headlamp.

She *promised* that she *would* be there.

The basic rule has an important exception: The *present* tense, rather than the past, is called for in the subordinate clause to express a continuing or timeless state of affairs. Consider: "He *said* the world *is* round." Applying the basic rule of sequence, *is* should be *was* because the main verb, *said*, is in the past tense. But that might make it sound as if the world no longer was round.

Exceptions to the basic rule of sequence are properly made to describe any condition that continues in effect at the time of writing. Here are some examples:

The surveyor *reported* that the terrain is (not *was*) rugged.

He *pointed out* that there are (not *were*) 75 to 80 independent government agencies, each of which *consumes* (not *consumed*) the president's time.

Although the basic rule of sequence applies properly to one sentence at a time, some writers allow succeeding sentences to be attracted into the past tense; for example, "The chances of Richard Roe, candidate for Congress, *were considered* good. Roe *was* a Catholic from a predominantly Catholic district."

Since Roe's candidacy continued at the time of writing, this gave the unintended impression that he might have changed his religion. Lapses like this, which can be prevented by understanding the rule of sequence and knowing when to make an exception to it, have drawn indignant protests to editors and have confused readers.

Split Infinitives

One might think the revered H. W. Fowler had the last word on the split infinitive more than 50 years ago when he divided the English-speaking world into five classes, namely, "(1) those who neither know nor care what a split infinitive is; (2) those who do not know, but care very much; (3) those who know and condemn; (4) those who know and approve; and (5) those who know and distinguish."

His conclusion remains the consensus of authorities on usage. In a nutshell: a split infinitive is not an error of itself. The acceptability of a split infinitive depends only on whether it damages the rhythm or meaning of the sentence.

Let's start from the beginning. An infinitive is a verb form containing *to*: to go, to run, to eat, to walk. It is split when *to* and the verb are separated: *to* quickly *go, to* clumsily *run.* Splitting an infinitive objectionably is only one of the many ways a sentence can be spoiled by poor arrangement. Yet many writers go to any lengths to avoid splitting, even though the cure may be worse than the disease.

Those who are impatient with grammatical distinctions may rely on the ear as a pretty good guide. If a sentence doesn't sound right it isn't any good, whether or not the infinitive is split.

These split infinitives are objectionable because they sound awkward: "I want to *consistently* enforce discipline"; "His purpose was to *effortlessly* be promoted"; "Jones was ordered to *immediately* embark." The adverb (italicized) fits easily at the end in each instance.

But look at this: "Production of food fats is expected to *moderately* exceed domestic use and commercial exports." Non-split fanatics are likely to do one of two things with it. They may make the sentence read ". . . is expected *moderately* to exceed. . . ." which is unsatisfactory because it raises doubt whether the expecting or the exceeding will be moderate; or they may move *moderately* to the end of the sentence, but that's too far away from *exceed*, which it modifies. The sentence is fine as it stands.

This sentence was criticized as containing an undesirable split: "This will permit the nation to *quietly* drop her violent opposition to the treaty." Although there was no other comfortable place for the adverb, rewording was prescribed. This kind of thing only illustrates Fowler's comment to the effect that reasons are not the strong point of the critics of split infinitives.

Infinitives of Purpose

Consider this sentence: "He made the trek in four days to arrive here exhausted." One might easily get the impression that the poor fellow had traveled with the intention of wearing himself out. That seems absurd, so you decide that what the writer really meant was "He made the trek in four days, arriving here exhausted."

Constructions like *to get* in "He went to the store *to get* some ice cream" are sometimes called infinitives of purpose. Obviously, they convey an intention. They ought to be saved for that purpose; if they are used when no intention exists, a double meaning results.

"Increased sales are announced by many companies, to confound the pessimists." One would think those diabolical companies announced increased sales just to confound the pesky pessimists. What seems more probable is that the confounding of the pessimists simply occurred after the announcements, such as would be expressed by "Increased sales are announced by many companies, confounding the pessimists."

Misleading Infinitives

Infinitives find their way into places where they are obtrusive, ambiguous, or both: "It was the largest maneuver *ever to be held.*" The writer could have achieved the purpose explicitly by leaving out *to be:* "It was the largest maneuver ever held in the South."

Sometimes an infinitive displaces a relative clause: "This is one of 19 communities *to have* such a program." Here, too, there is a suggestion of the future. The intended meaning, however, was *that have.*

"One of the most determined suicide attempts *to be* recorded locally was a failure yesterday." Again, the infinitive does nothing but give a misleading suggestion of the future; it should have been omitted. *Ever* would contribute emphasis, if that is desired.

"He was one of three speakers to address the meeting." Misinterpretation is unlikely here, although this might be understood as ". . . who were scheduled to address . . ." The writer meant ". . . one of three speakers who addressed the meeting."

Division of Compound Verbs

There is a widespread and mistaken idea, apparently prompted by the delusion that it is wrong to split an infinitive, that it is also wrong to put something between the parts of compound verbs like *has been, must approve,* and *will block.*

The budget was *(tentatively)* approved.

The matter was *(automatically)* delayed.

Experts are *(now)* pinning their hopes on the House.

The words in parentheses separate the parts of compound verbs, and some critics would place them elsewhere. But there is no reason for it, although the first two examples would be just as acceptable with the adverbs at the end.

Consider these points:

1. In many sentences, an adverb falls naturally between the parts of a compound verb. Juggling the quoted sentences around will show this.
2. The separation of compound verbs is essentially a question of word order. Considerations of emphasis, euphony, and meaning should govern.

Fowler was emphatic in refuting the superstition that division of compound verbs is undesirable, and he went so far as to say that putting the adverb anywhere except between the parts of the verb requires special justification.

Shall and *Will*, *Should* and *Would*

There is a formula for the use of the verbs *shall* and *will* and *should* and *would*. It goes like this: To express the simple future, or let us say to indicate a simple intention, use *shall* with the first person and *will* with the second and third persons. This gives us "I *shall* grow old one day" and "You (he, she, it) *will* grow old one day." Plurals follow the same pattern. "We *shall* . . ." but "You (they) *will* . . ." Then, to express determination or insistence, the pattern is reversed: "I *will* demand my share, no matter what they say" and "You *shall* obey the law like everyone else."

The mass mind that decides such matters appears to have rejected this method of making the distinction between simple future and determination, however. Usage now largely ignores it.

For better or worse, *shall* and *should* have taken on a precious overtone. The purists among the English lump Scots, Irishmen, and Americans together when they fix the blame for the downfall of *shall*.

"The story is a very old one," writes Sir Ernest Gowers, "of the drowning Scot who was misunderstood by English onlookers and was left to his fate because he cried, 'I will drown and nobody shall save me!' " Fowler mentioned the same story, calling it much too good to be true. In the story, the English, construing their grammar strictly, understood the Scot as insisting that he was determined to drown and would allow no one to save him.

Shall, then, seems well on the way to extinction, much like the hapless Scot, except in certain constructions where it is used idiomatically without hesitation, for example in questions, like "Shall I answer the telephone?" and "Shall we dance?" *Shall* also remains firmly entrenched as a means of expressing compulsion or obligation, especially in legal contexts: "The sum shall be repaid in monthly installments."

To the undiscriminating, *shall* is more elegant than *will,* and this causes them to put it in impossible contexts: "I look forward to the time when delegates like yourselves shall meet in every country of the world." The writer intended the simple future, which would have been conveyed by *will,* but with *shall* he expressed the idea *will be compelled to meet.*

Should has fallen under much the same shadow as *shall.* "I should like to attend the premiere" and "If the price fell, I should buy the property" grate on the ears of most Americans, who would say *would. Should* is generally used now only in the sense of *ought to:* "We should put the car in the garage before it rains."

The nice distinctions of determination vs. simple future that once hung on the choice between *shall* and *will* are now made by the tone of voice, in speaking, and by a choice of words that cannot be misunderstood ("you *must*" rather than "you *shall*"), in writing.

Passive Voice

The use of the passive voice ("The door *was opened"* rather than "Someone *opened* the door") is a frequent object of unjustified criticism. Sweeping indictments like this are meaningless.

Some critics say the passive is undesirable in description or narration. The real issue is whether the subject brought into prominence by use of the passive voice is important enough. "The door was closed quietly" and "The issue was discussed for an hour" are hardly objectionable if the closer of the door and the discussers of the issue are unimportant.

As a device for varying sentence structure, however, the passive is not only objectionable but conspicuous. In the course of a biographical sketch, "Further education *was received* at Brown University" is absurd because it places an unexplainable emphasis on *further education.* "France and Germany *were visited* next" illustrates the same fault. (The use of the passive in headlines has already been discussed in chapter 3.)

Problems of Reference

Pronouns are conveniences, but we often tend to shun them in favor of unnecessarily repeating nouns or using synonyms. Ambiguity, it is true, can result from using pronouns carelessly. But when the reference is unmistakable, it seems too bad to forego the terseness, naturalness, and ease of expression that come from writing simply *he* instead of *the waiter, she* instead of *the lawyer,* and *it* instead of *the proposal under discussion.*

Fear of pronouns is related to another idiosyncrasy, love of synonyms, or what Fowler called "sobriquets." The writer sometimes seems to want to astound the reader with the number of different names that can be given to the same thing. Thus a game becomes successively a *contest*, an *event*, a *match*, a *set-to*, a *tilt*, an *encounter*, and a *tussle* in as many paragraphs. Fear of pronouns is evident in the examples in the next three paragraphs:

"Three governors planning to attend the conference have stated their intention of turning public schools over to private hands. The three are . . ." Why not "*They* are"?

"A mechanic's helper shot and killed his estranged wife with a shotgun while she slept with one of the couple's three children." By saying the *couple's* instead of *their*, the writer avoided the smoother construction for the more awkward one.

"A spokesman said the group gave a vote of confidence to the negotiation committee and endorsed the latter's stand in refusing a wage increase." Why not *its* instead of the clumsy *the latter's?*

Sometimes repetition of a word grates on the ear and is therefore to be avoided. But a dozen sentences are spoiled by straining to avoid repetition for every one that is spoiled by repetition, as Fowler noted.

He, She (   )

"Jones said Smith had told him about the affair and that he (Smith) had denied taking part in it." The writer evidently decided that *he* might be ambiguous, and thus put *Smith* in parentheses beside it, as if to say, "*I* know who I mean, but I must give the reader some help." The writer may also be trying to avoid simply repeating the name, and in doing so commits the folly of *he (Smith)*, which is an example of editing that has been imposed on the reader. There is no reason to write *he (Smith)*. Here is the original example, sensibly amended: "Jones said Smith had told him about the affair and that Smith had denied taking part in it."

If ambiguity indeed exists, repeat the noun; the pronoun and the noun side by side are silly. "The governor decided to resign in favor of the secretary of state, so that he (the governor) could be appointed to the Senate." Not really ambiguous with *he* alone, but in any event the writer's fears could have been allayed by *the governor* alone.

The *he, she (   )* construction is called for only in a direct quotation when it is necessary to prevent ambiguity: "The observer reported, 'Some believe that he [Alexander] is only waiting for the right moment.' " Brackets, instead of parentheses, are used in such instances to indicate an editorial insertion.

Leapfrog

Another problem of reference is exemplified by a device we might call leapfrog. The object is to see if the reader can make the jump from one to the other of two related references that have been separated by the writer, as in this example:

> A prominent businessman criticized the city's proposals for off-street parking today as too expensive and poorly planned. Edward Kline spoke at a meeting of the Chamber of Commerce Traffic Committee, of which he is a member.

Is Kline the prominent businessman? Of course, the writer might reply. Yet the link between *prominent businessman* and *Edward Kline* has to be forged by the reader. Depending on a variety of factors, more or less hesitation ensues when the reader encounters such a gap in identification. Neglecting to show the relation between one thing and the next is an offense against the principle that calls for effective transitions. In the example, the second sentence should have been tied to the first by something like "The businessman, Edward Kline . . ." or "The criticism was expressed today by Edward Kline at . . ."

Let us go on to what might be called a three-stage example of the same kind of error: "Senator Francis Case, for one, is going to be definitely chary. The South Dakotan has too long a memory. When the newly elected solon heard about the incident, he laughed." There was nothing in what went before to identify Senator Case as either a South Dakotan or newly elected. The reader was expected to jump to the conclusion that all three designations referred to the same man. No doubt the reader did jump to the right conclusion after a confused moment or two. But why should the reader have to jump at all? It would have been better to write "The senator, who is newly elected from South Dakota, has too long a memory. When he heard about the incident, he laughed."

Here's another obstacle course: "The judge discharged a juror, after learning that William Roark was related by marriage to the defendant's cousin." Roark was the juror, but the reader could not be sure of this without looking for further clues. It would have been better to write "The judge discharged William Roark as a juror after learning that he. . . ."

Conclusion

In this, the concluding chapter on faults of writing common in journalism, we have considered the use of *like* and *while* as conjunctions; the pairs *as . . . as* and *not so . . . as;* omission of *that;* prepositions ending sentences; choice of prepositions; *on* as an all-purpose preposition; the decline of *whom; with* phrases; sequence of tenses; split infinitives; infinitives of purpose; misleading infinitives; division of compound verbs; and the uses of *shall/will* and *should/would.* We have also examined the passive voice; problems of reference; *he, she (   );* and leapfrog.

13 The Press and the Law

The guarantee of freedom of the press under the First Amendment is not absolute or unqualified. Absolute freedom of expression in print or by any other graphic means is curbed by a variety of laws. The most important of these to the copy editor are those laws aimed at deterring and punishing *libel,* that is, statements that damage a person's reputation or tend to cause ridicule or contempt.

But there are others. The publication of obscenity is punishable by law, but what constitutes obscenity has never been satisfactorily defined. Legal precedents in this field continue to shift. This shifting has occurred more rapidly in recent years, perhaps, than ever before because of swift changes in the public view of sexual morality. Copyright laws are aimed at protecting the ownership of what a writer has created. Invasion of privacy, a new and still foggy field, is regulated by law to protect people from unwarranted publicity concerning their private lives. Lotteries ordinarily may not be publicized under postal regulations. Each of these fields will be dealt with to the extent that fits their importance to the copy editor.

Libel

Sticks and stones/May break my bones/But names will never hurt me. So goes the old playground jingle, which makes the distinction between physical injury and hurt feelings or offense. Calling names, however, can not only hurt the victim but can subject the caller to lawsuit and the payment of damage.

Libel is a complicated subject, but it is unnecessary for editors to command a lawyer's knowledge of it. It is not possible, in any event, to deal with more than its highlights in this chapter. Schools of journalism invariably offer separate courses in law of the press. Every newswriter and editor should know enough about the basic principles of libel to be able to recognize instantly a statement in a news story or a headline that may present a danger of it.

If such danger arises, one of two courses of action is open. The potentially damaging matter may be struck out if it is of no importance. Or, if the statement is important and the newspaper feels that the public should have access to it, the editor may consult a lawyer before publishing it, to get advice on the extent of the danger. Large newspapers keep libel lawyers on retainer for such advice, and many newspapers carry libel insurance. Even though the lawyer may conclude that the danger of suit is great, the newspaper may decide to take a chance and publish the statement anyway if it feels that the public interest must be served.

Libel is a matter of state law, which means there are 50 sets of laws on the subject. Although they correspond pretty well on general principles, there are also some important differences, so it behooves journalists to be familiar with the libel laws of their respective states. Ultimately, libel, in a given case, is what the court or jury decides it to be. Although general principles can be deduced from the law and from precedents set in trials, identical sets of circumstances have been adjudged libelous in some cases and harmless in others.

To begin with, there are two classifications of libel, *civil* and *criminal,* which correspond to the classifications into which all court actions fall. Civil cases are those in which a person who feels wronged in some way by another (for example by breach of contract or failure to pay a debt) and sues the other person. In civil cases, the state provides the facilities (that is, the courts) and the referee (that is, the judge and jury). The parties to the action, represented by their lawyers, then fight it out. Criminal cases, on the other hand, are those in which a wrong against society is charged, such as murder, theft, rape, or any other act defined by the law as a crime. The overwhelming number of libel cases are civil suits, that is, actions in which one person is seeking amends from another. The number of criminal libel actions, in which the published statement is regarded as likely to prompt a breach of the peace, is negligible.

In civil suits, generally, the object of the person suing is the payment of money, the ownership of property, or the guarantee of certain rights that are in dispute. No one is fined (compelled to make a payment to the state) or sent to jail as the result of a civil suit, although the defendant may be required to pay a monetary penalty to the plaintiff. In criminal actions, the government takes the initiative on behalf of society, arresting and charging persons suspected of having committed crimes, trying them, and, if they are found guilty, fining or imprisoning them or both.

Libel may also be placed in one of two classifications other than civil and criminal: *per se* (on its face, or in and of itself) and *per quod* (under the circumstances). For many years it has been considered libelous to falsely call a person a Communist; doing so would be an example of libel *per se,* that is, libel on its face. In a case of libel *per quod* the plaintiff would have to show that damages to reputation occurred due to the circumstances. At the time when polygamy was a tenet of the Mormon Church, a published report in New York revealing the name of a man who had joined the church could have been the basis for a lawsuit on the grounds of libel *per quod,* since polygamy was an infraction of the law forbidding bigamy.

It may be useful at this point to define the terms *plaintiff* and *defendant.* The plaintiff (the term applies only to civil suits) is the one who feels wronged by someone and who does the suing. The defendant (the term is used in both civil and criminal actions) is the one being sued or, in criminal actions, prosecuted.

Bases for Libel

Libel is descended from and closely related to another legal concept, namely, *slander.* The essential difference between them is that slander is what has been spoken and libel is what has been printed or given some other graphic representation, such as writing on a wall. Usually, statements that have been transmitted by the broadcast media are regarded as libel rather than slander, because the audiences are so large.

The important thing to remember about libel is that it is *defamation;* that is, it damages the victim's reputation. A libelous statement may cause people to think less of the victim; it may cause people to shun the victim's society by saying the victim suffers from a contagious disease; it may undermine the victim's means of livelihood by questioning occupational competence. Hurt feelings or offense alone, which might be caused by an insulting but private letter, do not constitute grounds for a complaint of civil libel. It is the damage to one's standing in the eyes of others that counts here.

Libel is further defined by other conditions. To begin with, a libel must be *published.* The word is usually understood as meaning *printed,* but in the eyes of the law *published* means "exposed to public view." Thus, a typewritten sheet posted on a bulletin board or a photograph tacked to a telephone pole would also be regarded as having been published. Also, the victim must be *identified* in the statement complained of. This seems simple enough, because identification appears to hinge on whether the victim is named. But once again, the legal view goes farther. If a published statement refers to a person in such a way that a substantial number of readers can deduce who is meant, even though the person may not actually be named, identification may be presumed.

Because a newspaper is responsible for all its content, which includes advertising as well as news, ads should be as carefully scrutinized for possible libel as news stories. Letters to the editor can be dangerous. A newspaper is also responsible for printing a libelous letter, even though the letter may present a point of view with which the newspaper itself totally disagrees. The fact that a libelous statement is quoted, say, in a story based on an interview or the coverage of a speech, likewise offers no protection from suit.

A libel can be in the form of a photograph—for example, a photograph misidentifying a respectable citizen as a criminal or one that appears to depict the citizen in some questionable activity. The fact that the libel was the result of an accident, such as a typographical error, does not diminish the responsibility for it, though this will probably soften the judgment. Most libel suits grow out of carelessness with small facts, such as names and addresses, in stories about crimes. Some criminals deliberately give false addresses to the authorities. Libel suits have been filed by the innocent people living at those addresses. This is the reason why police stories often refer to an arrested person as one "who gave the address to police" as the location published. Some newspapers even avoid giving house numbers in such instances and give only the block number.

The concept of *malice* figures importantly in libel actions. In common parlance, malice is ill will or the intent to injure. Libel law, however, makes a distinction between malice, which is assumed to be present even though a defamation is unintentional, and *actual malice,* or the deliberate intent to injure.

Defenses Against Libel

Once a newspaper has been sued for libel, it must cast about for means of defending itself. Three primary defenses and several lesser ones may be invoked, depending on the circumstances. *Truth* is one of the three most important defenses. In most states, the suit will be dismissed if the statement complained of can be proven to be true. The difficulty here is that many true statements are not provable to the satisfaction of a court; a possible defendant contemplating this defense should consider carefully what evidence can be offered. It is up to the defendant to prove truth; the plaintiff need not prove untruth. In other states, truth is a defense only if the court determines that the statement was published with good motives and for justifiable ends. That is, the defendant must prove that a truthful statement was made with the public interest in mind—and *not* with the intent to injure the plaintiff. To put it another way, absence of actual malice must be evident.

The second of the three important defenses is known as *privilege*. Under certain circumstances, libelous statements may be freely published without danger of successful suit. Participants in a trial or legislators in session cannot be sued for any statements made in the course of the proceedings, whether those statements are true or false (though of course lying under oath is punishable as perjury). Public documents, such as official records of arrests and of ownership of property, are privileged. These immunities have been established so that fear of reprisal will not interfere with the pursuit of justice in a trial or with the process of lawmaking. The participants in these two kinds of proceedings enjoy *absolute privilege*. Newspapers and other publications enjoy *qualified privilege,* which means that they may report what has been said provided a balanced and fair account is given. If, for example, a newspaper favored one party in a lawsuit and reported only that party's side of the issue, it might lose the protection of privilege.

Statements made in places other than a court in session or on the floor of a legislature are not privileged, even though they may relate to a trial or a legislative issue. Reporters often obtain information from lawyers in the corridor or on the courthouse steps. Newspapers are not privileged to publish this information if the information is libelous. Lawmakers are sometimes challenged to repeat, away from the floor of the legislature, statements they have made there under the immunity of privilege. The purpose of such challenges is obviously to set the stage for a lawsuit.

The third of the three most important defenses against libel is *fair comment and criticism*. The point is that anyone who offers something for public approval (for example, a person who has written a book or performed on a stage) is open to criticism. Such criticisms may be sharp indeed, without endangering the critics. This defense offers the protection under which book, drama, music, movie, and other critics do their work. The rule of thumb is "Don't get personal." Critics may freely call a *book* the stupidest book ever written, but they may be on dangerous ground if they call the *author* stupid.

The doctrine of fair comment and criticism was greatly expanded in relation to public officials by the 1964 Supreme Court decision in *New York Times* v. *Sullivan*. The case grew out of civil rights activity in Montgomery, Alabama.

Under the heading "Heed Their Rising Voices," a civil rights group published a full-page advertisement in the *Times* on March 29, 1960. The ad contained a number of statements that L.B. Sullivan, commissioner of public affairs for the city of Montgomery, believed reflected adversely on him, although he was not named. Sullivan held the *New York Times* responsible for the several factual errors in the text of the advertisement. Among them were that police had ringed the Alabama State College campus during a demonstration; that students were expelled from school for demonstrating on the capitol steps; and that the college dining hall had been padlocked in an attempt to starve students into submission. Sullivan also charged that descriptions of attacks on Dr. Martin Luther King, the civil rights leader, implied that Sullivan was responsible.

Sullivan sued the *Times* and four black clergymen whose names appeared beneath the ad and won a $500,000 verdict in the Alabama courts. But the case was appealed and the decision reversed in the United States Supreme Court. This reversal had far-reaching influence on the effect of libel law on public officials. The most important conclusion was that statements about public officials may be false and still not libelous. To be considered libelous, the statements need only be intentional falsehoods or show reckless disregard of the truth. Where the line is drawn on "reckless disregard" is a matter that can only be decided case by case. But there is no question that the Sullivan decision sharply reduced the protection of the libel law for public officials. Some authorities believe it destroyed that protection and, in effect, made public officials fair game for any attack having to do with the performance of their duties.

It should also be noted that a "public figure" is not necessarily a "public official," and that the libel laws for public officials may or may not apply to public figures. The rule laid down in the Sullivan case has been subsequently applied in others where the plaintiffs were a well-known writer and a noted professor. Where the line is drawn on what constitutes a public figure must also be decided case by case, although in many instances the decision is obvious.

There are other defenses against libel, but they are less important because there are fewer occasions for using them. One such defense is consent; that is, if a person has given permission for the publication of personal statements, that individual cannot sue. Consent may be useful with respect to interviews. For evident reasons, it should always be obtained in writing.

The statute of limitations governs libel as it does other legal actions; that is, a suit must be started within a specified period, usually one or two years. The right of reply is another minor defense (in the sense that few cases occur in which it is invoked). It relates to the right to answer an attack in terms as vigorous as the attack itself.

Mitigation

The penalties in a libel suit may be reduced if the ~~plaintiff~~ *defendant* can show absence of actual malice, that is, of deliberate intent to injure. This is not difficult in cases where the libel results from accident, for example from a typographical error or other honest mistake. Damage to the plaintiff's reputation may have resulted, and the publisher of the libel may be penalized, but not as severely as if actual malice is evident.

People who think they have been libeled may demand a retraction, and if the newspaper decides it has made a mistake or could not defend itself against the lawsuit, the correction may willingly be granted. A retraction takes the form of a news story admitting the original account was in error and expressing regret for the mistake and any embarrassment or inconvenience it may have caused the victim. Generally speaking, a retraction does not necessarily forestall a libel suit, but it, too, may be a mitigating factor for the defense.

Since 1945, the state of California has provided that if a newspaper, broadcasting station, or press association (but *not* a magazine) has published a libel, the plaintiff may recover no more than actual personal monetary losses, unless the plantiff demanded a retraction within 20 days of the original publication. Publication of the retraction then removes grounds for suit. To qualify for this exemption, the paper must publish the retraction as conspicuously as the original article and within 21 days after the request has been made. Twenty other states have passed similar laws.

It is a widespread delusion among newspeople that use of the word *alleged* (alleged thief, alleged gangster) confers immunity from libel. This is not true. At most, it may be argued that the word was intended to soften the description and thus should be considered in mitigation. Under the same delusion, newspeople often use the word *accused* (accused murderer). This may not be libelous, but authorities on English usage have criticized it on the grounds that it may leave the reader with an impression of guilt, and not merely accusation.

Copy editors must handle headlines with care, since a headline itself may be adjudged libelous, notwithstanding the fuller explanation in the text beneath. The commonest danger is in characterizing as a criminal someone who has merely been charged with an offense and may be acquitted. Or the charges may later be dropped for lack of evidence. The difference between danger and safety may hinge on the choice of prepositions. "Man arrested for robbery," for example, convicts the defendant in advance on the specific charge of robbery. "Man arrested *in* robbery," on the other hand, safely says that a robbery occurred and an arrest has been made in connection with it.

Headline writers must also be careful to avoid characterizing suspects or defendants in such a way as to indicate they have been convicted. Obviously, a person who has simply been charged with or is being tried for a crime cannot be called a "killer" or "thief" or "swindler," in the headline. Such terms are safe to use only after a suspect's conviction; that is, after the defendant has been found guilty.

The fact of an arrest, although it is certainly defamatory, is a matter of public record, and reporting it does not cause exposure to suit for libel. This is true even though the defendant is found not guilty or if the charge is dropped. The danger in cases like this usually arises from lack of care on the part of the reporter. It is necessary to verify that a charge has been officially entered by the police before reporting it as fact. Documents should be checked. The police sometimes announce their intention of lodging a charge but then change their minds. An erroneous report that a person has been charged with an offense may expose a paper to suit.

Statements by the police concerning the probable guilt of someone they have arrested are not privileged, nor are the defendant's confessions or other statements privileged. Nevertheless, such statements are freely reported every day by the press. Few libel suits grow out of them, perhaps because a person charged with a crime, innocent or not, has other, more pressing matters at hand. Sometimes people who feel they have been injured by a published statement refrain from seeking a retraction that might easily be obtained, simply to avoid attracting further attention to the matter.

Damages

Damages that may be assessed against a newspaper or anyone else found to have published a libel are classified under three headings: compensatory (or general); punitive (or exemplary); and special.

Compensatory damages are intended, as the word implies, to atone to the injured victim. The reasoning is that although money will not heal all wounds, it may be an effective salve, and that the libeler owes it to the plaintiff. Compensatory damages may be nominal (in name only), and amount to as little as six cents. This was the judgment in a case many years ago in which Henry Ford, the founder of the Ford Motor Co., sued the *Chicago Tribune* for having called him an anarchist. Such an award may seem meaningless, but it does constitute a moral victory and may satisfy the plaintiff.

Punitive, or *exemplary,* damages, as the terms imply, are intended to punish the defendant and to make an example of him to others. Such damages may be assessed in addition to compensatory, or general, damages.

Special damages are levied to repay the victim for actual monetary losses suffered as the result of a libel. A merchant libeled by a statement that he was in the habit of overcharging his customers, for example, might be awarded special damages calculated on the extent to which his business suffered as a result of the charge. In a given case (for example, one in which a doctor was referred to in terms creating the impression that she was a quack, or one in which a lawyer was described as a shyster) all three kinds of damages might be assessed.

Who May Be Libeled?

Groups, as a general rule, cannot sue for civil libel unless it can be shown that the derogatory statements complained of are damaging to their members as individuals. Such cases are rare. Derogatory statements about a group, if they are found to tend to a breach of the peace, riot, or other unlawful act may be the basis for a suit for *criminal* libel, however. Corporations can be libeled, because under the law they are regarded as persons; cases involving damage to corporate reputations are sometimes referred to as trade libel. People who are dead cannot be the subjects of action for civil libel because their reputations are assumed to die with them. However, libel of the dead can be the subject of a charge of *criminal* libel on the grounds of the effect it may have on survivors.

Invasion of Privacy

This is a relatively new concept in law, having arisen from an article by Louis D. Brandeis and Samuel N. Warren in the *Harvard Law Review* in 1890. The idea is that people are entitled to protection from exposure of their private lives. Brandeis and Warren complained that "the press is overstepping in every direction the bounds of propriety and decency." This was at a time when large and growing circulations of newspapers were feeding to a great extent on sensation. The concept remains foggy, because not many court cases have been based on it, and definition depends on decisions in cases.

Court cases so far have largely involved the publication of pictures. There is no question that a person's picture may not be used in an *advertisement* without that person's permission, but the content of ads is not likely to concern the copy editor or the news editor. No question of invasion of privacy arises if a person is photographed at random in public for news purposes or in circumstances where the newsworthiness of the picture is beyond doubt. However, people in poverty areas whose pictures were published to illustrate their condition of life have filed suits on the grounds that such depictions held them up to scorn and ridicule.

If any doubt arises as to whether privacy has been invaded by pictures taken, say, at the subject's home, it is well to obtain written permission before their publication.

Copyright

Copyright laws resemble patent laws in that their purpose is to protect property rights in products of the mind—for example, an invention or a piece of writing, a photograph, or a musical composition. As copyright laws affect newspapers, perhaps the most important thing to realize is that facts (that is, information) as such cannot be protected by copyright. Copyright protects only the form in which the information is cast—the arrangement of the words. As the term itself suggests, copyright law is aimed at copying, or plagiarism.

Some information on which news stories are based is obtained from books, magazines, and other copyrighted sources. There is no danger of infringement of copyright as long as the facts are not repeated in the same words the source used. Courtesy and fair play require, however, that credit be given to the source of any substantial information even though it is not directly quoted.

A great deal of rewriting of other newspapers goes on in journalism, and all of it is considered fair play and is taken for granted. On well-regulated newspapers, stories from other papers are not rewritten without a check to make certain the statements in the original are accurate and to discover whether there are any new developments. In some instances newspapers have been embarrassed and even penalized under laws controlling unfair trade practices for regularly relying on the fact-gathering done by their competitors. In one such instance, the parasite was trapped because the victim deliberately included errors of fact in stories intended to corner the copying paper, which repeated them.

Direct quotation of copyrighted material requires not merely that the source be credited but that permission be obtained. Sometimes a fee may be charged for such permission. In all instances, the fact that permission was granted must be indicated in the form specified by the copyright holder.

The laws regarding permissions are modified, however, by what is referred to as the doctrine of "fair use." Under this principle, which has never been sharply defined, writers may quote briefly from copyrighted works without obtaining permission. How much may be quoted? This is where uncertainty comes in. No specific number of words has ever been established. Some authorities say up to 50 words, but this is just a guess. Two of the considerations that enter into quoting under the fair use principle are the proportion of the whole that is used and the purpose in quoting. Quoting to illustrate a point in a scholarly or academic work, for example, is considered safe; popular works such as fiction may be another matter. The source of whatever is quoted must be scrupulously identified. Passing off another's words as one's own is, of course, plagiarism, which is illegal as a form of theft from copyrighted material and immoral in any event.

As a practical matter, no suit for infringement is likely to arise from a reasonable quotation properly credited. Even if the author feels taken advantage of and thus presses a suit, the author's chances of recovering enough to make legal action worthwhile are usually remote. Many authors, on the other hand, are delighted to see their words quoted, within reason; it is a form of recognition and may have value as free advertising of the quoted work.

Book reviewers, however, have the prerogative of directly quoting a reasonable amount from a work being reviewed, for the purpose of illustrating a point. No permission is required in this circumstance. Publishers ordinarily are delighted to have their books reviewed, even adversely, and are more than willing to have them quoted in reviews.

Feature writers, particularly, sometimes have occasion to quote lyrics of popular songs, but if they do so without permission their newspapers are certain to hear from the copyright holders, very likely in none too agreeable terms. Great care must also be exercised in quoting poetry.

Problems of copyright seldom arise in newspaper work. When in doubt about the legality of quoting, however, request permission.

Lotteries

Lotteries, more commonly known as drawings, may not be publicized in newspapers under postal regulations. An offending newspaper is likely to receive a warning from postal authorities before any drastic action is taken, but by disregarding the law the paper may lose its second-class mailing privileges. Three requirements must be met for a drawing to constitute a lottery: (1) a prize must be offered; (2) there must be a consideration, that is, purchase of a ticket or some other investment; and (3) the prize or prizes must be awarded by chance.

Presumably the law forbids publicizing such activities in either ads or news stories as a means of discouraging gambling. Nevertheless, no such restraint is placed on horse racing, an occasion for betting compared with which most lotteries must be considered peanuts. In recent years, however, several states have instituted official lotteries as means of raising money for operating expenses, and these lotteries have been publicized despite the question of legality. Nevertheless, the postal regulations affecting lotteries have kept innumerable announcements of church bingo parties, turkey raffles, door prizes, and the like out of the newspaper.

Rulings have held, however, that lotteries may be mentioned when the circumstances constitute news of general interest for its own sake, and when publicity of the lottery is not the motive. This decision resulted from an incident in 1947 in North Carolina, when a black man turned out to be the winner of a Cadillac in a drawing that was sponsored by a service club. This was before the great civil rights advances of recent years, and the event had been regarded by its sponsors as restricted to whites. An unsuccessful effort was made to refund the winner's money; he insisted on the prize. Word of the imbroglio got into the press and it received national publicity. An attempt to penalize the *St. Louis Star-Times* (now defunct) for publishing the story led to a ruling that the law was not intended to punish publications in which the fact of a lottery is only incidental.

Freedom of the press is not absolute but is under legal restraints intended to protect people from certain kinds of injury. These restraints include laws governing invasion of privacy, publication of obscenity, protection of an author's rights and, perhaps most important of all for journalists, libel, or damage to one's reputation. Copy editors are expected to know enough about libel to detect the danger of it in the copy they handle.

Although libel falls into two classifications, civil and criminal, the overwhelming number of actions are for civil libel—that is, the libel for which one person sues another or a publication. Certain criteria are necessary to establish a libel: publication and identification. In another respect, libel may be defined as *per se* (in and of itself) or *per quod* (under the circumstances). Headlines and pictures, by themselves, can be libelous. Malice (the intent to injure) figures prominently in libel actions.

A publication being sued for libel has three principal defenses: truth (whose proof is up to the defendant and is a defense that is subject to modification in accordance with the laws of particular states), privilege, and fair comment and criticism. A libel suit known as the Sullivan case had an important effect on the application of libel law to public figures. Lesser defenses are consent, the statute of limitations, and the right of reply.

In some instances, publication of a retraction may satisfy the person libeled. The use of "alleged" offers no protection from suit. Headlines must be carefully composed since they can be particularly dangerous, especially on stories about crimes and arrests. The fact of an arrest, however, as long as it has been officially recorded, does not afford grounds for suit.

Damages that may be assessed in a successful libel suit fall into three categories: compensatory (or general), special, and punitive.

Groups such as organizations, for example, cannot sue for civil libel, but corporations can be libeled. Like a group, a dead person cannot be the subject of a suit for civil libel, but either can be the subject of an action for criminal libel.

Invasion of privacy is not yet a well-defined concept, and experience with it to date has largely involved pictures.

Copyright laws, as noted, protect the writer's or publisher's ownership of written composition, though the laws are modified by the doctrine of fair use. Facts themselves, however, cannot be copyrighted; the form in which facts are expressed can be copyrighted. Permission must be obtained to reprint copyrighted material.

Lotteries (drawings) may not be publicized under postal regulations.

14 The Editor and Printing

The technological developments that have been rapidly adopted were briefly described in chapters 1 and 2. Formerly, "hot type" ("hot metal") composition prevailed. The method was so called because the type was composed by injecting molten metal into molds. The process was expensive, slow, and dirty. Computerized systems, in which the composition and editing of stories take place at video display terminals operated by reporters and copy editors, produce photographic images of columns of type and headlines that can be used to make metal or plastic printing plates. This is known as "cold type" composition.

Computers are an essential element of this technology. Among other things, they are programmed to decide where words should be divided at the ends of lines. This process is known as *justification* (making lines equal in length), and under the old system it required line-by-line decisions by the operators of the typesetting machines. After the images of columns of type and headlines are produced as photographic prints, they are cut up and pasted onto cardboard sheets to form master pages of the paper in accordance with instructions on the *dummy*. The dummy is a small design laid out by the news editor that indicates the placement of stories on the page.

Logically enough, the process of assembling the cut-out stories on the cardboard sheets is known as *pasteup*. The new technology has moved the composition of type, as well as proofreading, into the editorial rooms, but pasteup is in the domain of the mechanical department. Computerized composition has given staff members of the newspaper much more control over—and responsibility for—mechanical accuracy. It has also greatly accelerated production and reduced its cost. In fact, lowered costs have been a major benefit of the adoption of the new technology.

Computer technology is used in different ways on various newspapers. Allen H. Neuharth, president of the Gannett Co., has predicted that "any wall between production and editorial is tumbling down . . ." Someday soon, he continued, "there will be no more than 10 minutes between copy and press." Already, in fact, pages are being assembled by electronic processes that are displacing manual pasteup.

Journalists, particularly those who function as editors, should understand the mechanics by which newspapers are produced. The process falls into two main subdivisions. First comes setting the type (composition), which we considered in chapter 2. The second subdivision is printing—impressing the image on paper and producing finished copies of the newspaper.

Printing, or presswork, is accomplished by three different methods in newspaper production. Printing methods are differentiated by the *surface* that transfers the image to the paper. The oldest method is known as *letterpress*, in which the image is transferred to paper from the raised surface of type and illustrations on which a film of ink has been laid. This method is almost universally used with hot-type composition. Letterpress printing is a hot-type method because the printing plates for entire pages are cast from molten metal. The huge presses necessary to print in this way are very expensive. The *Los Angeles Times* estimated several years ago that it had $65 million tied up in printing equipment. But the paper was planning to convert to offset printing, which is better adapted to computerized typesetting technology. Most papers have made the switch.

Offset printing, unlike letterpress, is done from a flat surface. It might seem that a flat printing plate could only transfer a rectangular blob of ink to the paper. But the plates have been treated in such a way that the image—the type and graphics—and the white space around it are separated. By means of chemical action, the image area attracts a film of ink and the white-space area attracts a film of moisture. Figure 14.1 shows how the process works. Better-quality printing is produced by offset presses than by newspaper letterpresses.

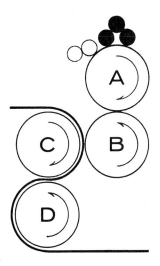

Figure 14.1 This diagram shows how offset lithography works. The plate wraps around cylinder *A* and picks up the dampening agent from the small rollers *(top left)* and ink from the small black rollers. The plate transfers its image to the rubber blanket wrapped around cylinder *B*, which retransfers it to the sheet of paper coming around the impression cylinder *(C)*. The sheet transfer cylinder *(D)* delivers the paper from the press.

The third printing method is known as *gravure*, or intaglio. Here, the surface that transfers the image is depressed. Indentations in the surface (known as *wells*) contain varying amounts of ink, depending on their depth. Gravure printing is particularly desirable for the reproduction of photographs. Special magazine inserts and sometimes single-page advertising inserts are printed by the gravure process.

Computer Editing: Advantages and Disadvantages

Professor Larry Kurtz of the University of Arizona reported in 1978 that "papers [in a four-state area] which have converted [to electronic newsrooms] generally reported gaining an hour or more in routine deadline flexibility because of the production advantages of computer systems. *However, the actual editing process takes more time.*"

Computer editing takes more time than noncomputer editing because it requires more mechanical dexterity and it encourages more editing—for instance, the editing of wire-service copy, which had almost become obsolete with the introduction of punched-tape transmission and teletypesetting. Still, even with VDTs, many editors continue to send wire-service copy right through. They have neither the time nor the staff to edit it.

Computer editing may take more time, but Daniel Hayes, managing editor of the *Davenport* (Iowa) *Quad-City Times*, says that it improves the editing process. Hayes offers three reasons:

1. Computer editing gives papers greater flexibility. Editors are able to update stories quickly; change type sizes, column widths, and spacing; edit one way for one edition, another way for the next; and quickly determine story lengths and headline fittings.

2. Editing and rewriting are easier because the computer allows greater attention to detail.

3. Editors have more control of their operations because they are no longer dependent on printers and compositors. Since papers no longer have proofrooms, editors "are forced to do what [they] should have been doing all along. [They] are forced to be better copy editors. In short, [they] are forced to pay more attention to detail."

Computers can identify misspelled words and incorrect hyphenation for editors to correct (although computers can also be the source of incorrect hyphenation). Editors can even work out programs to automatically reduce the length of stories, but no computer can exercise judgment. On screens that monitor wire-service copy, the computer can identify stories that would appeal to local readers.

Using the VDT's file directory, editors can call up any story at any time and check it. But some papers that have converted to

Figure 14.2 The Teleram P-1888 portable editing terminal allows reporters to develop stories in the field, edit them, and then transmit them to typesetting systems over telephone lines.

Figure 14.3 The Teleram 2277 is a stand-alone terminal that operates independently of the newspaper's main computer system. It offers a full range of editing possibilities, and it can transmit or receive over regular phone lines, special lines, or direct cables to sending or receiving devices. Editors and reporters using it can store up to 84,000 characters (about 14,000 words) on each diskette.

VDTs have complained about inadequate storage capacities and a shortage of screens in the newsroom. And papers that converted to computers early must make do with equipment that, compared to the latest units, seems outmoded. Still, one estimate is that an electronic system will pay for itself in three years.

Some writers and editors using terminals complain of eye-strain, and a few think that typographical errors are more elusive on a screen than on paper. Furthermore, rearranging a story can be difficult if the whole thing cannot be seen at once on the screen.

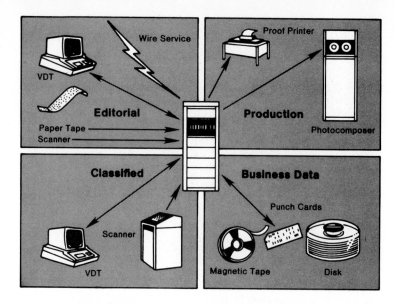

Figure 14.4 This schematic drawing illustrates the interrelation of elements in an electronic editing and composition system. Here a central computer serves classified advertising and business as well as the editorial departments. Various combinations of such equipment are possible. (Drawing courtesy of Tal-Star Computer Systems, Inc.)

Professor Will Lindley of Idaho State University, who has worked in both pencil-editing and VDT-editing newsrooms, says that VDT rooms have one disadvantage for copydesk chiefs: they can't see what their copy editors have taken out of a story. With pencil editing, they can still make out what has been deleted.

Most papers that convert to VDTs continue to use hard copy (typescript) for reference. "But the expansion of high-speed, computer-to-computer delivery bodes ill for hard copy," Kurtz reports. "Many newspapers, given the economic foundation underlying judgments on new technology, will operate fully electronically, rather than invest five-figure sums in high-speed printers just to have hard copy."

Kurtz says an unexpected advantage of conversion is that "placing production quality control in the newsroom has removed a traditional source of conflict between newsroom and back shop, thereby giving video systems a staff popularity transcending any operational complaints." And computers do more than help set type and make up pages. By 1966, according to an American Newspaper Publishers Association survey, the computer—or at least electronic technology—had been applied to 17 different newspaper functions in advertising, business, and circulation departments, as well as in news departments.

On some newspapers, a central computer system embraces all departments. In others, a series of computers does the work. An advantage of a central system is that it allows one department ready access to information from another department. A disadvantage is that a breakdown affects all departments. Also, a system that attempts to serve many departments could end up serving none of them very well. An advantage of a series of computers—a distributed processing system—is that a newspaper can invest in the system gradually and develop it according to need.

Figure 14.5 A close-up of one of the *Eugene Register-Guard*'s editing terminals, a DEC. The strip just above the keyboard is an in-house guide to commands that the terminal responds to. (Photo by Joe Matheson.)

Figure 14.6 This is the 8400 Autokon II laser graphics unit. By turning a few dials, you can convert line or continuous tone art to a negative or print, ready for production. A single pass of its laser scanning system can modify artwork in any number of ways.

Despite the complications, reporters and editors can quickly pick up the skills necessary to operate computerized equipment. And because systems vary so much from paper to paper, new staff members must get on-the-job training. Journalism schools and textbooks readying students for newspaper editing jobs cannot hope to cover all the ground.

The Reproduction of Art

The term *art* refers to any form of illustration used in printing. From the standpoint of reproduction, art for a newspaper falls into two categories: line art and halftone art. Line art is any drawing done in ink or dark pencil on white paper. Cartoons, maps, charts, and many illustrations for news and feature stories qualify as line art. Halftone art includes photographs, wash drawings, paintings, and some pencil drawings—anything, in fact, that involves shading. Reproducing halftone art can be complicated because of its tonal values. Such art is also referred to as "continuous-tone art."

Editors like line art because it reproduces exactly as it is drawn: crisply, with solid black areas. There are no surprises in the reproduction. An editor is uncertain how a piece of continuous-tone art destined to become a halftone will turn out.

In either case, the art is shot by a camera to produce a negative. If the art is continuous-tone, a screen (cross-hatched lines on glass) goes in front of the negative and behind the lens to break the picture into a dot pattern. What you see in a halftone, then, are dots of different sizes and in different densities, creating the effect of gradations of tone. You are fooled into thinking you are seeing grays; halftones are an optical illusion.

No matter what the printing process, art must be photographed in order to make a printing plate.

The Use of Color

Some editors have tried color and found it wanting. Perhaps their printers had trouble providing the correct shades. Perhaps the register was off, as when red appeared too high on a subject's upper lip. Color printing involves the use of different plates for different colors; if the plates are incorrectly aligned, the picture is said to be "out of register." Billy Watson of the *Macon Telegraph & News* reports an editor saying, "If God had meant newspaper pictures to be colored, He would have passed out crayons to subscribers." But Watson thinks editors should give more thought to using color. Editors, he says, should "raise the color consciousness of everybody. . . . One way to go about this is to establish a Color Use Committee. A committee provides the vehicle to get people involved, to make them a part of the effort to use more and more color."

Studies show that color not only attracts attention but also helps readers remember a feature. The novelty of the color helps. But as color becomes more commonplace on papers, its effectiveness is likely to become less pronounced. A remarkable black and white photograph might well be more memorable.

The secret of good color in newspapers lies in its restrained use. Color only occasionally used, and then used dramatically, will make more of an impression on the reader than page after page of color. And restricted use results in cost savings.

An advantage of editorial color is that it stimulates advertisers to use color, too. And advertisers, of course, pay more for color advertising than for black and white advertising. Sometimes it is the advertiser who gives the editorial side its chance to use color. If an advertiser buys color, the press setup allows the editors to use the same color elsewhere.

The best color may take extra hours or days to prepare. This makes it difficult for some papers to run timely news photos in color. The best use of color in newspapers often involves planned photographs.

So far as the composing room is concerned, color plates take about three times as long to process as black and white plates. That means about three hours.

Figure 14.7 These are some of the effects you can get with the 8400 Autokon II.

Newspapers use two kinds of color: process color and spot color. Process color usually involves the use of several plates to create the illusion of full color, as when a color photograph is reproduced. The printer, working from a slide or transparency or, less commonly, a color print, makes separation negatives from which the plates are made. The various plates print single colors that, when combined, produce a full-color image.

Full-color art does not come solely from photography. It can come from oil or watercolor paintings, too, and even from chalk or crayon drawings. Color separations for this kind of art are made in the same way as separations for color transparencies.

The best process color requires four plates: one each for the three primary colors and one for black. Papers that are unable to include a black plate end up with color photography that looks washed out or muddy. On many papers, process color is confined mostly to the food and grocery pages, where the art comes from outside the paper.

Photographing in Color

Color costs more than black and white for both processing and printing. Tom Schumaker of the *Grand Forks* (Neb.) *Herald* says that at the photographer's end you can save some money by comparing prices for film and supplies, by purchasing film in bulk, and by using 16- and 20-exposure (or 24-exposure) rolls instead of 36-exposure rolls. Seldom are all 36 exposures used on any given assignment.

Today you do not need to worry about extra light for your color shots. If you can get the shot in black and white, chances are you can get it in color.

As in black and white photography, you can use any good 35mm camera. But some papers prefer the larger 2¼″ × 2¼″ reflex cameras. You can get greater detail in your color-separation blowups if the transparencies you start with are bigger.

Planning for Color

With color available, it is easy to fall into the trap of using the same kind of photograph over and over. Sunsets are popular as feature shots, and fire scenes as news shots. And editors love to show off their color with shots of people in costume.

The high standards of content and composition in black and white photography should hold for color photography, too. The paper needs to plan for feature photographs that lend themselves to color. A local art show or a circus coming to town, for instance, provides plenty of opportunity for color shots. A file of clippings from other papers can suggest even more color possibilities.

Where reproduction of process color may be a problem, as in a letterpress operation, editors turn to line art and spot color (the kind of color one finds in the Sunday comics). These colors appear in artwork as solid splashes, and they are lively enough to catch and hold the eye of the reader. One bright color put next to normal black, for instance, can provide real contrast on a page.

Rather than use a second color only for a headline or for the lines making a box, consider using it as a large solid or screened mass. For instance, you can use a light color as the full background for a boxed story or article on a tabloid page, stopping the color at the boxed edge in order to leave a margin of white all around. The contrast of the white with the color will give the color more prominence. If a photo is used, you can inset it in a white block.

You can also use a second color to fill in empty space around a silhouetted drawing or cartoon, making the drawing stand out better. The color would form its own borders all around, squaring off the art.

Conclusion

Whether or not they have adopted computerized technology, most newspapers have their own printing facilities and nearly every newspaper does its own typesetting. The printing of most papers these days is done by the offset method. Pasteup, the assembling of composition and design into pages, is done in a room adjacent to the newsroom.

Reporters and copyreaders today are involved in typesetting in that they operate computer-assisted machinery in the newsrooms. They set type as they write their stories.

People who work in the newsrooms need to know how type is set, how pages are pasted up, how art is produced and reproduced, and how printing is accomplished, for these people must make decisions about all this. They should also become familiar with the computer because it is very much a part of today's newsroom. Computers improve the copy editing process. They justify the lines. Increasingly, they aid editors in laying out pages. But computers cause problems, too. They can fail at crucial times. They demand a dexterity that some reporters and editors may not have. There is some evidence that staring too long into a computer terminal screen causes eyestrain. Though computers may not save time in the copy editing process they do save time in composition.

15 Typography

Editors need to know about type—about how it's measured, what face to choose, and how to keep it readable. Choosing typefaces these days is harder than it used to be because so many are now available. Once editors settle on a few faces, they stay with them and find variety in the various settings these faces offer.

The whole idea is to choose sizes, faces, and arrangements of faces that are harmonious and readable, not just pretty or unusual. In fact, the more familiar the face, the more likely it is to be readable.

The Measurement of Type

Editors measure the height of type in points (72 to the inch) and the width of lines in picas (6 to the inch). Note that there are 12 points to a pica. On some papers the editors measure the depth of the story not in picas but in lines (*BLS* for "body lines" or simply *LS*). The full-size layout or pasteup sheets may be calibrated in lines. A *BL* or *L* would be the type size used plus the standard space between lines (called *leading,* after *lead,* the metal). For instance, if the type is 9 point set on a 10-point slug or base (or with 1 point of leading), *BL* adds up to 10 points. Lengths of stories, however, are oftener given in inches.

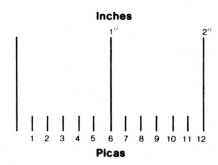

Opened

Figure 15.1 You can't tell the point size of type simply by measuring the height of the capital letters. This is 72-point Bodoni Bold Condensed. The rules shown are exactly 72 points apart. For mechanical reasons all letters are shorter than their point size.

Even though hot metal composition is nearly extinct, the original terminology continues to be used. An *em* of space is equal to a square of the type size, or the width of an *M*. An *en* is half an *em*. *Ems* and *ens* are useful in designating space for paragraph indentations. An *em* or an *en* in 9-point type would be smaller than an *em* or an *en* in 10-point type. Printers imprecisely use *ems* as a synonym for *picas*. The term in this context should be *pica ems* or *picas*.

Long ago, type sizes went by names, not numbers. Agate type, for instance was 5 1/2-point type, about the smallest you could find. You could get 14 lines to the column inch. Advertising is still measured by agate lines. A one-column by one-inch ad would be a 14-line ad. The actual number of lines of type in the ad (no doubt the type would be bigger than agate) would make no difference. Ten-point type was once elite type, and 12-point was pica type. These terms have survived in designating two common sizes of typewriter type.

Categories of Typefaces

Typefaces are divided basically into romans and sans serifs. Roman faces use thick and thin strokes in their design and have short cross lines, or *serifs,* at the ends of strokes. Nearly all sans serif faces have strokes of uniform thickness, and, as the name indicates, they have no serifs. The presence or absence of serifs creates the essential difference between roman (with serifs) and sans serif (lacking serifs) typefaces.

Less useful categories, at least for newspapers, include slab serif faces (often referred to as "Egyptian" and having names taken from ancient Egypt), Old English faces, scripts, and ornamental faces. Slab serif faces are like sans serif faces in that the letters are formed from strokes of uniform thickness; however, they have serifs, unlike sans serif faces. Old English faces (correctly called "text" or "black-letter") are thick and thin, ornate, and are used almost exclusively in the nameplates of newspapers. Scripts look like handwriting, and they find their way into newspapers only as column headings. Ornamental faces, which range from letters that look as though they were built from sticks and stones to letters that just don't fit into the other categories, enjoy use only occasionally on feature pages to help create moods or simply to afford variety.

Palatino
PALATINO
Palatino Italic
PALATINO ITALIC

Melior
MELIOR
Melior Italic
MELIOR ITALIC

Helvetica
HELVETICA
Helvetica Italic
HELVETICA ITALIC

Optima
OPTIMA
Optima Italic
OPTIMA ITALIC

Each of these basic categories can claim many families of type. For instance, among the romans you have Garamond, Caslon, Bodoni, Baskerville, Times Roman, and many others, including their imitators. Among the sans serifs you have Futura, News Gothic, Franklin Gothic, and Helvetica.

The term *roman* causes confusion in printing because it is also used to designate any typeface that is upright, distinguishing it from its slanted version, italic. Most typefaces have an italic version (see fig. 15.2). In many faces, italics are narrower than upright letters. To some people, italics suggest action or speed (after all, they are designed on the diagonal). In body sizes, italics provide emphasis. They are also used by some newspapers for names of publications, plays, and so on.

The following three examples give you some idea of the variety of faces that fall into the roman category. "Choice" represents an old-style roman: the differences between the thick and thin strokes are not distinct, and the serifs merge gradually into the main strokes. "Three" is a more modern roman, and is in a condensed form. Note the distinct serifs on the *T*. In this face, the lowercase *h* is taller than the capital letter. This face has an unusually large *x*-height. The *x*-height represents the height of a lowercase *x*, that is, the height of a lowercase letter without any ascending or descending strokes. The third example, "Alternative," is a recent roman with design peculiarities. For instance, some of the thick strokes seem to extend past the point where the thin strokes begin, almost as if the design of the letter were still in progress.

Choice

Three

Alternative

Sometimes the serifs on a roman are so subtle that you can't tell right off whether the type is a roman. The all-caps "FRESH" is such a typeface. The slight swellings at the terminals of the strong strokes, which do vary in thickness (the cross strokes are thinner than the up-and-down strokes), qualify the face as a roman. The word "smoking" uses a similar face, but in lowercase.

Some people refer to sans serif type as "gothic" type, while others use "gothic" as a synonym for Old English. Obviously, "sans serif" causes less confusion. There are actually some slight variations in the stroke thicknesses of many of the sans serifs. The "Northwest" example set in a sans serif with a big *x*-height shows clearly how some strokes thin down as they join other strokes. Notice the *r*. This face is designed to keep ink from clogging at some of the stroke intersections. A chip of white works its way up under the top left intersection of the *N* and down into the bottom right. The letterspacing in this elegant sans serif is tight, but not so tight that it hurts readability.

The typeface in "Senate approves catch-all funding" represents one of the modern sans serifs widely used for headlines; close spacing provides for good readability. The letters are clean and crisp, not too dark, not too light. The face has a large *x*-height.

Two versions of slab serif or Egyptian faces follow. The close-fitting "Made" looks a little like typewriter type. And the serifs are slightly rounded. The word "summer" represents a more normal slab serif. At one time, slab serifs were popular as headline faces. Once in a while in books you see a slab serif type used for body copy.

Scripts come in formal as well as informal styles, designed in such a way as to neatly join at the same height, letter after letter, to create the appearance of handwriting. You see both a formal and an informal script in the "leadership" examples. It is as if one script were done with a pen, the other with a brush. You would never letterspace a script because that would disconnect the letters. Nor would you run a script in all caps, which are extremely difficult to read. This is true, also, of Old English or text faces. In general, all-cap setting diminishes readability. It is used sometimes for contrast in headlines, but body type should never be set all caps.

The "Promises" heading serves as an example of Old English type. This type should be tightly spaced: the heavy vertical strokes were originally meant to create a strong pattern or texture. It is best to avoid the outlines or shadows some papers add to text faces used in their nameplates.

FRESH

smoking

Northwest

Senate approves
catch-all funding

Made
summer

CLOTHES

LABORATORY

The Lighter Side

CONTOURS

NEW

The stencil type in "CLOTHES" is one of hundreds of decorative, or display, faces available. Many of the decorative faces come only in capital letters, and they often lack italic versions. The "LABORATORY" example is a decorative type that has a contemporary look. Note that the letters do not appear to line up at the bottom, and some of the letters look incomplete. Even their sizes may seem different. The faces used for "The Lighter Side," "CONTOURS," and "NEW" are also decorative. They are basically standard faces in outline, black-with-outline, and outline-with-perspective forms.

Some faces come only as display faces, and others as both display and regular, distinguished only by the size in which they are used.

Formerly, you could look at any typeface and immediately recognize it. But since the advent of phototypesetting and press-on letters, typefaces have multiplied into the thousands, and many duplicate characteristics of earlier faces. For instance, it is almost impossible to tell a true Palatino, designed in the 1950s by Hermann Zapf, from an imitation, Paladium.

Fortunately, on a newspaper you pick a face or two for your headlines and another for your body copy, and your task is finished. Only for feature pages, ordinarily, would you experiment with other faces.

Settling on a single typeface, you still have plenty of chance for variety. Consider these factors:

1. size (in points)
2. weight (light, medium, bold, ultrabold, etc.)
3. width (regular, condensed, expanded)
4. stance (upright or italic)
5. case (capitals, small caps, caps and lowercase, all lowercase)

6 pt. CAPITALS and lowercase

7 pt. CAPITALS and lowercase

8 pt. CAPITALS and lowercase

9 pt. CAPITALS and lowercase

10 pt. CAPITALS and lowercase

11 pt. CAPITALS and lowercase

12 pt. CAPITALS and lowercase

14 pt. CAPITALS and lowercase

18 pt. CAPITALS and lowercase

24 pt. CAPITALS and lowercase

30 pt. CAPITALS and lowercase

36 pt. CAPITALS and lowe

42 pt. CAPITALS and

48 pt. CAPITALS ar

60 pt. CAPITAL

72 pt. CAPIT

Figure 15.3 In this chart, Times Roman appears in the most commonly used sizes, starting with 6 points and moving up to 72 points. Times Roman is a widely used body type, designed originally for the *Times* of London. Like many faces, it can also be used for headlines

Helvetica Light

Helvetica Light Italic

Helvetica Medium

Helvetica Medium Italic

Helvetica Bold

Helvetica Bold Italic

Helvetica Extra Bold

Helvetica Extra Bold Italic

HELVETICA LIGHT ALL CAPS

HELVETICA LIGHT ALL CAPS ITALIC

HELVETICA MEDIUM ALL CAPS

HELVETICA MEDIUM ALL CAPS ITALIC

HELVETICA BOLD ALL CAPS

HELVETICA BOLD ALL CAPS ITALIC

HELVETICA EXTRA BOLD ALL CAPS

HELVETICA EXTRA BOLD ALL CAPS ITALIC

Figure 15.4 These are just some of the variations you can get in a single typeface in a single size (in this case, 18 points). Many faces come in a greater variety of weights than shown here. In addition, they come in a variety of widths, including regular, expanded, condensed, and others. Some faces come with novelty treatments in addition to regular treatments: for instance, outlined letters and letters with shadows.

phone tulip fine rent

Readability and Legibility

It might be useful here to distinguish between readability and legibility, although the distinction is not universally observed. Readability has to do with the broad aspects of how easily the reader gets through the material. Legibility takes into account the design of the individual letter and the ease with which the reader recognizes it, even from a distance. (We have all had experience with illegible handwriting.) Readability mostly concerns body copy; legibility, headlines.

Roman faces are thought to be more readable than sans serif faces. But sans serifs are more legible, which is why so many papers use them for headlines. Some authorities believe the greater readability of roman faces grows out of the fact that because they are the predominant faces used, readers are more accustomed to seeing them.

Figure 15.5 Many typefaces come in more than one width system. Each of these four words is set in 42-point Franklin Gothic. The first is set in a regular version; the second in a condensed version; the third in an extra-condensed version; and the fourth in a wide, or extended, version.

Publisher

Figure 15.6 Palatino, a classic roman face used here to set the word "Publisher," is considered a *readable* face because of its subtly thick and thin strokes, which bring some variety to the letters, and because of its serifs, which help move the reader from letter to letter. Faces like Palatino are especially useful in body-copy sizes.

Safely

Futura (in a medium weight), used to set "Safely," is considered a *legible* face because the sans serif letters, constructed from same-width strokes, can be made out easily from a distance. Sans serifs like Futura have long been popular as headline faces.

House

The face becomes even better suited as a headline face, many editors believe, when it becomes bolder, as seen in "House," set in Futura Demibold. Such boldness can bring sparkle to an otherwise gray page.

Body Type

Too often the attention to typography all goes to headline type. But body type is what readers see the most of. If you want readers to stick with you, you will make their reading of body copy as effortless as possible. This means:

1. Set odd-measure lines narrow enough so that readers do not lose their place as they move from one line to the next. This used to mean setting lines to a width that measured no more than an alphabet and a half of lowercase letters, but with wider columns now on newspapers, editors are willing to relax that rule a bit.
2. Set stories in type big enough to be read by older as well as younger readers. Few newspapers go below 9-point type in size. Some papers change type sizes for special sections. For instance, in 1978 the *Buffalo* (N.Y.) *Courier-Express* launched a large-type section for older readers in its Sunday issues. Until the 1960s, 8-point type was the universal standard, but now most papers have gone to 9-point or slightly larger to improve readability. Whatever the size, lines of type should be leaded a point or two to make reading comfortable.

The typeface should be familiar enough to *not* call attention to itself and appropriate to the printing process and paper used. Some faces with dainty strokes and fragile serifs do not lend themselves to reproduction on newsprint. Type houses have introduced special "new faces" especially appropriate to the printing and production facilities of newspapers.

Italicizing

Centuries ago, italics (slanted letters) were designed as imitations of handwriting. Because they were narrower than upright (roman) letters, italic letters could be fitted more closely together. Italics became popular, then, because they made possible a saving in paper. In more recent times, italic versions were designed for most upright typefaces, to give editors more choices. The italic version of a typeface can consist of narrower letters, same-width letters, or wider letters.

Not all faces have italic versions, however. Some body-copy typesetting systems offer regular and italic versions in one size or regular and boldface, but not both. If your typesetting system does not have italics, you obviously do not have the option of italicizing publications' names. If you underline names of publications on your typewritten copy, you are likely to get boldface, the only change available; however, you don't want names of publications popping out from the page. The great value of italics is that you can designate publications' names, titles of books, plays, movies, and the like without upsetting the pattern of the columns of copy. If no

Typography

italics are available, you should be content to present names of publications as you would any proper names—by capitalizing the important words. Some newspapers use quotation marks to set off the names of books, plays, and so on. The practice to be used is designated by the newspaper's stylebook, which lists writing and editing rules.

Italics can also be used for emphasis. But some writers rely too much on such emphasis, just as some writers rely too much on exclamation points to convey excitement, importance, and surprise.

Ordinarily, editors avoid setting copy in all-italics, because italics are unfamiliar to the eye. They are more difficult to read in text matter.

Italics can be used to set some headlines apart from others on a page. It is not a good idea, though, to mix italics with upright letters in a single headline. This breaks down the visual unity of the headline. The names of publications mentioned in headlines are not italicized as they would be in body copy.

Leading

The design of body faces does not allow for enough space between lines (in newspaper use, at least). The columns appear crowded, so the type is set to allow a little extra space—called leading (pronounced "ledding")—between lines. Nine-point type, for instance, may be ordered set on a 10-point slug (to use hot-type terminology). In short, the type is set 9/10 (spoken: "nine on ten"). Figure 15.7 provides examples of 9-point type with three different leadings.

shows shocks

Some faces have built-in leading in that they have small x-heights. The words "shows" and "shocks" illustrate how a difference in x-heights in typefaces of the same size can change the type's appearance. You have 24-point Garamond on the left and 24-point Times Roman on the right.

Typefaces designed to be used as body copy for newspapers have large x-heights to make them appear larger. Set *solid* (meaning set with no extra leading), these faces are too hard to read. It is necessary, then, to lead newspaper copy slightly. You can add a mere half point of space if you wish. But the leading must be consistent. Generally speaking, the wider the column, the greater the leading. In the days of hot type and letterpress, backshop people spaced out too-short columns with extra leads between lines, working usually from the top. When the column was spaced out enough, the leading stopped. As a result, the first parts of stories looked different from the last parts.

Pasteup operations also employ corrective spacing, but because single cut-out paper lines are hard to handle, spacing is usually done between paragraphs. Such spacing should be consistent.

Palatino

9 Point   1 Pt. Leaded

In the Old Bailey, on this day in 1663, one John Twynn, printer, was condemned to death for high treason for the printing of a "seditious, poisonous, and scandalous book, entitled *A Treatise on the execution of Justice is as well the people's as the magistrate's duty, and if the magistrates prevent judgment, then the people are bound by the law of God to execute judgment without them, and upon them."*

The sentence upon Printer Twynn was, "That he be led back to the place from whence he came, and from thence to be drawn upon an hurdle to the place of execution; and there to be hanged by the neck, and being alive, to be cut down, and his privy members to be cut off, his entrails to be taken out of his body, and he living, the same to be burnt before his eyes; his head to be cut off, his body to be divided into four quarters, and his head and quarters to be disposed of at the pleasure of the king's majesty."

Palatino

9 Point   2 Pt. Leaded

In the Old Bailey, on this day in 1663, one John Twynn, printer, was condemned to death for high treason for the printing of a "seditious, poisonous, and scandalous book, entitled *A Treatise on the execution of Justice is as well the people's as the magistrate's duty, and if the magistrates prevent judgment, then the people are bound by the law of God to execute judgment without them, and upon them."*

The sentence upon Printer Twynn was, "That he be led back to the place from whence he came, and from thence to be drawn upon an hurdle to the place of execution; and there to be hanged by the neck, and being alive, to be cut down, and his privy members to be cut off, his entrails to be taken out of his body, and he living, the same to be burnt before his eyes; his head to be cut off, his body to be divided into four quarters, and his head and quarters to be disposed of at the pleasure of the king's majesty."

Palatino

9 Point   3 Pt. Leaded

In the Old Bailey, on this day in 1663, one John Twynn, printer, was condemned to death for high treason for the printing of a "seditious, poisonous, and scandalous book, entitled *A Treatise on the execution of Justice is as well the people's as the magistrate's duty, and if the magistrates prevent judgment, then the people are bound by the law of God to execute judgment without them, and upon them."*

The sentence upon Printer Twynn was, "That he be led back to the place from whence he came, and from thence to be drawn upon an hurdle to the place of execution; and there to be hanged by the neck, and being alive, to be cut down, and his privy members to be cut off, his entrails to be taken out of his body, and he living, the same to be burnt before his eyes; his head to be cut off, his body to be divided into four quarters, and his head and quarters to be disposed of at the pleasure of the king's majesty."

Figure 15.7 Most body-copy faces require a little extra spacing between lines during the setting. The extra space, called leading (pronounced "ledding"), makes the type more readable. Leading, once decided upon, must be kept consistent throughout the setting (and probably throughout the newspaper).

Compare these three different leadings and notice how leading increases the depth of the columns. A newspaper strikes a balance between the need to make type readable and the need to conserve space.

the role, according to Robert Lindstrom, music critic for the Oregonian, Portland's morning newspaper.

After a few measures of "(We've Got) Trouble," in which O'Conner skipped over and left out lyrics, he stopped conductor Fevrel Pratt with the explanation, "This is such a lovely song, I hate to louse it up."

Lindstrom said the restart was no more successful than the initial attempt and words continued to be mangled and unconvincingly improvised. But the audience tried to stay with their star in anticipation of improvement — which never came, Lindstrom said.

Figure 15.8 An example of poor body-copy setting. The "to be mangled and" line is letterspaced in the interest of justification but at the expense of body-copy pattern. Obviously some resetting is called for here.

Ragged-Right Setting

Although many magazines and book publishers have used it, ragged-right, or unjustified, setting of body copy has not caught on with newspapers. And yet, ragged-right setting can be faster, more economical, and even more pleasing to the eye. You get a better pattern in the body copy, and you need less hyphenation (in some systems, none) at the ends of lines.

You also can make corrections more easily. A correction that changes the width of a justified line can mean resetting a whole paragraph, but in ragged-right setting the space at the ends of lines enables corrections to be made with less resetting. Ragged-right setting becomes especially functional when you go to narrow widths for columns. The narrower the width, the more awkward the spacing between words when you justify right-hand margins. Figure 15.8 illustrates a problem often encountered in justified columns.

The Denver *Post* experimented with ragged-right setting in the 1960s. One of the few papers that have adopted ragged-right setting is the *New Haven* (Conn.) *Journal Courier.* It made its move in 1979, when it went through a redesign. Apparently readers did not notice the ragged-right setting. No one called in to complain. But no one called in to praise it, either.

It is not our intention to promote ragged-right setting but merely to suggest that it is not the monster some make it out to be. Type may also be set ragged *left,* but this is usually done only for special effect in advertising copy.

Subheads, Bylines, Credit Lines

Breaking a long story into shallow, equal segments and spreading those segments over several columns appears to shorten the story. If this is not possible, and you have one long column of material, you can at least allow the reader to pause at an occasional subhead. The subhead can be flush left or centered in a bolder face to set it apart from the story. It should have some extra space above and below, especially above, to give it adequate display.

For some newspapers, the subhead consists of the first few words of a paragraph set in boldface and in all caps. A little extra space above this kind of subhead helps set it off from the preceding paragraph. Such a subhead has the advantage of writing itself; it has the disadvantage of being set before the page is made up, which means it may fall at the top of a column if the first column carries over. The subhead doesn't do much good there.

A separate subhead can be set anytime. Sometimes the subhead is written after the story is in place, but more often it is added in copy editing. Subheads can also be used to space out a column if it falls short of the bottom of the page.

Bylines typographically resemble subheads in that they are set in a type slightly bolder than the type used for stories. Credit lines that tell who took the picture under photographs or running up the sides can be smaller. They should be distinctive enough so as not to become confused with the cutlines.

Cutlines

Newspaper editors call captions *cutlines*. Cutlines run under photographs and art work to explain them. The term derived from the letterpress process, in which photographs were reproduced as cuts (engravings). Because the term was well established when offset printing came along, there was no inclination to change it.

Because art often runs across several columns, cutlines may run wider than one column. But when they stretch across two or more columns, editors often break them into two or more segments (two 1½-column segments across three columns, for example). Type set too wide is difficult to read. Cutlines are usually set in a typeface different from the body copy as an aid to readers, and perhaps also to gain typographical variety. They may be set in italic or boldface versions of the body copy, or in a smaller size. A few editors have also experimented with cutlines set in sizes larger than body copy. Often, as in the "TAKING COVER" example, the cutlines are preceded by boldface, all-cap summaries. Some editors use one style for cutlines on pictures that stand by themselves and another style for pictures that accompany stories.

TAKING COVER — Sandinista guerrillas watch a National Guard plane pass overhead during fighting in Managua, Nicaragua, Tuesday. The guerrillas claim to have captured about 30 percent of the country.

In the *Boston Globe,* photographs accompanying stories carry boldface cutlines in a type size smaller than body copy. A photograph without a story gets an all-caps lead-in, followed by a dash. Mug shots (head portraits) get the person's name in all caps on one line, then a brief one-line description preceded by three periods.

Cutlines do not necessarily have to go under the photographs. They can go in a narrow space to the left or above the photograph. Some editors create extra white space by running cutlines narrower than the picture. Some newspapers fill out the last lines to make them even with the other lines. That means counting the letters in the last lines of cutlines and maybe resetting them to make them fit, a time-wasting process. The *New York Times* centers a shorter last line.

The pasteup artist can cause grievous cutline errors by mixing the cutlines. A main job at the page proof stage is to check cutlines against art. The *Annapolis* (Md.) *Evening Capital* once had to run this correction: "Francis Moreland was misidentified in a photo appearing in Tuesday's *Evening Capital*. The photo was of the new Amberly water treatment plant. The newspaper regrets the error."

Newspapers today run headlines with fewer lines than in the past. And where subordinate headings in smaller type (decks or banks) were once thought to be needed, a single set does well enough now. But decks are often used under big headlines as a transition to the small body type. Three-line headlines have been giving way to two- and even one-line headlines. Where appropriate, especially in horizontal layout, one-line headlines are a perfect solution to the problem of display. Readers see all the words in one glance. They get the feeling of a single sentence.

Headlines

Some newspapers make the mistake of running headlines too large in relation to the space they occupy. This makes the letter count too short, which complicates the problem of fitting the headline to the space. It also results in a crowded-looking page. You can achieve display that is just as good by using smaller headlines and allowing extra white space (often referred to as "air") to set them off.

Editors continue to argue the merits of all-lowercase, or so-called downstyle, headlines—or headlines which capitalize only the first word and proper names. The downstyle system, patterned after the practice used for sentences in text, is almost universal in magazines and is catching on with newspapers. Still, a lot of newspapers prefer the upstyle—the traditional style of capitalizing every important word. Downstyle headlines look more contemporary. Such headlines are not to be confused with headlines entirely in lowercase, including the first word *and* proper names. Such headlines are unnatural, and their novelty wore out a long time ago.

Another option, all-cap headlines, is used occasionally for typographical variety, but all caps are harder to read than lowercase letters and they take more space. All-cap headlines were popular at a time when papers had few choices of type and fewer large sizes. All caps have the advantage of commanding attention, and they are used sparingly, like italics.

One might expect that italics would be used only for certain kinds of stories, for soft news, say, rather than hard news. That way, italics would act to sort out the news for readers. But shifting between romans and italics on most newspapers is arbitrary. It is done mostly to bring variety to the page or to keep side-by-side headlines from tombstoning, or reading into each other.

While headlines are written to conform to the head schedule (described in an earlier chapter), headlines for some of the special sections of the paper may be written more freely, as titles for magazine articles are written. The editor or designer sketches in the headline in the desired size, then orders or sets type to fit. Or the headline is written and set without regard to the space it might take; the design accommodates itself to the set headline. And, of course, these special sections of the paper are more likely than news sections to engage in typographic experimentation.

Many newspapers use kickers—the short, small-type, one-line headlines above main headlines. The two examples that follow show one newspaper's style. The headline face is the popular Bodoni bold. The "Lima beans" example has an underlined kicker whose typeface is a bolder, fatter Bodoni, with the first word left uncapitalized. The "Woman" example has an italicized kicker and the face is in the same boldness as the regular headline face, but smaller. In each case the kicker starts to the left of the main headline. Sometimes kickers are flush left with main headlines.

cook it your way
Lima beans, franks hearty duo

Declined escort
Woman told PCC
she feared man

Papers depending heavily on newsstand sales—and other papers as well—continue to use *banner* (also known as *streamer*) headlines that run all the way across the front page and sometimes on inside pages. Not only do these headlines run in giant sizes, but they also often run in all caps. No doubt about it, banner headlines can help sell newspapers. At the *New York Post,* the circulation manager is involved with the banner head, not necessarily helping to write it but at least finding out what it will say. If the banner head looks promising, the manager will order a larger press run because the *Post* depends largely on newsstand sales. On June 13, 1979, for instance, the head read, "Carter: If Kennedy runs, I'll whip his ass." It sold 66,000 more copies than usual.

In choosing a typeface for headlines you must consider your production capabilities, printing facilities, and paper quality. Some typefaces, like the regular or lightface Bodonis, do not reproduce well in offset on low-quality papers. The thin strokes are too fragile. Bolder Bodonis may be called for. Some faces, like Bookman and Cheltenham (strong romans), and most of the sans serifs, reproduce well on almost anything by almost any process.

You must also take into account the width of the letters. Faces having wide letters could crowd you on head counts.

Some of the display faces come with ligatures (two or more letters blended into single units), alternative characters (more than one version of some of the letters), and swash characters (characters with extra swirls and curlicues). You see the word "Note" set in italics with a swash *N*. Swashes and other character deviations are best confined to nameplates and column headings.

The design of the face can make it obviously appropriate or inappropriate to the subject matter. Among the variety of faces available are those that look strong, fragile, graceful, bold, businesslike, informal, hurried, modern, and old-fashioned. Picking the right face becomes a matter not only of taste but also of function. Novelty faces are good only occasionally, usually for features rather than hard-news stories. One of the advantages of the old standby typefaces—the classic Garamonds, Caslons, Bodonis, and even the new Futuras and Helveticas—is that because they are not gaudy or self-conscious they can be used for any heading. They allow the words to convey their meanings without distraction.

On Mixing Type

Ideally, a publication would use only a single typeface in various sizes for everything: headlines, cutlines, body copy, and even nameplate. That way, each element would show its relationship to the others. Variety could come from different sizes and weights, not from different faces. But the result could be monotonous. So far, few if any newspapers have tried it. And why should they, with so many inviting typefaces available? Of course there is danger in abundance, as mentioned earlier. Some inexperienced or unsophisticated editors are tempted to try a little of everything, and their publications turn out to be hodgepodges.

Probably the best approach is to use only a few faces: one main face for headlines, another for body copy, and maybe an occasional oddball face for a feature headline. The nameplate is hand-drawn or at least doctored somewhat from available faces. And the cutlines, to set them apart from the body copy, are set in a smaller version (or maybe a bigger version) of the body copy, or in a bolder version, or in italics.

It is an inviolable rule that the principal styles of typefaces (roman and sans serif) should not be mixed in the type dress (that is, the range of faces used) of headlines in a newspaper. Mixing is regarded as creating an unharmonious, distracting effect. The worst offenses against this rule are commonly committed by small newspapers that also do job, or commercial, printing and thus have a large stock of different faces; they may use many of these faces indiscriminately for newspaper headlines, creating an unattractive jumble.

If a newspaper is big enough, however, it may go to a contrasting typeface for a particular section. Some large papers uniformly use sans serif faces for headlines, except in special sections, such as those devoted to features, editorials, and news of entertainment, whose headlines may be in, say, Bodoni, a traditional roman face.

It should be noted, however, that the use of a roman face for body type and sans serif for headlines is not considered a violation of the mixed-faces rule. Very few newspapers use sans serif body faces. Some typographers consider it difficult to read. If this assumption has any validity, it is probably because the eye is unaccustomed to sans serif body type, just as the eye is unaccustomed to italics.

Playing with Type

Among some editors the notion persists that in special sections stories must have some supporting artwork. Without appropriate photographs or illustrations, the editor turns to display type, figuring out something clever to do with the letters. Most of these experiments fail. They only make things harder for the reader. The headline becomes cute, or worse, unreadable. Often the best look comes from quietly and attractively arranged typography in a generous area of white space.

Desk editors are sometimes tempted to play with type. An early edition of the *New York Times* ran the following headline over a story about the mayor's pitch to the Democratic party to hold its convention at Madison Square Garden. An editor saw it, called it sophomoric, and ordered it changed for later editions. The paper already had too many typographic dingbats, the editor said.

Koch Gives Pitch to Party to ♡ the Garden

Unfortunately, the new typesetting technology has made type trickery easy. The letter "A" shown here is one example. A little of this trickery goes a long way. Photocomposition and press-on letters have made available many unusual typefaces, some of them only marginally readable.

One good way to get the feeling of art from display type alone is to run it in a giant size. Choose a face that is beautifully designed. Because lowercase letters are more interesting than all caps (lowercase design is more complicated) you may want to use lowercase in your blowups. Look at all the interesting stroke changes, angular thrusts, and space divisions in the oversize lowercase roman word "perfect."

perfect

Large letters, especially in sans serif, can cheapen a page, however. One way to make them less gaudy is to screen them to a medium percentage of black or run them in color—even a light color—or in outline form. The *Boston Globe,* among other papers, runs section heads in giant outline type. Without having to resort to unusual faces, you can also experiment with type by arranging lines of headlines in patterns different from those on straight-news pages. For instance, instead of using flush-left headlines, you can center each line. You can draw your inspiration from the editorial content of magazines and even from advertisements there. Consider this headline from an ad for a book called *Everest* (Oxford University Press, 1979).

The "impossible" climb.

Figure 15.9 The color block into which this heading was reversed helps tie the words together, but the fact remains that stacked letters reading from top to bottom make for difficult reading.

LET'S PULL TOGETHER

You have short lines—one-word lines, in fact—which give you more space than usual at the right, perhaps. The lines are flush left, but the punctuation marks at the left go outside the axis (or lineup) formed by the flush-left setting. The axis is stronger that way. The heading ends with a period. You probably would want to leave such a style to the advertisers, but it does have some lessons for us. At least the designer has not used several typefaces. Nor has the designer underlined or otherwise doctored any words to give them emphasis. The headline speaks for itself.

Most typographic trickery and variety centers on display faces, or faces used for headlines. But occasionally, editors play with body copy, too, and readability inevitably suffers. Practices you should avoid with body copy include:

1. setting type in a silhouette to draw a picture of, say, a tree or an automobile. Set the type instead in a normal block and run a picture—a real picture—nearby.
2. running a photograph or even a line drawing behind the type. Even screening the art to a light gray impairs the readability of the type. If you must do this, at least use a bold sans serif typeface for the overprinting.
3. reversing (printing white letters) in black areas. A little of this might work; a lot of it is a disaster. Again, for reversing, use bold sans serifs. The commonest mistake with reversing is doing it against too light a background (a halftone, say, that contains light gray areas) and destroying legibility.

No time for deploring, wishing

How can any nation that since 1884 has taken so much pride in the Statue of Liberty continue to delay, discuss and defer rescue of the homeless and wretched masses of Vietnamese boat people yearning to breathe free?

Few other nations profess such a human rights stance. Few other nations have such wealth that they can do something immediately. Is the stance one of high-sounding inscriptions but not action?

Is the wealth "just enough for me but not to help you"?

That they are wretched cannot be denied. People do not sell all possessions, risk capture or death, board leaky boats and flee their homelands just because they have heard they might survive and might be settled in America. They do so because freedom is gone, because life is unbearable.

Vietnam righteously argues Western nations could stop the flow of refugees if they announced they would not accept any more. Would that save those at sea now? Would that stop others from fleeing a heartless government, though flight does not guarantee something better, or even life? It is not the West's promise, but Vietnam's oppression, that has created this human tragedy.

Action, not indignant or even sympathetic words, are needed to save the refugees. Two boatloads of Vietnamese broke through a naval blockade and landed on the Malaysian coast Tuesday, but the government said it would send them back to sea, as it has nearly 13,000 others in the past week. Almost 55,000 refugees in some 330 boats have been expelled from Ma-

"Give me your tired, your poor,
Your huddled masses yearning to breathe free,
The wretched refuse of your teeming shore.
Send these, the homeless, tempest-tost to me,
I lift my lamp beside the golden door."

laysia this year. No reliable information recounts their fate, but relief officials say thousands have drowned when their overcrowded, unseaworthy craft sank.

President Carter is considering allowing an additional 5,000 Indochinese refugees into the United States this year, for a total of 89,000. The Senate has approved $7.2 million to pay the costs for the additional 5,000, and Congress has before it a bipartisan resolution urging Carter to allow even more refugees into the country. With that encouragement, Carter could do much more. Even without it, he should do more.

Many in this country would tie U.S. aid to that of other countries. Sen. Ted Kennedy has urged that any international conference seek a cease-fire in Cambodia and international guarantees of peace, neutrality and independence for Cambodia and Laos. U.N. Secretary General Kurt Waldheim has begun seeking pledges from 52 countries to accept refugees or provide some aid. He will sponsor an international conference in July on the refugee problem.

All might save lives eventually, but none would save them now.

A massive rescue operation, for which only the United States has the logistics and technical ability, must be started. The pressure on Malaysia must be relieved. Afterward, settlement on a worldwide basis can be determined. Afterward, the Vietnamese government might be persuaded to end its repressive policies.

But now, there is no afterward for thousands of human beings adrift on the China Sea.

Figure 15.10 You can use a blurb or an area of type as though it were a piece of art. Here the *Oregonian* of Portland inserts a familiar quotation inside an editorial, because it touches on the same subject. That the copy must wrap around the insert creates a bit of a problem in justification, as you can see at the left where a one-word line in the third paragraph doesn't quite make it across. The narrow setting also results in some poor word spacing elsewhere.

Conclusion

The attractiveness and, more important, the readability of a newspaper is determined not so much by the typeface or the type size used, but by the way spacing is handled. Lines are leaded to improve readability. The leading is done as the type is set.

Headlines can use one face, body copy another, but sans serif and roman typefaces should not be mixed within either element. You can achieve variety through variations in size and weight of a single style—sans serif or roman.

Body type does not necessarily have to be justified to be readable; it may be set ragged right.

It is a good idea to avoid tricks with type. Good typography is typography that is readable. Readability comes with typefaces that are familiar and set large enough in column widths that are normal. The best faces for most uses are those without any affectations—faces that do not call attention to themselves. Novelty faces are good only occasionally as headlines for feature stories.

16 Photographs and Drawings

Editors know what they like when it comes to art, and that is the art readers get. But readers' tastes vary, and art styles multiply as new techniques evolve and as technology improves. It is a good idea for editors to broaden their art bases. This chapter encourages that.

Photographs and drawings or paintings represent the two basic kinds of art, but within these two categories are many variations. Obviously, locally produced photographs and custom-made art are best, but sometimes editors must turn to syndicates, press associations, and stock-art sources.

Some art can be improved through such editing processes as cropping, retouching, and even flopping (reversing the photo, right to left). But editing should not be automatic. Good photographers edit as they choose their subjects and as they bring their subjects into focus. The photograph may already be a well-composed piece of art when you get it and it may say exactly what you want it to say.

Selecting Art

To journalists, anything in the news columns that is not type is "art." Art consists of photographs, drawings, and paintings. One of the editor's jobs is to make choices among pieces of art. On newspapers today, the choices are endless.

Ethics often enters into the choices. How much can a newspaper show before it intrudes on the rights of someone caught up in the news? How much violence is too much? When is tragedy not photogenic?

An ethical problem can arise at the moment the photo is taken. When a photographer stepped up to take a picture of Robert Kennedy as he lay dying on the floor of a Los Angeles hotel where he had been shot, another photographer yelled, "Don't take pictures! Don't take pictures! I'm a photographer and I'm not taking pictures!" The other photographer yelled back, "Goddammit, this is history!" And the picture was taken.

Figure 16.1 A photograph covering a murder-suicide need not be grisly. This Duncan McDonald photograph quietly tells it all: a husband chases his wife away from a beauty shop and shoots her, then himself. We come upon the scene to see the covered bodies, the sign, and the police car. The covered bodies are silhouetted against the dark gray background. That all these details are included in a single photograph is no accident.

Which photographer was right? One felt more the duty to inform. The other felt more the obligation to let a man die with dignity. Questions such as this cannot easily be answered.

Most of the time the art coming to a newspaper will be informative or elaborative, but sometimes it may seek only to establish a mood. It may be more abstract than realistic. The editor may decide to dispense with cutlines and let the picture tell its own story. On the other hand, journalistic art—art that is informative, argumentative, representational—does need cutlines. Readers want the details of pictures: who is being shown and what is going on in the picture. There is no need to insult the reader's intelligence but no reason, either, to fail to answer all the questions.

Cutlines can add to the appreciation of the art even when they do not increase the reader's understanding. In 1979, the *Eugene* (Ore.) *Register-Guard* ran an AP photo, larger than it deserved, of Great Britain's Prince Charles being surprised by an embrace and kiss from a woman in a bikini. "Security guards were either too far away to intervene," said the cutlines, "or perhaps were convinced the woman carried no concealed weapons." The reader, looking at the woman and seeing mostly flesh, could appreciate the understatement.

Art comes to the newspaper from many sources: from staff members, from freelancers, from wire services, from syndicates, from public relations people, and from stock-art houses. On non-unionized newspapers, especially weeklies, reporters are likely to take their own pictures. On unionized newspapers, editors may have to live with a rule that says no reporter can take a picture within 300 miles of the plant. A photographer must accompany the reporter on closer assignments. Occasionally you find a reporter who doubles as a cartoonist-illustrator when needed; this combination

Figure 16.2 A man caught going through a stop sign in the small town of Veneta, Ore., demanded, and got, a jury trial. Photographer Duncan McDonald covered it, coming up with a two-page series of pictures, "Judgment Night," for the tabloid *West Lane News.* In this shot he captures the reactions of the jury to the testimony of the arresting officer.

is especially useful in the production of feature stories. Smaller newspapers without staff artists sometimes turn to their advertising departments for help. Using an advertising artist to illustrate a news or feature story is not always a good idea, however. An advertising staffer is not likely to have the right feel for news or feature stories. When you hire an artist for the newsroom or when you line up a freelancer, you should be as concerned about journalistic know-how as artistic ability. Freelancers are less useful to newspaper editors than to magazine editors because of the tighter deadlines on newspapers. Occasionally, freelancers turn up with spot news photographs because they were on the scene.

The wire services supply both photographs and illustrations. The AP, for instance, noting in its July 17, 1978 *AP Log* an increased interest among editors in sketches for feature stories, reported that it staffs two art departments: one concentrating on spot news, another on features. The *Log* listed a total of 16 persons that turn out drawings for member papers.

The feature syndicates supply not only bylined columns but also, and especially, comic strips, cartoon panels, and editorial cartoons. Syndicates like the Tribune Company and Newspaper Enterprise Association offer charts and graphs and other art that dramatize current events and social and economic conditions.

Public relations people supply their material, including photographs, without charge, in the hope that they will benefit from the resultant publicity. Much of what they supply is pure puffery and hence is of little use.

Some papers face a problem with wedding pictures taken by various studios in town, all insisting on credit lines. If the newspaper complies, and it runs the pictures all in small sizes, the credit lines will dominate the page and give the appearance of an orgy of advertising.

Stock-art houses supply both photographs and drawings, but newspaper people find the drawings of more value. The price usually is reasonable. The trouble with such illustrations is that they are not exclusive to the paper, they have a look-alike quality to them, and, most disheartening, they are not tailored to the local stories. Stock art is best used in advertising. If the news editorial side of one paper uses a stock illustration, it can get the best effects by having a staff artist doctor it, add to it, or combine it with other pieces. An imaginative artist can make stock art a significant contribution to the paper.

Illustration or Photography?

Once there was no choice: papers used only illustrations to relieve the monotony of gray columns of type. The illustrations had to be carved from wood or metal. They took so long to produce that editors saved them, and once in a while, to illustrate, say, a fire, an old illustration got called back into service. A fire was a fire.

Photographs presented interesting possibilities, but it took photoengraving, which came along late in the last century and enabled papers to publish photographs, to make them competitive with cartoons and illustrations. For a time illustrations and photographs vied for reader attention, but eventually photographs won. Nonphotographic art serves mostly where photographs are not available.

Photographs are faster, cheaper, easier to produce, and, to most readers, more believable than illustrations, although editors and photographers appreciate the fact that photographs can lie, too: they can catch subjects in uncharacteristic poses. And with all the new lenses available, photographers can distort their subjects as much as illustrators can.

Cutlines

Cutlines are often dashed off with little thought, and often they sound like it. Sometimes cutlines do not tell readers what they deserve to have explained about a picture. Then again, sometimes cutlines insult the intelligence of readers by noting in the picture the presence of some commonplace object that is plainly visible. Many picture editors for the wire services and on metropolitan newspapers give careful consideration to cutlines, however, and the following instructions for writing cutlines have been assembled from their experience.

Do not use such descriptives as *is pictured* or *is shown* (doing something). Use the present tense to describe action obviously in progress in the picture: use *gestures,* not *is pictured* or *is shown gesturing.* The present tense generally enhances the immediacy of the picture. But avoid the jarring effect caused by a past time element in the same sentence with a present-tense verb describing the action: "William Willis *stands* aboard his balsa raft as it *moves* off the Peruvian coast *yesterday*." If the time element is essential, work it into another sentence where it does not clash with a present tense verb. Nor should the tense be shifted within a sentence, as often happens ("William Willis *stands* aboard his balsa raft as it *moved* . . ." Correctly, *moves*).

Everyone appearing prominently in a picture should be identified. The number of people in the picture should be double-checked against the number of names in the cutlines. This often turns up a missing identification. Identifications should be in the same form in cutlines and in an accompanying story.

For the sake of concision and uniformity in cutlines, write *from left,* not *left to right.* Or, when two people are pictured, write "E. G. Marshall, *left.*" Do not labor the obvious; if the president is shaking hands with a kilted Scot, it is superfluous to identify the president as the man on the left. Sometimes the monotony of the *left* designation may be avoided by reference to distinctive attire, gesture, direction of gaze, and the like.

The place where the picture was taken should be mentioned in the cutlines even if the picture is running with a story. Many readers are attracted by pictures and read the cutlines but do not read the accompanying stories.

Conspicuous and unusual objects in the scene that would be noticed by the reader should be explained; the reader should not be left wondering about them. Often a publicity shot shows some prop without telling what it is or what it is for. Important or interesting but inconspicuous details that are likely to be missed by the reader should be pointed out.

Descriptions of what is a matter of opinion or self-evident should be omitted. Do not comment on the appearance of people; do not call them beautiful, handsome, attractive, or homely. Do not call a person old; give the age, as the occasion requires, and let the reader judge. Do not insult the reader's intelligence by commenting on size: "a 10-lb. ball of wax" is OK, but not *a huge* or *a small ball.* . . . Similarly, avoid describing self-evident action such as *smiles, points, kicks,* and *waves.*

You must have the picture before you when writing the cutlines. The detail that cries out for explanation is one you often miss when you rely on your memory of the picture.

Cutlines should be written from the version of the story to be used, not from another wire service's version; writing cutlines from another version leads to inconsistencies. Keep such details as the toll in accidents out of the cutlines in a developing story; correction of the cutlines tends to be overlooked when the figure is updated in the story.

Cutlines under pictures accompanying stories should do no more than identify the people (or the scene) and tell what is going on. Do not repeat in the cutlines a large chunk of the information in the accompanying story that has no necessary relevance to the

Figure 16.3 Proof sheet for Duncan McDonald's series of photographs about a hospital emergency ward. A photographer, editor, or art director studies these actual-size prints with a magnifying glass, then picks out the useful ones for 5-by-7-inch or 8-by-10-inch blowups.

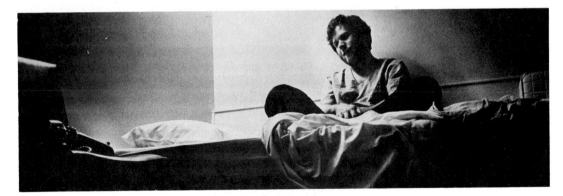

Figure 16.4 A photograph, chosen from the proof sheet shown on this page, blown up and cropped to a severe horizontal. The cropping in this case improves the composition and better displays the subject, an emergency room doctor in his room waiting for the next call from the admitting room. (Photo by Duncan McDonald.)

Photographs and Drawings

picture; the repetition annoys the reader. In extreme cases of repetition you sometimes get the same thing set forth in the same words in (1) the story headline, (2) the cutlines, and (3) the lead or somewhere else in the story. The heading should not be repeated verbatim in the cutlines. Cutlines beneath pictures standing alone should not get too windy, either. Extensive explanation is the business of a story, not of cutlines.

Cutlines should not start out like news stories, giving a summary of the situation, then telling what is happening in the picture. Such cutlines should be revised to bring the subject of the picture to the fore.

Avoid numerous parenthetical details concerning names, titles, places, and the like; they make for difficult reading. Deal straightforwardly with the action and then fill in the necessary details. Sentences should be reasonably short.

Libel is as great a danger in cutlines and captions as elsewhere. In cutlines and captions, as in headlines, lack of space is not an excuse for lack of necessary attribution. An innocuous and provable descriptive like *held* or *booked* is safer than *murder suspect*.

Triteness and Art

A picture can be more compelling and more informative than a story. With its great power, though, goes a great weakness: a picture can be painfully trite. That great or cute idea that comes too readily to mind probably came as readily to some editor or photographer weeks earlier. And so busy do newspaper people become that they forget their earlier inspirations. They use the same idea again and again. The usual ideas that appear around a holiday are especially tiresome. When will a truly new picture show up for Christmas or the Fourth of July?

You can be reasonably sure that these photographs have been seen before by readers:

1. the one showing the first baby born on Jan. 1, too late to provide a tax exemption;
2. the one showing a cadet lying unnoticed in the sun while his fellows, still in line and standing at attention, stare straight ahead;
3. the one showing from the back a girl, a boy, and another boy on a bench. The girl is holding hands not with the boy next to her but with the boy sitting next to him;
4. the one showing the child who has taken his clothes off to escape the heat (rear view only).

Even worse are the pictures that are so dull and overused that they have become known as cliché shots. The most glaring examples are those showing someone handing someone else a check

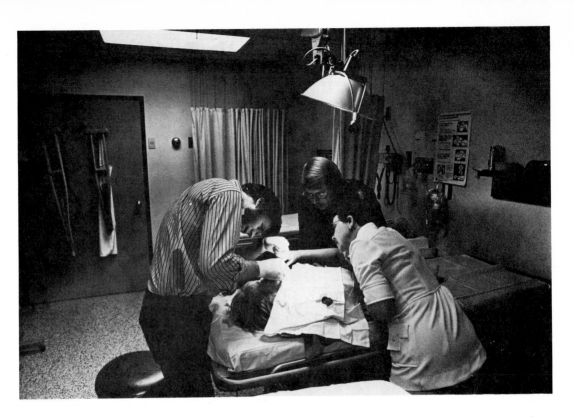

(as a prize or a contribution), a trophy, or some other award; a committee seated around a table; and perhaps the worst, a committee standing in a pose that critical photographers deride as "the police lineup."

Cliché shots and trite shots are too often the familiar solutions to the problems of busy photographers. Cartoonists and serious illustrators tend to rely on familiar solutions to art problems, too. Staying on the alert against triteness becomes one of the editor's chief jobs.

The Art of Cropping

As an editor you sometimes need to change a piece of art to make it better fit your page or to redirect its emphasis. You might also be able to improve its composition. So you crop it, slicing away part of it and keeping what you like. Often you crop to change a horizontal picture to a vertical one, or vice versa.

For impact you might occasionally crop a picture to an extreme vertical or horizontal and run it larger than usual. Maybe the shot is of a tall pole with a person at the top. By making the picture itself tall, you dramatize the tallness.

Portraits or mug shots usually work best as deep verticals, which can be run in column width or as half-column inserts. But you can crop a mug shot into a horizontal, too, when background

Figure 16.5 Close cropping sometimes can ruin a picture's story. Sometimes a full-frame picture is best. This Duncan McDonald photograph needs the background and props to establish the fact that a doctor in an emergency ward, aided by a nurse, is working over a girl injured in a fall. The father *(center)* looks on earnestly.

Figure 16.6 Victims of cerebral palsy, this couple met at a nursing home. Photographer Duncan McDonald caught them at their wedding, the new bride about to kiss the bashful groom. The facial expressions on the newlywed couple and the witness in the background make this picture. The picture was part of a two-page newspaper feature in the *Eugene* (Ore.) *Register-Guard.*

in the picture is useful in putting the person in some context. Also, when you have several mug shots that will appear together, crop them so that the heads will all be the same size when published; also make sure that the amount of space above the heads is the same as the amount below the necks. Once in a while, a portrait or a series of portraits can be cropped close as horizontals, getting rid of some forehead and chin. But such occasions are rare.

You would also avoid cropping exactly at the neck or ankles. Give the subject a little chest if what you want is a regular mug shot; give the subject feet if you have a full figure.

As editor, you enjoy the right of cropping and you can insist that the photographer give you full-frame shots capable of taking cropping; however, you must not crop recklessly. You might ruin the photograph's beauty. The usual practice is to cut away unneeded foreground or background, but these could be exactly what give the photograph its superior composition. Perhaps by consulting with your photographer you could gain a better understanding of what makes a picture well composed and exercise your right of cropping with the kind of restraint a photographer can appreciate.

Put your crop marks in the margins of the photograph, using a grease crayon. Someone else may want to use the photograph later, with a different cropping. The grease crayon marks can easily be rubbed away with a rag.

Reduction

Art is almost always reduced from the original size for reproduction, and it must always be reduced proportionately. For example, if the original photograph is 8 by 12 inches, the final reduced version as it appears in print would have to be 4 by 6 inches or 6 by

Figure 16.7 A tough shot to get: Bob Hall, head down, winning a wheelchair track event sponsored by Nike-Oregon Track Club. Hall, of Boston, is the world record holder. (Photographed by Duncan McDonald.)

9 inches, or any such proportion. The reduction is based on a simple ratio, which may be expressed by

$$\frac{\text{width of the original}}{\text{depth of the original}} = \frac{\text{width of the final version}}{\text{depth of the final version}}$$

This can be worked out by simple arithmetic; three of the four elements in the equation are already known. These are the width and depth of the original, and the width desired (almost always in terms of columns) in the final version. The unknown element is the depth of the final version.

The problem often is solved not by arithmetic but by using a circular scale made of cardboard. Such scales give not only the dimension sought, but also the reduction in terms of percentage: 50 percent, 80 percent, and so on. The percentage is a sufficient instruction to the printer.

There is also a geometrical method of solving the problem. A diagonal from one corner to the other is drawn lightly on the back of the picture. Then a horizontal line representing the final desired width is drawn from the left edge of the picture to the diagonal. The distance between the point at which this line intersects the diagonal and the bottom of the picture will be the final depth. This method is faster and easier than using arithmetic, although it is not as precise. But it is close enough for newspaper work, where a little juggling is always required to make things come out even.

A good photograph for a newspaper is one that says something clearly. A good photograph also provides visual pleasure. You do not have a good photograph when, say, you have two people pointing to something that is not in the picture. Your story is not complete. Your reader feels cheated. Some kind of reference to size in

A Good Photograph: Composition and Printing

Figure 16.8 A feature in the *Rochester* (N.Y.) *Times-Union* about the problems politicians face after they win elections said, "Take George Washington. Take Albert Schweitzer or Florence Nightingale. Put them in office and in six months the rabble will be calling them scoundrels because they voted for or against gun control, capital punishment, abortion, raising taxes or cutting funds for something." There was no need to show clear photographs of these people; decorative or abstract art would work just as well. The paper decided to use line conversions of ordinary photographs or paintings, and closely crop the conversions to horizontals. It was an inexpensive but effective way to provide art for the feature.

ALBERT SCHWEITZER

FLORENCE NIGHTINGALE

GEORGE WASHINGTON

the photograph may be necessary to tell your story. Often this means the inclusion of a familiar prop that the reader can use as a basis of comparison.

When people are pictured, you would want to show them in context with their surroundings, if possible, and engaged in an appropriate activity. The photograph should be nicely composed, with a center of interest or a point of emphasis and some contrast in the sizes of various areas within the picture.

Glossy-finish 8-by-10-inch prints reproduce best. A 35mm camera produces a negative that will allow an 8-by-10-inch enlargement. Make sure there is no graininess in the print, that the focus is sharp, and that there are plenty of intermediate tones. You don't want a print too gray, but you don't want one with too much contrast, either.

With its use of finer screens for halftones, offset lithography makes better definition possible in photographs. The detail of a photograph is far clearer in offset lithography than in the letterpress process. But to use offset lithography, you need better photography to begin with. This has put pressure on wirephotos, which are fuzzier than original prints. The Associated Press has tried to solve this problem with its laserphoto service.

Figure 16.9 A section of a piece of art used by the National Association of Manufacturers in one of its publications. Can you figure out how it was done? It is a line drawing, drawn with a brush and ink (for the solid black areas) and a grease crayon (for the patterned, or "gray," areas). The artist used a rough-textured paper specially made for this kind of technique.

Sometimes editors stuck with poor photographs try to salvage them with unusual handling. For instance, they treat the photographs as though they were pieces of line art, which gets rid of all the middle tones. This process is called *line conversion*. The process works once in a while to give you the illusion of art drawn with shadows, but it can be overused. It is also possible to make a photograph look different by using a pattern other than the usual dot screen.

Editing Photographs

The editing of photographs starts with the selections made from the many proof prints—or full-size prints, for that matter—offered by the photographer. Editing also includes decisions on size and shape. A photograph best fits a rectangle or square. Only occasionally, as for a feature section, would you run a photograph as a silhouette, its background stripped away. Seldom would you run a photograph in a circular shape. And you would never take a photograph and cut it up into some strange shape, such as a star, in order to give it—what? Character? Some critics deride such photos as "cookie cutter" pictures.

Photographs should not be cut into to make room for heads or captions. That a photograph contains some neutral area should not be an invitation to invade it with other material.

Some editors have experimented with rounding the corners of their photographs, a harmless enough practice. For consistency's sake, all photographs used on the same page, along with any boxes, should have rounded corners.

Photographs can be retouched to eliminate unfortunate inclusions or to add essentials, but retouching should be attempted infrequently. Retouching was more a part of the letterpress scene, when editors had fewer photographs to choose from. A weak photograph could often be strengthened, and the coarse screens used in letterpress printing hid the retouching nicely. The finer screens used in offset printing make retouching more detectable. Anyway, with 35mm, natural-light photography, editors have many photographs to choose from. A useful adaptation of retouching involves putting arrows and labels on photographs where pinpointing is necessary; for example, in the scene of a crime or accident.

One of the simplest changes an editor can make is to flop a picture, ordering the platemaker or cameraman to reverse it right to left. No harm is done to certain scenes and pattern shots. Maybe the change is necessary to correct a wrong facing on the page.

But flopping can be dangerous. Often it makes a lie out of the picture. You know this from studying your face in the mirror; in mirror reverse it is a different face from what the camera produces. You would never flop a picture where, say, a sign or a part in a person's hair is shown. Pictures of people wearing double-breasted suits are unfloppable, too. The *Elyria* (Ohio) *Chronicle-Telegram* learned an embarrassing lesson on March 8, 1979, when it flopped a UPI picture of a Navy ship with the name *John Hancock* being painted by a sailor. The name that has become America's most famous signature had to be read backwards by the newspaper's readers that day.

What Illustrations Can Do

When the circumstances call for it, a photographer goes out with the reporter. Or the person who goes out is both a reporter and photographer. But sometimes an illustrator must accompany the reporter. Illustrators can do things photographers cannot do. Illustrators can show a scene in a courtroom, for instance; many states bar photographers from courtrooms. (The unreasonable barring of photographs from courtrooms dates from the time when taking pictures caused commotion, as when flash power helped light things up for slow film exposure.) Illustrators can reconstruct a scene photographers missed. Illustrators can ignore seasons. They can make the person pictured merely representative, thus avoiding libel or other embarrassment. They can show cross sections and simplify locations. Better than photographers, illustrators (we'll call them that rather than "artists," because both photographers and illustrators can be artists) can focus the reader's attention.

Figure 16.10 An illustration does not have to be large to be effective. If it's simple enough, it can serve as an insert in a column of type. This illustration, shown actual size, helped a story to emphasize the tax bite on the salary earned by the average U.S. worker.

Kinds of Illustrations

Chapter 14 looked at illustrations from the standpoint of reproduction. Let's look at the subject again—from the standpoint of the originals.

You have continuous-tone illustrations and line illustrations to consider. Continuous-tone illustrations include photographs, primarily, as well as occasional wash drawings, paintings, and pencil, chalk, or felt-marker drawings with various tones. Such art requires halftone reproduction, like photographs. Wash drawings are really water-colors done in watered-down india ink or lamp-black pigments. Paintings can be done in any medium, opaque or transparent. If they are in color and reproduction is to be in black and white, the original art is treated as though it were an ordinary black-and-white photograph and shot as a regular halftone. If color is to be printed, color separations will have to be made, as previously explained. Pencil, chalk, and gray marker drawings with delicate middle tones must be halftoned to retain the detail. It is also possible to illustrate a story with a photograph of a piece of sculpture, giving it halftone reproduction because it is continuous-tone art.

Line art, in contrast to continuous-tone art, is black and crisp and more easily reproduced; a screen to change tones to a dot pattern is unnecessary. Do not feel that you are stuck with just line and pure black-on-white paper in a line drawing. You can have your artist add tone to the drawing through use of grease-crayon shading or the application of Zipatone (a preprinted shading that can be cut up), in which case you would have a piece of art still eligible for line reproduction. You should reduce line art to minimize imperfections in drawing. Fortunately, in a line drawing, patches, scratches, and white retouches fade in reproduction.

Sometimes, for a startling effect, an editor will blow up a small drawing to emphasize its strength of line or crudeness of drawing. The practice makes for a good change of pace.

Figure 16.11 Pictures of the columnists help direct readers to their favorites. The pictures, usually inset in the column to conserve space, can be photographs, line-conversions, or drawings. The drawings must be first-rate, worthy of being seen day after day. Line drawings, like this one of Russell Baker, taken from the *Oregonian,* stand up better than pencil or wash drawings, even when the line drawings carry a lot of parallel lines and crosshatch shading.

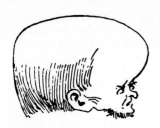

Figure 16.12 Caricatures probably would not work as well as realistic drawings to accompany regular columns. The humor of caricatures seen every day might grow tiresome. But, of course, caricatures work well as one-time illustrations elsewhere, as when something on the page deals on a one-time basis with a public official.

Pick line art over continuous-tone art whenever possible because you can better control its reproduction. What you see with line art is what you get in printing, even when you change its size. The halftone process, on the other hand, is fickle.

Cartoons

Newspapers make more use of cartoons than other print media do, except for comic magazines. What is a cartoon? How does it differ from an ordinary drawing or illustration? A cartoon is a drawing that depends upon humor or exaggeration to make its point. If the cartoon is self-contained satire that holds a politician up to ridicule and it appears on the editorial page (or, rarely now, on the front page), it is an *editorial* or *political cartoon*. If the cartoon appears as a series of three or four panels on a page with several other panels, and it concentrates on the same fictional characters day after day with conversation appearing in balloons over their heads, it is a *comic strip*. If the cartoon is a regular one-panel feature with a light or humorous touch, it is a *cartoon panel*. If, instead of standing by itself, it merely illustrates a news or feature story, but in a humorous way, it is a *cartoon illustration*. A non-cartoon illustration used with more serious stories would look more photographic, drawn possibly in shadows and tone rather than in mere line.

Editorial cartoons can be locally produced or purchased from a syndicate, which charges the newspaper a fee based on its circulation. Syndicated editorial cartoons usually originate with a big-city paper, then are sold to other newspapers. They are cheap, considering what the paper would have to pay its own editorial cartoonist; many newspapers subscribe to the work of several big-name editorial cartoonists and use only those that catch the editors' fancies. Syndicated editorial cartoons have the disadvantage of never dealing with local issues.

Comic strips almost always come from syndicates. Compared to what the paper would have to pay for an exclusive strip locally produced, the cost of syndicated comic strips is minimal, so the paper can afford to subscribe to a number of strips from several syndicates. Usually the strips appear together on a single page, much reduced in size from what they were during the earlier and golden years of comic strips. Sometimes a strip has special appeal to readers of a section, such as the sports section, so it appears there as a change of pace. Occasionally, a strip is controversial enough or opinionated enough to appear on the editorial page, as *Doonesbury* does in a number of papers.

Panel cartoons consist of single frames and, like comic strips, feature reappearing characters, as in *Dennis the Menace,* or they center on a theme, as in *They'll Do It Every Time.* Some panel cartoons are gag cartoons, with the joke set in type below the drawing.

Name that plane

By SEYMOUR CRANE
Junction City Air Raid Warden

That's not a bogey at twelve o'clock high, fellahs, that's the IRS!

That's right, aircraft owners--if you failed to pay a federal use tax for using those "navigable U.S. airways" you'll be getting your delinquency notice from IRS soon.

Federal Aviation Administration registrations are matched with tax returns on file. Nearly 4,000 Oregonians are being contacted through this returns-compliance program.

IRS Form 4638 "Federal Use Tax Return on Civil Aircraft" is due on August 31. The tax year for the use tax begins July 1 and continues through June 30 of the following year.

The tax includes a $25 annual fee for each aircraft plus a tax of 3½ cents for each pound of maximum certificated take-off weight for turbine powered aircraft and 2 cents for each pound of maximum certificated take-off weight over 2,500 pounds for piston powered aircraft.

The tax revenue is used for the expansion and improvement of airport and airway systems throughout the United States.

IRS Publication 582, "Federal Use Tax on Civil Aircraft" and the Use Tax form are available from all IRS offices.

Figure 16.13 An example of too-playful handling of art and typography. The photograph does not lend itself to silhouette treatment; the facial expression is not appropriate; the spacing between lines in the headline is uneven; and the mortise for the byline is irregular and crowded.

Figure 16.14 One way to produce the art for two-color printing. First, the artist (in this case Jim Bodoh) makes a master drawing in line. Second, the artist draws an overlay in black or red on a sheet of frosted acetate. The third unit, which you see here, is what results from the two-impression printing. (Think of the gray area as color.) (Reproduced by courtesy of *Old Oregon*.)

Figure 16.15 Editorial cartoons may express an opinion different from the opinion of editorials, or they may complement editorials. James D. Sneddon's "Gov. Brendan Byrne sings the nuclear litany" editorial in the *Weekly Herald* of Mount Holly, N.J., was given added impact by a Steve Barr editorial cartoon, around which the editorial was wrapped.

Syndicated cartoons, whether editorial cartoons, comic strips, or panel cartoons, do not lend themselves to editing. They may only be omitted entirely, and sometimes are, if the editor dares to incur the wrath of the loyal fans.

Illustrative cartoons are most often locally produced and do lend themselves to editing and even dictation by the editor. But, like self-contained cartoons, illustrative cartoons—the best of them—have ideas behind them. The cartoons either capture the theme of the stories they illustrate or pick out scenes or facts and depict them to entice readers. Just what to illustrate requires a good understanding of the story. In some cases, the editor supplies the idea; in most cases the cartoonist does.

Thinking clearly can be a more important attribute for the cartoonist than drawing well. The trouble with many illustrative cartoons is that they are cute, not clever. They exaggerate self-consciously. They add little to an appreciation of the stories they illustrate. How often must the reader face lightbulbs over heads, crossed eyes, big feet, or sweat marks? The real questions the editor should ask of the cartoon illustration are, How, exactly, does it fit the story? and Does it add a dimension?

Cartoons work well for feature stories and news items with a light touch, but for more serious stories or stories of tragedy, other kinds of art are more appropriate. A woman who wrote an angry letter recently to the editor of a big daily about a cartoon illustration accompanying an article on rape was right in her outrage; rape is nothing to laugh about.

Local editorial cartoonists, doing their work for editorial pages, often work under a system where they submit two or three rough sketches with their ideas for the day and then finish off the roughs that are OK'd by the editors. Ideas dreamed up by editors and passed along to their cartoonists do not work very well because the ideas are almost always literal. An editorial cartoon is a figure of speech in graphic form, and it has to come across simply and mercilessly. It is a vehicle for condemnation, not praise.

In this age of euphemism, some editors like to blur the distinctions of art with the term "graphics." Anything that is not a photograph is a "graphic." Somebody does a cartoon, for instance, and the credit line says, "*News-Times* Graphic" or "Graphic by George Jones." This is ridiculous. If it is a cartoon, call it a cartoon.

If the cartoonist signs the work, you do not need a credit line. A credit line is for a piece of work—usually a photograph—that otherwise would go uncredited. You would also use a credit line for a set of cartoons illustrating a story. You would not want the cartoonist to sign each one of them.

Maps

Just telling readers where something happened may not be enough. You may have to show them on a map. Many maps are copyrighted, so you cannot photograph sections of them and pinpoint the areas in the news. Nor is it a good idea to use government-made maps. They may be in the public domain, so the price is right, but often they are drawn in such a way as to defy good reproduction in newspapers. Sometimes they carry too much detail. Your artist can refer to existing maps, though, and then draw new versions, which ordinarily would be greatly simplified and strengthened.

The *New York Times, Chicago Tribune,* and *St. Petersburg Times,* leaders in the use of newspaper art, each have at least one artist who does nothing but maps. To prepare for map-making, your artists need a large file of maps from all kinds of sources to refer to. Artists would also save the maps they make with the thought of using them later with revisions as necessary. Mapmakers need a careful filing system.

Most artists make maps larger than the reproduction calls for: twice as large is common. That way, any imperfections of line or hand lettering are minimized. But that means, too, that your artists must put down lines and patterns with enough strength to take the reduction. A reducing glass is useful in checking how a piece of art will take a reduction.

If your map artists understand letterform or are calligraphers, they can letter in the names of places. Otherwise, they can use press-on letters. It is a good idea to encourage a consistent style in maps so that regular readers can learn to read them quickly. For instance, bodies of water could always be black or screened to a percentage of black. Main roads could be double-lined.

Sometimes it is appropriate to show a map that is personalized, exaggerated, and in perspective. Let's say you want to describe visually a recently developed park with its various facilities. A cartoonist could do the map, drawing it as though from the top of a high building. The reader would get the illusion of looking down on various park activities. The figures would be out of scale and the facilities crowded together, but they would be correctly placed. Such a map could say more about the place than a flat, correctly scaled rendering.

Jim Green, managing editor of the *Lexington* (Ky.) *Herald,* complains about the quality of maps supplied to his newspaper by the AP. He calls them dull. Green asks that wire-service maps be made with the thought that they will be reworked at the receiving newspaper to conform them to house style. Type, he says, should be put down with the thought that it will be removed to make room for the newspaper's own type. Units in a chart should be put down with the thought that they will be cut apart and replaced to change the proportions of the chart. Green also argues against the use of condensed type because many papers today reduce the width of the page (to save newsprint) but not the depth (to preserve the depth of the advertising). This results in super-condensed type that clogs up. Green likes Helvetica because it stands up under a shrink lens and looks good with any other type.

Charts

Knowing that many readers cannot grasp sets of figures presented in news stories, editors supplement these figures with charts and graphs whenever they can. To describe chains of commands and manufacturing processes, editors use organization charts and flow charts. To show the makeup of some product, editors show cutaway drawings and cross sections. All these require the services of a dedicated, accurate artist with a good, tight style. Using ruling pen, compass, press-on letters, and special printed tapes, the artist makes a useful contribution. Three basic charts can be used for figures and percentages: pie charts, bar charts, and line graphs or charts.

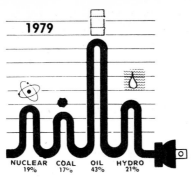

Charts show percentages of fuels used to generate electricity in New York State now . . .

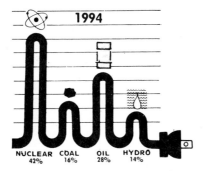

. . .and industry projections for a decade and a half from now.

Figure 16.16 To compare percentages of fuels used to generate electricity in New York State in 1979 with fuels likely to be used in 1994, the *Rochester* (N.Y.) *Times-Union* used line charts. The line charts were dressed up for visual impact. The line in each case became an electrical cord. Symbols at each bend helped identify the fuel sources.

Like maps, charts can be embellished to make them more inviting. A pie chart showing how money is disbursed can be shown as a dollar instead of a plain circle, and the wedges can be three-dimensional. A bar chart can show people in place of the bars. A line graph can be superimposed on a photograph that shows what is being measured. Even a table of figures can be dressed up with tones, colors, and sidebar drawings.

A word of caution: in dressing up charts, your artist may inadvertently distort the statistics. Let's say that in a bar chart, one standing figure represents 1,000 workers, while a second standing figure represents 2,000 workers. Should the second figure be twice as high as the first figure? Not really. A figure twice as high as another is also twice as wide and twice as thick. The second drawing of a figure, then, would appear to be much more than twice as big as the first.

Another error occurs when the artist, in doing a bar or line chart, cuts away a center section to save depth. The cutaway section is marked well enough, but it distorts the proportions, and the reader gets the wrong impression. A good book to consult about these matters is Darrell Huff's *How to Lie with Statistics.*

Figure 16.17 A clean, readable chart from the Cleveland *Plain Dealer*. The chart is flawed, however, in that it suggests the "Number of Patrolmen" is separate from the "Total Police Force." It would be better to show the "Number of Patrolmen" for each year as a section of the "Total Police Force."

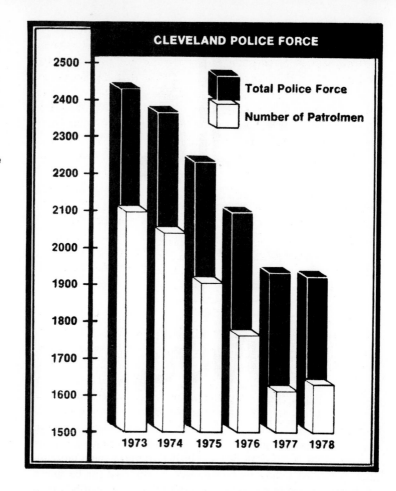

Arranging Art on the Page

Picking art is one thing. Arranging it on the page is another. A few rules can provide some guidance. For instance, allow photographs to face inward in order to hold the reader on the page. Also, run the art large so it can be seen and appreciated. But give the reader lots of art, and lots of variety. There you have a dilemma. *Large* pictures and *many* pictures do not mix.

One way out is to cluster your photographs on a page, not only to better organize them but also to create larger units of visual interest. It is not necessarily a good idea to scatter photographs.

When Do You Go Big with Art?

To avoid overkill, you run your photographs in giant sizes only occasionally and only when they deserve attention: when they are beautifully composed or important. This is not to say that artistic mood shots or even abstractions should not enjoy some sprawl from time to time.

Sometimes you have photographs that stand by themselves, needing only cutlines and maybe their own headings. They do not illustrate stories. Such photographs are said to "run wild." It is necessary, then, to arrange the page to show that the pictures are self-contained units. Perhaps they should be boxed, or a rule should separate them or their cutlines from adjacent headlines. Too often, a headline of an unrelated story is mistaken by the reader to include the photograph, and improbable connections are made.

Some papers run photo pages that bring certain kinds of photographs together and display them without interference of columns of copy or advertisements. Typically, the page carries, in addition to photographs of various sizes, a headline, a small block of copy, and necessary cutlines. Such pages are good outlets for photographers who like to put on one-person shows dealing with single subjects, such as beach scenes or personalities. Sometimes a disaster covered elsewhere in the paper gets such full-page treatment as a sort of sidebar to the main story.

Conclusion

A heightened visual sense among readers and the flexibility of offset lithography have made art of all kinds more important in newspapers. Typically, art runs bigger these day, and you find more of it. Frequently, color is involved.

Many photographs and most drawings and paintings probably should be run without cropping, retouching, or other doctoring; however, editors do find it necessary to edit the art, at least to the extent of changing sizes (while holding proportions) and eliminating unnecessary or unwanted detail. Sometimes it is necessary to change the proportions of a piece of art to dramatize it or to make it fit an assigned space.

Because of their realistic quality and availability, photographs remain as the art staple of newspapers, but often, a line or wash drawing does the job better. In some cases, a drawing is the *only* answer.

When you think of ordering a drawing, you should remember the numerous techniques available to the artist. A cartoon may be the answer, but for a more serious illustration you may want to turn to a scratchboard drawing, a grease-crayon drawing, or some other rendering. How the drawings are to reproduce is always a consideration. Only experience will show you what kinds of art reproduce best.

17 Designing and Laying Out the Newspaper

Design is the term usually applied to the permanent aspects of the paper—the width and number of columns on a page, the presence or absence of column rules, the typography, the nameplate, and the new horizontal arrangement of elements on a page vs. the traditional vertical arrangement. *Layout* (or *makeup*) refers to the daily display of news and pictures.

A newspaper can go many years without changing its basic design, but in recent years many newspapers have been redesigned. They have widened their columns, necessitating six or fewer columns to the page in place of the former eight. They have adopted the new horizontal display, spreading stories sidewise under multicolumn headlines in place of the old vertical display (in the old display, headlines seldom exceeded two columns in width, except for headlines on the one or two leading stories of the day). Changes like these have been aimed at improving the appearance of newspapers and making them more inviting.

Who designs the newspaper? In the past, editors have done the job. But increasingly, specially trained people called *art directors* are taking over. Even so, word-oriented editors need to know something about design because design helps establish a newspaper's overall personality. The personality should be evident at once to readers, even from several feet away on a newsstand.

It is possible to categorize newspaper design as either loose or orderly. Obviously, a strong case can be made for orderly design because it makes things easy to find and promotes readability, but some looseness is useful, too, to enliven the pages.

Newspaper Sizes

The Full-Size Newspaper

The usual size for a newspaper front page is, roughly, 15 inches wide by 23 inches deep.

The six-column format does not have to confine the stories to a single width. Stories can be set in widths that approximate two columns or even 1½ columns and can be arranged as modular units stretching across the page. Stories can appear on the page, then, in several widths.

Figure 17.1 The front page of the first issue of *Stars and Stripes*, published in 1918, gives you an idea of what newspapers looked like earlier in this century. Notice the many decks for headlines, the all-caps type used for the top heads, and the vertical lineup of stories. Those are "ears" on each side of the nameplate.

Some papers, in offering stories set wider than normal, put extra space between the columns, giving them further distinctiveness. Space between columns should be wide enough at a minimum so that the reader doesn't wander into the column next door by mistake, but not so wide as to make the space intrusive. Two picas is probably too much. One pica is more like it. Too much space between columns often means too-narrow setting of columns, and that means poor letter- and word-spacing.

The Format and Printing Material Standards Committee of the American Newspaper Publishers Association has worked on standardizing column widths and spacing, mostly as an aid to national advertisers and their agencies, who have been inconvenienced by all the varieties because they could not standardize on ad sizes.

Designing and Laying Out the Newspaper   **203**

The eight-column format makes possible a greater variety of arrangements than the six-column format, especially when you explore the possibilities of horizontal layout. But the endless possibilities also call for more decisions, thus slowing down the layout process. Faced with so many columns, editors tend to crowd more and smaller items on the page.

At any rate, the six-column format, at least for the front page, has become almost standard for the full-size newspaper as an aid to readability, since it makes larger body type possible. And editors have shown that even with fewer columns, the possibilities for innovation are still there.

Willingness to accommodate advertising sometimes leads to varied column widths for news matter. And a few front pages have 7½ columns, 6 of uniform width and 1 a column and one-half wide. The wider column may be used for a standing, bylined column or a combination table of contents and news digest.

The Tabloid Newspaper

The tabloid, an 11½-by-16-inch newspaper, looks more like a magazine than a newspaper in that it comes closer to magazine size. There are fewer stories on its smaller pages, and it even has a center spread that can be spanned easily with a piece of art, a single featured story, or a double-truck ad. But unlike a magazine, a tabloid is not bound.

The tabloid came along in the 1920s to serve readers who bought papers to read on streetcars, subways, and buses. Because the early tabloids appealed to working people, they stressed what editors thought would interest such readers: sensation, froth, and misplaced sentiment. "Tot Kills Mom and Dad" typifies their headlines. Consequently, the tabloid format came to be associated with the worst in American journalism. But lately, more serious publications, including the *Christian Science Monitor,* have seen its value as a format. In some respects the tabloid is easier to lay out than a full-size newspaper.

Newspaper Art Directors

As noted, newspapers are giving more attention to layout these days. With the move from letterpress to offset and with the availability of cheaper, higher-fidelity process color, newspapers use more photographs in larger sizes and often in color. And editors give more careful consideration to how the photographs are displayed.

Design and layout no longer represent merely a sideline interest of the editor. On many large newspapers today, one person works solely on design and art problems. Some newspapers call that person the "art director"; on other newspapers that person is a "graphics editor."

Designing and Laying Out the Newspaper

Louis Silverstein, assistant managing editor of the *New York Times* and art director of the Times Company, considers the new emphasis on graphics part of a revolution that involves three forces coming together at the same time: "The *first* is the technological revolution—the computer, cold type and the rest. The *second* is the . . . adjustment to changing markets. . . . The *third* force is newspapers' belated discovery of the usefulness of the professional designer. Newspapers are the last major medium by far to discover and use the art director or the professional designer."

In 1979, people primarily involved in newspaper design and layout formed the Society of Newspaper Designers. By that year's end, 130 persons had joined.

Newspaper art directors usually do not have professional design backgrounds. They have not attended art schools. They have come through the ranks as writers or editors or, increasingly now, photographers or illustrators. With so much emphasis on art, the photographer or illustrator seems a logical choice for art director, but how can the newspaper be sure such a person really understands graphic design? More important, how can the newspaper be sure that the new art director understands typography, which is possibly the most important aspect of graphic design?

Newspapers can't expect much help from journalism schools, which are too word-oriented, or from art and design schools, which are too advertising-oriented.

Whether they come to newspapers with news, art, or advertising backgrounds, art directors must be as much newspersons as artists. For that reason, many newspapers are content to have their design decisions made largely by word-oriented people. After all, design is as much a matter of organization as it is a matter of esthetics. Perhaps it is more a matter of organization. To design means to plan. Editors are close to things. They understand the relative importance of the various stories and photographs that go into their papers each day.

More Than Good Looks

Good newspaper design allows flexibility, last-minute changes, and economies in production. Good design is also good printing on paper made to take the impression.

To readers, good design is not so much a matter of looks as it is of placement. Will readers be able to find what they're looking for? Will the editorial page be in the same location each day? Is the guide to TV programs easy to follow? Harold Evans, editor of the *Sunday Times,* London, summed it up nicely: "Design is not decoration. It is communication."

The problem in design, as Evans sees it, "is to communicate within the same physical context not one message but a series of disconnected messages of infinitely varying significance, and to do this with speed, ease and economy in a recognizably consistent style."

Figure 17.2 A page in a newspaper may start out with no more promise than what is shown here. This gridded 6½-by-9-inch sheet shows the scribblings of a *Seattle Times* editor planning the page. The small sheet represents a full-size page. The calibrations read from bottom to top at the right edge to make distances from the bottom easy to figure, too.

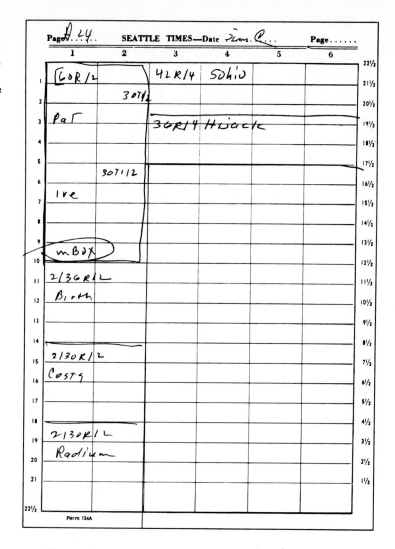

Some editors ask too much of design. With their newspapers facing declining circulations and a lack of interest among young people, editors think new typefaces, wider columns, and better display will do the job. Good design may help rescue a failing newspaper, but it can only help. As McCrohon says, "Design does nothing for you unless you have content."

Developing a Personality

The few design school graduates who end up on newspapers get there probably by way of advertising. Many of the big-name consultants brought in by newspapers to conduct redesign programs (more about this later) have had most of their experience designing ads for advertising agencies.

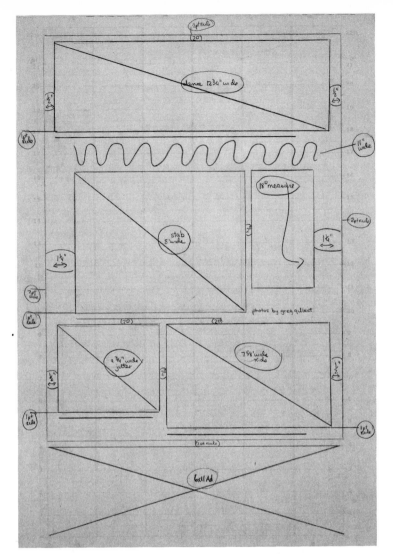

Figure 17.3 In the final planning stage, the editor uses a full-size gridded sheet (18 by 24 inches), blocking in columns of copy and photographs carefully. This serves as a blueprint or guide for the person doing the actual pasteup. That wavy line near the top represents an across-the-page headline.

The agency designer's idea of a good-looking newspaper is one that looks like a magazine. There is much to be said for introducing magazine concepts into newspaper design, but why shouldn't a newspaper, in the final analysis, *look* like a newspaper?

Newspapers stick pretty close to a basic pattern, one that is necessarily crowded, with space assignments rather uniformly applied. The number of columns per page is set on any given newspaper (although some papers change widths to make the columns fit around the ads). The distance between headline and story is set. The handling of cutlines under photographs is set. That does not mean basic patterns can't be changed or that variations within the pattern can't occur.

A newspaper maintains a design personality that sets it apart from other newspapers. The distinctiveness comes from the combination of the nameplate, which is specially designed for the paper, the headline type style, the way art is displayed, and the orderliness of the page. Put one paper next to another, and from several feet away constant readers should be able at once to pick out their own papers.

The Influence of the Underground Papers

The 1960s saw papers spring up in various cities to rally against the Establishment—to break the rules of makeup that newspaper people had developed and guarded for so many years. Known as "underground" papers, they served rebellious youth as the more staid traditional newspapers could not. These papers' interests seemed to center on drugs, explicit sex, bodily functions, and politics. Some treated genuinely important subjects seriously. Almost all of them experimented with typography, art, and color.

The growing popularity of offset lithography and the availability of cheap, cold-type composition systems made it all possible. Some of the display was grotesque and made the paper difficult to read, but occasionally a page cried out successfully for attention. There is no question that underground papers, with their uninhibited attitudes toward design, influenced redesign of traditional newspapers in the 1970s. Newspaper redesign was also prompted by the advertising competition from television, a visual medium, causing newspapers to give unprecedented attention to their appearance.

The Rules of Design: Are They Important?

It is much easier to defend the rules of grammar than the rules of design. The rules of grammar make the language precise. They aid readability. In contrast, the rules of design do not all aid readability. Many simply impose upon us the tastes of those who first established rules. But some of the rules of design are universal enough and logical enough to merit our serious consideration. One of the rules asks us to make things easy for readers, to simplify, to set up some kind of order.

Another rule asks that we divide our pages into pleasing segments for the reader, segments that vary in size to maintain interest. For instance, we would not present readers with nothing but same-size stories. Nor would we publish photographs that were monotonously uniform. We would not divide pages perfectly into halves or quarters. We would work for more subtle proportions.

Another rule asks that we adopt a style of design that is consistent. Art and type should work together in harmony. Readers should get the idea that the pages all go together. On a single page, readers should feel that all elements are related.

Consistency extends to the use of bylines, datelines, and other elements that appear daily throughout the paper. Bylines, for instance, need to stand out slightly from the stories. The *Christian*

Science Monitor's style is to center its bylines in boldface and, just below, to center body-face lines identifying the writers. The paper runs its datelines in boldface type, too, just beneath and at the right. Most other papers incorporate datelines into the first paragraph, using all-caps instead of boldface. The initials of the wire service follow, in parentheses; then comes a dash, and the story begins.

The designer establishes spacing standards for such units, as well as for headlines, decks, subheads, credit lines, boxes, etc., and the person doing the pasteup follows these standards.

One more rule asks that on each page one item stand out to capture the reader's attention. A little contrast in a sea of sameness makes for good design.

Few would argue against these suggestions. It is when the rules of design become arbitrary and restrictive that we rightly question them.

Some editors continue to insist that large headlines always appear higher on the page than small headlines, that similar-size headlines should *never* run next to each other; that each line of a headline must extend at least two-thirds of the way across the column; that the main display must be on the upper half of the page; that the No. 1 story must start at the upper right corner of the front page; that no photograph cross the fold on the front page; and that all four corners of the front page be "anchored" with art of some kind (as if the corners would blow away otherwise).

Some of these rules came about for good reasons. For instance, when newspapers depended largely on newsstand sales, it was necessary to display the best front-page stories above the fold, where they would catch the attention of passersby. But many of the rules should be reexamined. If the rules make for consistency of design, fine. If they are there only because that is the way the paper has been doing things through the years, maybe it's time to open up a bit.

Designers on Design

Professor Daryl Moen of the University of Missouri School of Journalism thinks that four basic steps are essential to good newspaper design. Moen aired his views on design in four articles in *Editor & Publisher* (Sept. 23, Oct. 28, Dec. 9, and Dec. 23, 1978).

1. Present your material in modules. That is, use only rectangular shapes to contain news stories. Under the old system many stories would start out two columns wide, then narrow to one. Another story would appear completely under the two-column umbrella.
2. Make it more obvious to the reader that certain stories and pictures are related. Organize material by content.

3. Run related pictures together to give them more impact. Use several good pictures of the same event.
4. Use illustrations correctly. They should call attention to the copy, not to the design of the paper. The temptation these days is to give art too much space and to play tricks with it—and with type—at the expense of readability.

A measure of how strongly editors held to attitudes about design—for instance, is horizontal, modular layout really more serviceable than the more traditional vertical-column format?—could be seen in the spirited letters to the editor responding to this series.

What do designers themselves say about how a newspaper should look? They generally agree that a well-designed newspaper page should be simple, with at least some white space for visual relief, and that the page should carry large photographs and probably only a few stories. The overall look should be orderly yet inviting, without typographic gimmickry.

At a 1978 Seminar on Newspaper Design sponsored by the American Press Institute, Professor Edmund Arnold of Virginia Commonwealth University said he was concerned about the danger of overdesigning newspapers. Newspapers, Arnold said, have to work with a standard pattern that sets column widths, type sizes for headlines, and the like. The design has to be prefabricated. But Arnold saw dangers in making design so standardized (through computers) that the newspaper look and feel would be lost. A paper should not be given over wholly to artists and computer people. "A newspaper should be put out by *news* people," Arnold said.

Paul Back, director of design at *Newsday* (Long Island, N.Y.), another speaker, said that most newspapers are still put together by rules dating to the 18th and 19th centuries. Newspapers have not really taken advantage of photocomposition. Back said a newspaper's personality should be expressed through design as well as through editorial content.

But Harold Evans, editor of the *Sunday Times* of London and author of a number of books on newspaper design, pointed out that many newspapers in America have forgotten their function and become faddish. For instance, headlines are too large for their stories, white space has become distracting, ads have taken over some pages with their unusual shapes, and typefaces have been distorted by the new technology.

Kinds of Newspaper Design

If you have to categorize newspapers by their design, it is probably best to use two broad headings: *orderly* and *loose*.

Orderly

An orderly newspaper strives to be consistent in its use of type, art, white space, and decorative elements. It has a clean, well-planned, almost austere look. Probably the look is modular. That is, stories, with or without pictures, fit into rectangular blocks.

Loose

A loose newspaper would look more lively, more daring, and maybe a bit amateurish in its enthusiasm. The reader might get the idea that the paper is less serious about things. Items might be harder to locate because of the clutter, but there would be an excitement there.

    This is not to say that one approach is necessarily better than the other. Your approach would depend upon the personality you wanted to convey.

Horizontal/Vertical

Another way of classifying newspapers by their appearance is to put them into either horizontal or vertical categories. Newspapers with a horizontal look (plenty of multicolumn heads, stories that run several columns wide, horizontal pictures, and perhaps even horizontally-ruled lines) have a more modern look than more vertical newspapers (columns largely unbroken by headlines or pictures stretching across the columns). Vertical-format newspapers once used several headline decks or banks for each story, which further increased the effect of depth rather than width. Most newspapers today strive for the horizontal look.

A number of scholars have attempted to measure reader reaction to design and design changes. The results of these studies have appeared mostly in the *Journalism Quarterly* and in publications sponsored by the American Newspaper Publishers Association. One such study, conducted by Theresa G. Siskind at the University of South Carolina, showed that readers not only prefer contemporary to traditional design, but also well-designed contemporary pages to ordinary contemporary pages. Siskind commented, "Prospective newspaper readers rated those papers defined as contemporary and/or well-designed as more informative and interesting than those defined as traditional or of average design. . . ."

    David Weaver and others, in a study of competing daily newspapers published by ANPA in 1974, found that leading newspapers tended to rely on traditional design while the second newspapers in those cities went to the contemporary look, using fewer stories on the front page, larger photos, and a horizontal thrust.

Impact of Newspaper Design

Design Elements

The Nameplate

Perhaps the most important single element of design in a newspaper is the nameplate. Mistakenly called the "masthead" by some people, the nameplate quickly establishes the paper's identity. Meant to be bold and to be read from a distance, the nameplate appears near or at the top of the page. In the old days it was set invariably in Old English; more correctly, the name was *drawn* in Old English, then made into a plate that could be used again and again, hence name*plate*. Old English, preferred by the old papers, is still used on some papers because it conveys tradition and dignity.

Often appearing with the type was a small piece of art appropriate to the area where the paper was published or symbolic of the newspaper's editorial policy. Some nameplates became outrageously ornate. The trend in recent years has been to simplify them.

Nameplates do not have to be run in the same place every day, or in the same size. A paper may have several varieties available, including, say, one in reverse letters (white letters in a black rectangle). On special occasions a newspaper can even doctor its nameplate slightly, as when it shows icicles during a cold spell.

Directly under the nameplate goes a set of short lines, usually referred to as the *folio,* running the width of the page and giving the volume and number, the name of the publishing firm, the day and date, maybe the telephone number, and the price. Often this information is set off with a ruled line above and below. The *Los Angeles Times* runs both its daily and Sunday circulation figures there. With figures so impressive, why not? Sometimes a slogan is used. The *Chicago Defender* runs this all-caps slogan under its Old English nameplate: "Chicago's Daily Picture Newspaper."

The space on each side of the centered nameplate often carries *ears*—small messages, sometimes boxed, or headline and copy units that advertise something inside the paper or that carry condensed weather reports. One of the ears may give the edition of the paper. Some authorities regard ears as old-fashioned clutter, and in fact they seem to be disappearing. The *Los Angeles Times* runs nothing at the sides of its Old English nameplate. That way the nameplate gets no competition. The *Milwaukee Journal* treats its roman, all-caps nameplate the same way.

CORVALLIS GAZETTE-TIMES

Some papers spread their nameplates all the way across their pages, leaving no room for ears. The *Corvallis* (Ore.) *Gazette-Times* runs its all-caps nameplate in an expanded sans serif, with the name of the city on one line, in a smaller type, and "Gazette-Times" on the line below. A "GT" logo, often in color, accompanies the nameplate. The *Medford* (Ore.) *Mail Tribune* has an outlined roman italic for its nameplate and uses no other decoration—except for a little line of type underneath reminding readers that the paper once won a Pulitzer prize.

Medford Mail Tribune

A Pulitzer Award Newspaper

The name of a daily sometimes changes on Sunday, with "Sunday" added as part of the title. The *New York Daily News* runs a bigger nameplate, reversed in a color block.

The name itself could make a difference in the design of a nameplate. It could affect the choice of typeface. It could suggest an accompanying piece of art.

Often a paper, for its name, takes a city name and adds *Times, News, Gazette, Star, Post, Tribune, Press,* or the name of a political party. But sometimes a name is less usual, and even peculiar. Union Lake, Mich., has a *Spinal Column,* named by a chiropractor. Early issues carried the slogan, "The backbone of suburban livers." Linn, Mo., has an *Unterrified Democrat,* named at a time when being a Democrat there was something of a danger. In Texas you can read the *Ferris Wheel,* and in Arkansas you can read *DeQueen Bee.* In California there are other *Bees,* parts of the same group—in Sacramento, Modesto, and Fresno.

Some newspapers like to give prominence to the *day* the paper appears. Such papers may use a different nameplate each day; for instance, "Monday's News-Herald," "Tuesday's News-Herald," and the like.

The nameplate should stand out from other display type on the page. If the paper uses a slab serif for headlines, like Bookman or Clarendon, the nameplate could be in Bookman or Clarendon *outline* letters and could be considerably bigger than the large headlines on the page.

The nameplate can be set in type; then a staff artist can adjust the spacing and otherwise change the setting to make it unique. In other cases, a letterform artist or calligrapher would be called in. It is worth paying a high price for the design, for you will live with it for a long time. Nothing looks worse than a bargain nameplate lettered by, say, a show-card sign painter or a cartoonist.

If you add art to the nameplate or place the nameplate in some kind of box or frame, make sure the extra touches do not overpower the name itself. And don't overdecorate the type. Old English, for instance, looks best tightly fitted and condensed; outlining the letters or giving them shadows destroys the character of the original design.

Related to the nameplate is the "story logo," a typographic design that gives special distinction to a continuing expose or interpretive story. A temporary story logo placed inside or above the story each day helps the reader find the story and recognize it as part of a series. The logo that follows is what the *Lewiston* (Idaho) *Morning Tribune* used each day for a three-part series on the effects of herbicides.

HERBICIDES
What are they killing?

Column Rules and Boxes

Many newspapers recently have discontinued use of column rules and minimized their use of boxes. Interestingly, as newspapers move away from these devices magazines pick them up.

Some editors use horizontal lines to separate stories. In some cases the lines are heavy enough to be considered bars. Another possibility is to use thin rules between related stories and thick ones between collections of stories. Or use thin rules vertically and thick rules horizontally. Thick rules (3 points or larger) don't have to be black. They can be screened to gray. Editors call them "Benday rules" after Benjamin Day, who invented a screening process to bring tone to line drawings. Thick rules or bars and wavy lines can be used for boxes, but most designers agree that clean, thin straight lines are best.

Editors can box in some of their shorter, lighthearted stories and use the boxes to help separate large headlines or to add some variety to their pages. The boxed stories are set in a narrower measure to make room for the lines or rules. Some editors who use modular design put everything in boxes. The result is a collection of obvious rectangles. Such an arrangement works better on a tabloid than on a full-size newspaper simply because there are fewer boxes.

On any newspaper, a box can be useful in gathering art, cutlines, headline, and story and separating the unit from other units on the page. The box need not be complete on all four sides. One side could be open, as in a box wrapping around three sides of a standing head, which is often referred to as a "hood." A tint block can serve as a variation of the box. The tint—a screened background—should be light enough for the type to remain legible.

Boxes can be used also to house line drawings, although the irregular silhouette of a line drawing gives the drawing some of its character. Boxes can also house silhouetted photographs. The silhouette—photographed or drawn—can extend outside the box, as though the box is not big enough to contain it. Such treatment breaks up the box, making the photograph more interesting.

Redesign

A paper that did a lot of redesigning in the 1970s, especially in its special sections, is the *New York Times*. Its book review, magazine, and week-in-review sections, especially, earned praise from many in the industry. These sections are not only handsome, but they are also easy for readers to get into and follow. "Significant improvements in design seem to come easier and better in the context of 'How can we give the reader a better paper?' than in the context of 'How can we make what we are doing better-looking?' " says Silverstein, who played a major role in the redesign.

Most papers, when they consider redesign, call in a consultant who studies production facilities, suitable typefaces, and staff assignments, as well as the paper's place in the community: matching all this with the prejudices of the owners and editors, the consultant comes up with a master plan. With that done, the consultant may leave the details to the newspaper's own art director.

A format set up by a consultant must be easy to follow. "I try to give editors something that has very close confines," says Peter Palazzo, a design consultant, "yet I also try to give them the elements with which they can give the paper some excitement, too."

Figure 17.4 In an effort to build and hold readership in this visual age, *The Herald*, a daily and Sunday newspaper published at Everett, Wash., follows a trend toward fewer and wider columns, along with large photographs run in full color. An example of the new horizontal design.

But what often happens is that the instructions are followed and design standards are honored for a time, then little modifications set in. Gradually, the master plan erodes, and one day it will probably be necessary to call in a consultant again to get things squared away and, perhaps, to take advantage of new technology.

Add to the problems of redesign the fact that the design of ads often remains uninspired. The newspaper may adopt a compelling format and administer it thoughtfully and esthetically, day after day, but if its display advertising department continues to turn out schlock design for retailers, the overall look of the paper suffers.

Arkansas City Traveler

107TH YEAR   NUMBER 120   ARKANSAS CITY, KANSAS, FRIDAY, JANUARY 7, 1977   18 PAGES   PRICE 15¢

Arkansas City Traveler

15¢
Monday, December 18, 1978

109th Year   No. 104   Arkansas City, Kansas   22 Pages   2 Sections

---

Arkansas City **Traveler**

15¢
Wednesday, February 7, 1979

109th Year   No. 146   Arkansas City, Kansas   24 Pages   2 Sections

---

Arkansas City **Traveler**

15¢
Monday, February 12, 1979

109th Year   No. 150   Arkansas City, Kansas   14 Pages   1 Section

---

The Arkansas City **Traveler**

15¢
Saturday, February 24, 1979

109th Year   No. 161   Arkansas City, Kansas   14 Pages   1 Section

---

The Arkansas City **Traveler**

109th Year, No. 180   Monday, March 18, 1979   Arkansas City, Kansas   15¢   12 Pages   1 Section

---

Figure 17.5 When the *Arkansas City* (Kan.) *Traveler* changed its nameplate in 1979, it changed it gradually, over a two-month period, to avoid surprising the reader. You see the progression here, from the original to the new. Donald Brazeal, editor, said, "As we hoped, only when the final flag appeared did we hear comments, and then only about the [bird] logo." The bird appears inside, too, on section headings. In the nameplate, the bird often appears in two colors: the top half blue, the bottom red.

Designing and Laying Out the Newspaper

217

By redesigning, newspapers often set out to capture younger readers. Such readers, having grown up on television and films, expect exciting visual treatment. There is no question that the great surge of redesign was prompted by the growth of television as a news medium and as a formidable competitor for advertising.

Whether or not newsstand sales are important to the paper would further influence the consultant. Newspapers that depend largely on newsstand sales need more visual excitement than papers delivered to the home. A newspaper that issues at least one edition each day for the newsstand buyer is a newspaper with two very different looks: one for the home-delivered subscriber and one for the newsstand buyer.

Newspapers follow one of two practices in effecting redesign. Some papers spring a brand new look on their readers. Others make their changes gradually.

What is real change to an editor might not even be noticed by the reader. Decide to eliminate the period after the nameplate (an old-fashioned device) as one major newspaper did after agonizing discussion, then announce the coming change and watch readers yawn. And really, who *does* care? Decide even to change your column setting to ragged right, after listening to the experts argue whether justified or unjustified lines are more readable, and readers probably won't even notice.

It is a good idea to take your readers into your confidence during the redesign period, though. Let them know the paper is contemplating some changes. Maybe they can offer some suggestions; these may not pertain to typefaces or spacing considerations, but they may pertain to organization of the pages, for instance. Too much design is based on the taste and whim of the designer rather than on research. Too often the design flirts with esthetics instead of dealing with readability.

Conclusion

Watching what has been happening to America's newspapers, you get the impression that editors everywhere are paying more attention to design. Television and other visual media have heightened interest in design and made readers more conscious of it.

A few basic principles can help editors achieve better design. Generally, it can be said that a newspaper is well-designed when the design is simple; when pleasing proportions have been worked out; when typefaces, spacing, and art have been used consistently; and when each page manages to emphasize one feature or story.

When a newspaper decides on a redesign program, it should do it with the idea of improving readability, not just with the idea of making pages more attractive.

Designing and Laying Out the Newspaper

Laying Out the Front Page

18

The personality of a newspaper is most evident on its front page. The most important stories start there; and although a basic pattern may have been adopted, each day offers readers a visual surprise. Sometimes the page may be mostly pictures. Sometimes extra large headlines may be in order. The very name of the paper—the nameplate—may move about to make room for urgent news stories.

Each section of a paper has its own front page. Each may be laid out differently, to appeal to specific audiences and to reflect the mood of the section; still, a design relationship ties them together.

Front pages offer the best layout possibilities because usually they are not burdened with advertising. On some papers, however, advertising is a consideration on the front page. A few papers still sell space there—at highly inflated rates—to advertisers who want first crack at readers. Even the *New York Times* runs advertising on the front page. The ads are not large; they are more like classifieds. But there they are, right at the bottom of the Sunday front page, used as if they were fillers.

The front page increasingly has become a place to display color photograpy. If cheaper color is needed, or if there is no color photography, the paper may put its nameplate or a banner headline in color.

If a newspaper publishes several editions, the layout will be changed from edition to edition. The street-sales edition will be splashier than the final, home-delivered edition because headlines on the former are intended to catch the eye of the passerby.

Layout Categories

Textbooks formerly put newspaper layouts into a number of distinct categories. For instance, if the main story was displayed under a large headline at the upper right and lesser stories appeared beneath the main story (forming a pattern that resembled a shelf supported by a bracket), the layout was referred to as a "brace" or "focus and brace" arrangement. There were other categories, such as the "circus," in which many large splashy headlines were used and no particular pattern was discernible. The *Denver Post*

Figure 18.1 For a class assignment, Nina Berkey redesigned a front page of the *Seattle Times*. She was told she could make whatever changes she wished, even changes that might not be practical. The page at the right was what she came up with. Note the strong logo, the bold date and price, the cluster of photos, the recropping, the use of bold horizontal bars, and the line art around which the copy wraps. The redesign does give the paper a more contemporary look.

was known for this makeup in its earlier days. The idea was said to be to give the reader the impression that *all* the stories on the page were important. But that was a simpler era, with less-educated and less-discriminating readers. Another category was the so-called "quadrant," in which the page was divided into imaginary quarters with a strong element—a large headline or a picture—dominating each quarter.

The Seattle Times

Sunday

May 20, 1979   .50

New leader under fire

China cruise
gets off to a
shaky start

N-plant probe
called a joke

Burgers with a bite

Still another pattern was known as "perfect balance." An imaginary line divided the front page into vertical halves, mirroring each other in the placement of their elements—pictures and headlines—so that symmetry resulted. This arrangement was associated primarily with the *New York Times*. Generally, it was regarded as somewhat artificial and could be used only on a day when the run of the news did not include a story of overriding importance.

Balance remains an important consideration in newspaper layout. But *perfect* balance, as described in the foregoing, never was popular. Instead, the balance that is striven for is asymmetrical—perhaps a large photo on one side, a smaller one on the other,

Figure 18.2 Good front page design does not confine itself to the dailies. This full-size weekly consistently runs a strong, well-designed front page and uses more than a single-column width for stories. The star symbol in the nameplate runs in red. The area over the nameplate is used as an illustrated index to what's inside.

a heavy headline on one side with perhaps several smaller ones on the other, etc. The page is *informally* balanced, but balanced nevertheless.

Starting the Layout

One of the makeup editor's main jobs is to help the reader determine what is really important in the news for that day. The importance of a given story is shown by the page it goes on, where it goes on the page, how long it is, how big a headline it gets, and sometimes by what art accompanies it. The editor makes some of

Figure 18.3 This front page of a full-size paper published in Brazil combines formal balance at the top with informal balance below. The large photograph gives the page its impact. One of the blurbs at the right carries its own art—on a diagonal.

these decisions early. Other decisions are made at the last minute.

Louis Silverstein, art director for the *New York Times*, suggests starting page layouts with a pencil. Makeup editors, he says, should make thumbnail sketches of pages. The sketches should run side by side, showing a complete section of the paper as it progresses. Staffers can look at these and make suggestions for changes. Silverstein believes in establishing beginnings, middles, and ends for sections of a newspaper, treating these sections as a magazine treats its sequence of pages. All the good art need not be crowded into the front section. Pages should not be considered

Laying Out the Front Page   223

separate units, according to Silverstein. There is no reason why stories and art cannot cross the gutter, as they do in magazines.

All this may be easier to do in a tabloid than in a full-size newspaper. And of course a full-size newspaper like the *New York Times*, a "newspaper of record" with its national following, may be in a better position to do it than a smaller newspaper with mostly hard news, and most of that local.

Ordinarily, you would not work up your layout pattern first, then look for stories and photographs to fit. You would consider the stories and photographs available, and let their news importance, subject matter, and mood dictate the layout.

Other advice worth considering: do not allow a margin between columns to extend all the way down a page without being interrupted by a crossover headline or photograph. Do not place headlines of identical size and style beside each other (a placement known as "tombstoning"), or jam them close together; headlines should be separated by a couple of inches of type to prevent a crowded, cluttered look. At the top of the page, of course, there is often no avoiding side-by-side headlines. But they can sometimes be separated by pictures or boxes. If an unrelated picture appears above a story, separate them with a horizontal cutoff rule so that the reader will not assume they go together.

The makeup editor indicates the layout of the pages on small sheets. Once the editor has sketched the positions of stories and pictures on these sheets, they are known as "dummies" and serve as road maps for the pasteup artists, who position the type and pictures. The pasted-up page, known as a *repro*, or *repro copy*, is then photographed, and a printing plate is produced from the negative by a chemical process.

Sample Layouts

The rough sketches of Issues A–R show a few of the arrangements you can get with an ordinary all-caps nameplate and three photographs. These sketches should suggest other arrangements, and when you consider that on other days you would have a different number of photographs and perhaps other kinds of art, including drawings, maps, and charts, you begin to appreciate the possibilities of layout innovation, even with a six-column format.

Dotted lines in these sketches remind you where the columns would be if you wanted to follow them.

Issue A uses two of the photos in a boxed skyline story above the nameplate and puts the third photo, a large one, near the center of the area below the nameplate. The nameplate does not quite

Issue A   Issue B   Issue C

stretch to cover six columns. Instead, a sixth-column story takes off at its immediate right, carrying a one-column, three-line headline. This issue makes limited use of the brace principle. The long story at the left runs to the bottom of the first column, then continues in short segments—sometimes called "joints"—in the next four columns, forming a sort of shelf. Under the shelf goes the four-column photograph. The page also features a "bridge" story, at the bottom; the segments narrow for two columns, allowing the insertion of another short story.

Issue B puts two photos above the nameplate, giving them about half the available space and carrying the cutlines for both immediately below and to the right. The third picture appears at the very bottom. A single ear appears at the right of the nameplate. The ear is boxed to match another, slightly bigger box below. This page assumes that the art merits all that space. There is little room for the stories. Most of the stories will have to jump to another page. The main story and its multicolumn headline are at the right.

Issue C puts everything in boxes, one of which is large enough to house the nameplate as well as the largest story on the page. That the boxes are of various sizes and shapes (verticals, horizontals, and squares) keeps the page interesting. A page like this needs to give lots of attention to the rules of good proportion. You could say that such a page owes some of its inspiration to the abstract paintings of Piet Mondrian. An all-boxes approach such as this is likely to be used consistently, but each day's set of shapes would change. It would not be necessary to continue the all-boxes motif on the inside pages.

Issue D

Issue E

Issue F

Issue D uses heavy rules or bars, both horizontally and vertically, also in a Mondrian style. The art is cropped to form a large rectangle near the top and is broken up only by the rules. This page carries a banner above the nameplate that, let's say, calls attention to a story inside. Note that the downstroke of the *T* lines up with one of the vertical rules. Presumably, the nameplate width would change from issue to issue to allow a similar lineup each time.

Issue E offers a formally balanced front page: all the items are centered along a vertical axis. The nameplate breaks into two units to better dramatize the arrangement. This particular page asks for some severe cropping to present the strong horizontal art at the bottom. Even the lines of the headlines and the cutlines are centered.

Issue F runs three index boxes (they are shadow boxes) and uses line art to lure the reader inside. The outline-letters nameplate picks up the same shadowing to bring some unity to the page. A more detailed index or a table of contents appears below at the left.

Laying Out the Front Page

| Issue G | Issue H | Issue I |

Issue G features a giant photograph in which the nameplate is reversed, presumably in an unimportant part of the picture. The other two photographs, which are much smaller, appear with one of the two stories on the front page.

Issue H uses heavy horizontal rules or bars to segregate elements on the page and features one story set in columns of a different width and, probably, a different type size. Thin *vertical* rules could be used between the columns of this unit to make it even more different from other material on the page.

Issue I, putting the photos together into an irregular unit, leaves enough space so that part of one of the photographs can jut out of the rectangular confines. What you see just below the far-right photo are cutlines and, below them, an index set off by thick horizontal rules.

Issue J   Issue K   Issue L

Issue J separates items with thick horizontal rules, uses a skyline story, and gives big, deep display to one of the photographs.

Issue K puts one story and a photograph in a box and offers wide-measure copy. A second photograph gets silhouette treatment.

Issue L offers a piece of line art and a flush-right ear with the nameplate, which is flush left. Horizontal rules divide the page. This is an example of modular layout.

Issue M uses a banner headline for a one-column story that extends down column three instead of column six. One story on this page (upper right) is set in wider measure.

Issue N uses three braces. Under one of the shelves is a photo; under another shelf, another story; under the third, a box with ruled lines only above and below. The large photograph stands by itself with its own headline to the left of the cutlines. This page manages to crowd in a lot of stories.

Issue O experiments by using photographs put together in a single large block and stories that do not line up at the top. The irregular white space adds interest to the page, nicely sets off the photographs, and eases fitting problems, but most editors would look upon such layout with suspicion. An index is at the bottom left.

Issue P reverses the nameplate in a color, black, or tint block and offers three banner heads above. One could refer to the lead story below, the others to stories inside. The lead story is set in a wide measure. The photographs, again, are gathered in a single block. The story below is blocked. The page has strength; the design would work, too, for a tabloid page.

Laying Out the Front Page

Issue M

Issue N

Issue O

Issue P

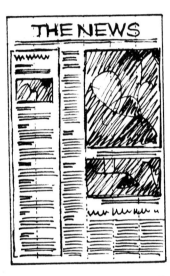

Issue Q

Issue R

Issue Q puts one of the photographs in a box (at the left) that summarizes the news and acts as an index.

Issue R is probably the most unconventional front page of the lot, with its up-the-side nameplate and its concentration of art into an irregular shape at the top. The chief innovation, though, comes from the generous doses of white space at the outside edges.

Laying Out the Front Page   **229**

Figure 18.4 A high school paper, *West Side Story,* published by West High School, Iowa City, Iowa, shows how to make a tabloid front page magazine-like: one headline, one story, one strong piece of art, and heavy column rules. The nameplate runs sideways in the first narrow column, with publishing information at the top. There is plenty of blank space to carry the address label. Many papers would find this modern, unorthodox front page wasteful of space, but it is a page worth studying for its impact and lack of clutter. Note that the story is a feature, not hard news.

WEST HIGH SCHOOL
2901 Melrose Ave.
Iowa City, IA 52240
January 19, 1979
Vol. 11 No. 6

Ski the prairie

While many students travel as far as Minnesota or Colorado for the chance to ski, an increasing number are finding that skiing isn't just confined to the slopes. Iowa's flat countryside and occasional rolling hills provide the ideal conditions for cross country skiing. "There are few hassles involved because it can be done right around your house. This kind of skiing is also very suitable to the type of terrain that we have in Iowa," said Steve Howe of Bivouac.

Not only is Iowa suited to this sport, but the price is also right for students without a lot of money to spend. The cost of a cross country ski package is one half that of downhill. For the less serious skiers who don't want to buy their own, Bivouac, The Bicycle Peddlers and the University of Iowa have skis available for rental. The price of these range from $6.50 to $7 per day and $10 for the weekend.

But cross country skiing should not be considered a less costly substitute for the downhill variety. It provides many students with a kind of satisfaction that can be found nowhere else. Unlike downhill skiers, their cross country counterparts don't have to contend with slopes or long lift lines. They can, in fact, go an entire afternoon seeing only a few other skiers. "Cross country skiing is a good way to be on your own out in nature when there's snow," said Chris Goerdt '79. "It's a great way to get outside to exercise in the winter and have fun at the same time," said Caroline Hale '81.

In recent years this sport has become very popular in Iowa City. According to Ken Meerdink of The Bicycle Peddlers, "It has been building slowly over the past couple years. Now it's come to the point where almost everyone knows someone who cross country skis." Iowa City has many locations that accommodate the increase in skiers. Hickory Hill Park, Lake MacBride, the Coralville Reservoir and Finkbine golf course are among the most popular skiing sports.

Another advantage to cross country skiing is the exercise it provides. "It tends to condition a person more than downhill skiing would. It's similar to jogging in the respect that you can take it as hard as you want. It can be very relaxed or you can cross country ski to the level where essentially you're a long distance runner on skis," explained Howe. "One of the reasons I like it is because it burns off 600 calories an hour and it's easy to do," said Nicole Hardt '79.

WEST SIDE STORY

The Tabloid

The front page of a tabloid is likely to be quite different from the front page of a full-size newspaper because it has only half the space a full-size newspaper has. Tabloids tend to devote more of their front pages to art and headlines, they offer fewer columns. The *Christian Science Monitor*, a four-column tabloid, ends up usually with a front page that is about one-third art. But then, full-size newspapers often use that ratio, too.

The tabloid front page very often is no more than a poster advertising what's inside: a photograph with a caption or blurb, a banner head, and several smaller heads, possibly with page numbers below.

Layout Decisions

Jumps

The editor has to choose between a wealth of stories beginning on the front page and jumping to inside pages, or just a few stories running in their entirety on the front page. The many-stories approach stands a better chance of serving all readers because it caters to a wide range of interests. But it is a nuisance for readers following stories to inside pages. And maybe the reader won't return to the front page (research shows that many do not). The few-stories approach makes for simpler design and increases the chance that the stories displayed will be read all the way through. But it creates a problem for the editor, who must decide which stories will appear on the page.

Jumps are widely recognized as a necessary evil. Some papers limit the number of jumps to three or four. Others, notably the *Los Angeles Times*, jump long interpretive stories to page after page.

If a story is to jump, it needs a *continued* line. Such a line would appear only when the story resumes on another page, and never when it merely moves to the next column.

Figure 18.5 *Bucknell World,* an alumni tabloid published by Bucknell University, starts off with an orderly, attractive front page *(left)* and uses plenty of white space at the top to display the nameplate. The table of contents is mostly illustration. The page at the right is typical of inside design of this publication.

Figure 18.6 The *Journal-Courier* of New Haven, Conn., runs its nameplate in color all the way across the page. The heavy underline, also in color, is repeated below to make some short items and an index stand out. Unusual among dailies, the *Journal-Courier* uses unjustified sans serif type for its body copy.

Continued lines do not necessarily have to have the word *continued* in them. The *Boston Globe* simply stops its stories abruptly on the front page, then, on the next line, flush left, runs a key word in all caps followed by a comma and *page* plus the number. The continued part of the story carries a new headline, but the story restarts on the same key word with a *continued from* . . . line underneath.

The *Los Angeles Times* asks you to *Please turn to page —, col. —.*

Laying Out the Front Page

If stories are to jump, should they jump just anywhere? Or should they all jump to one place? Should they repeat their original headlines, run shorter versions of them, or carry new headlines? Also, should the jump heads be set in smaller type? These are some of the details governed by the overall design.

Tables of Contents

In the past, newspapers confined their tables of contents to small boxes, called *indexes*, on the front page. These indexes directed the reader to the various sections of the paper and perhaps to a column or two, such as "Dear Abby" or the daily horoscope. But now newspapers are making these indexes more elaborate or are combining them with real tables of contents, complete with illustrations and summaries. These boxes become an important design element on the page.

The *San Francisco Chronicle* summarizes the news each day at the top half of the front page in a "Top of the News" section. Each summary sentence is followed by the number of the page where the reader can get the details.

The Bishop family tree grows in twos and threes	Government regulation: The costs and the causes	St. Andrews fits golfers to a tee
ACCENT G 1	MARKETPLACE E 1	SPORTS C 1

The *Lewiston Morning Tribune*, like a number of other papers, runs a promotional table of contents across the top of the page. A bold black or color bar appears underneath. The logo goes below the bar. A small boxed index elsewhere on the page lists sections or special pages. The *Louisville Courier-Journal* uses a similar style and placement.

5B Is there room for two recycling centers at Lewiston?

1E Can two South American llamas find happiness here? Sunday A.M.

1F A favorite tourist spot on the Snake has new owners. Business.

1C The minor leagues have been good and bad to former UI pitcher Ken Schrom.

Front-Page Boxes and Rules

Boxes and rules are especially useful in laying out front pages. For its front-page boxes, the *San Francisco Chronicle* uses wavy lines and also lines formed by heavy dots. Many papers have formed boxes by using only horizontal rules top and bottom, and indenting the text.

Knepper's

3-Hitter

Beats Braves

See Sports

When made from rules that are thick enough, the box can say, "This is an obituary." When the U.S. Senate voted to give the Panama Canal to the Republic of Panama, the *Arizona Daily Sun* of Flagstaff ran the story on the front page, above the nameplate, inside an obit box. The headline read, "U.S. Flag, Panama Canal Zone, 1914–1978." But most papers would consider this impermissible editorializing.

Running an oversize thin-line box on the page is another possibility. It gives you a chance to run a page within a page. The design inside the box can be quite different from the design outside. A full-color photo can be inside, for instance, with a headline reversed in an unimportant part of the photo. The story can be set in a wider measure than usual.

Front Pages for Sections

The front pages of the various sections of a newspaper deserve as much thought as the main front page. Sections have their nameplates, too— "Sports," "Living," and the like. Logic suggests that these nameplates should be smaller and less dramatic than the main nameplates, but section editors often get carried away with the importance of their sections and give their nameplates unusual flair.

In addition to their own nameplates, the sections are likely to also carry the main nameplate, but in a smaller size, to remind readers what newspaper they're reading. The front pages for sections deserve their own tables of contents, too. Some newspapers give initials to the sections—*B, C, D,* etc.—and restart the numbering of the pages. The *Milwaukee Journal* uses green paper (four pages—or a large sheet folded once) for one of its sections and calls it "Green Sheet." The section carries features and comics.

Although advertising is kept off the main front page, some newspapers sell space on the front pages of sections. Perhaps the paper reserves space for one ad for the front page of "Section Two," and a preferred long-term advertiser shows up there, day after day.

Sometimes a newspaper puts a "front" page *inside* a section, as, let's say, a page 3 "front" page that carries local news when page 1 carries mostly national and international news. The *Los Angeles Times* does this. The page may have its own nameplate.

The back page of the first or main section of a newspaper would make a good editorial page, but most newspapers give their back pages over to advertisers. There are newspapers, however, that use the back page as a local front page and jump stories from it backwards—to the inside of the paper. This practice is startling to those who have not seen it before, but is easy to grow accustomed to.

Conclusion

More attention goes to the layout of front pages than to the layout of inside pages because front pages are the papers' showcases, uninterrupted, usually, by advertising. These pages serve readers immediately and also get them to the inside stories. As newspapers pay more attention to design and layout they no doubt will put more effort into making inside pages as attractive as front pages.

In the old days, front page layouts used to fall into several rather restrictive categories such as brace, circus, quadrant, and perfect balance, but these categories are largely ignored today.

It is important to remember that a layout pattern should not be allowed to dictate news placement. The day's news should dictate the arrangement.

Whether to run only a few stories in their entirety on the front page or to start many stories and continue them inside is a policy an editor must decide. Arguments can be made for either approach. When stories do jump to inside pages, readers should be able to follow them effortlessly. And if the newspaper is thick and in several sections, a table of contents should be provided.

Laying Out Inside Pages

19

The advertisements, which fill much of the space inside the newspaper, go into place first and news-editorial material fills the remaining space. That space not only is small but, because the ads are stacked in a sort of staircase, it is also irregular. It is almost impossible to lay out these news holes with any real flair. Still, today's newspapers are giving more attention to inside pages, trying to bring to them the kind of attention that goes into the layout of front pages. Some inside pages are free or almost free of advertising, and some of the pages carry advertising that is arranged in rectangles rather than half pyramids. Laying out the news and features on these pages can be as satisfying as laying out front pages.

Of the special inside pages, the editorial page deserves the most attention. The layout of this page should attract readers and also should make the page, where opinion is expressed, different from all the other pages.

Feature pages also are given a different look from other pages. The design of these pages resembles the design of magazines—design that is less bound by preset standards.

Laying out inside pages can be especially difficult on pages where some advertisers are able to buy nearly full-page spaces, which leave only a narrow band across the top or down the side for news matter. The *Seattle Times,* for instance, sells partial double trucks, with thin *L*-shaped news holes on either side. Dick Pryne, when he was senior assistant news editor of the paper, called these units "elbows" and complained that there was little anyone could do to lay them out attractively. For instance, you cannot run photos with much depth across the tops of such pages. And your cutlines cannot be long. Some papers partially solve this problem by running "side saddle" cutlines.

Coping with Advertising

Figure 19.1 The *Weekly*, a handsome tabloid-size alternative newspaper that calls itself "Seattle's Newsmagazine," shows what can be done with inside pages dominated by advertising. The "Weekly Wash," a regular feature, wraps around an illustrated ad on the left-hand page. Letters to the editor and a table of contents appear in a tint block and spread over two same-size ads on the right-hand page. The vertical and horizontal rules help organize material throughout the tabloid.

There is little chance of moving the advertising. There is no chance of eliminating it. A business deal is a business deal. The editors must work around the ads.

The half pyramiding got started in the days when advertisers believed their advertising would not be read unless it touched editorial matter. That way, they thought, unwary readers would wander into the advertising almost as though by mistake. Small ads went on top of larger ads to give each of the ads—even the small ones—nearness to stories on the page. Some papers have done away with half pyramiding, arranging ads instead in modules. A few papers confine ads to all-ads pages. The inside pages then can be designed with the kind of freedom and flair you find on front pages.

Figure 19.2 The *Hastings Star Gazette,* a Minnesota weekly, stacks its ads in rectangles rather than putting them into a stairstep arrangement, leaving large rectangles for easy layout of news and editorial matter. The art for the "Divorce" feature is an example of line conversion of a photograph.

One solution to design problems brought about by the half-pyramid ad page is to fill the news hole with a series of horizontal blocks that grow successively narrower as they go down the page. Each headline would be an across-the-story one-liner.

Solutions to filling shallow news holes include (1) (center sketch) running a headline that stretches only part of the way over a story and (2) (right sketch) making a bridge of one story and fitting another, shorter story under it.

When advertising shares the stage with stories on inside pages, the editor makes every effort to keep the news content different in appearance from the advertising. If the ads are black and garish, the news hole should look somewhat lighter and quieter. The point here is that the layout should help the reader distinguish between news and advertising. The design of the advertising itself can affect the looks of the paper. But the editor cannot do much about that except to complain to the publisher, who could take the matter up with the display advertising department, which is responsible for preparing many of the ads for local advertisers. Some ads are prepared outside the newspaper, but it is unlikely that a newspaper would reject an ad simply because it was poorly designed. That is a luxury only a magazine—one like *The New Yorker*—could afford.

Like front pages, inside pages need to end evenly at the bottoms of columns. One way of doing this is to add a little space at points where inconsistencies will not be noticed. For instance, you can sometimes get away with a little extra space between paragraphs, around some of the subheads, and between headlines and stories. It is better, though, to reduce or enlarge photographs to make your adjustments. Sometimes, to make things even, the makeup editor drops in a house ad selling people on the idea of

subscriptions or promoting a current or planned feature. A few papers continue to use one-line or one-paragraph timeless fillers— pieces of general information—to fill the column, a practice not recommended.

Newspapers should give some thought to allowing columns at the bottom of the page to stop where they may, and not rely on fillers or space padding. Is it really necessary that the columns line up against an imaginary base line? Some magazines have allowed nonalignment for years.

As you design inside pages, look for pieces of art to bring some graphic relief. Photographs and cartoons are the usual choice. Comic strips usually congregate on a single page that has a few features, but some papers have tried scattering comic strips to bring added interest to many parts of the paper. Panel cartoons, especially one-column drop-ins, probably work best for scattering. They are particularly useful in preventing the tombstoning of headlines.

Editors who care about the looks of their papers apply to inside pages most of the design principles they use for front pages— despite the advertising on inside pages. And some of the inside pages—those without advertising—turn out to be as exciting visually as the front pages.

Good design can be especially useful in helping readers find their favorite pages or sections. To help differentiate sports news, the Milford (Mass.) *Daily News,* in a weekly "Sports Extra" section on Fridays, runs news of professional sports one way and news

Figure 19.3 That small rectangle of white space in the middle shows you what happens sometimes when a newspaper adopts an inside format that gives advertisements a set of widths different from that given to stories.

Figure 19.4 The weekly *Chico News & Review* (Chico, Calif.) shows that it is possible to bring good design to an inside page, at least in a tabloid, even when the page carries some advertising. But this example suggests that the advertising should be blocked off in a rectangle and that the editorial art should be kept at a distance from the advertising. The reader starts at the upper right on this page because that is where the initial letter is.

of local sports another. When readers get to the end of one area of coverage, they must turn the paper upside down to get to the other. "Now . . . [readers] can read only what they want and don't have to wade through a lot of needless information to get it," says Thomas C. Sawyer of the paper's marketing department. Many designers, though, forbid presentation of material that requires the reader to turn the page in any way.

Some papers start numbering pages anew with each section. Others number pages consecutively, no matter how many. Each inside page should carry the name of the newspaper, the date, and the section and page number. This not only reminds readers where they are, but also helps researchers cite their sources correctly. A line carrying this information can cut into a couple of columns; the remaining columns can start at the top of the page.

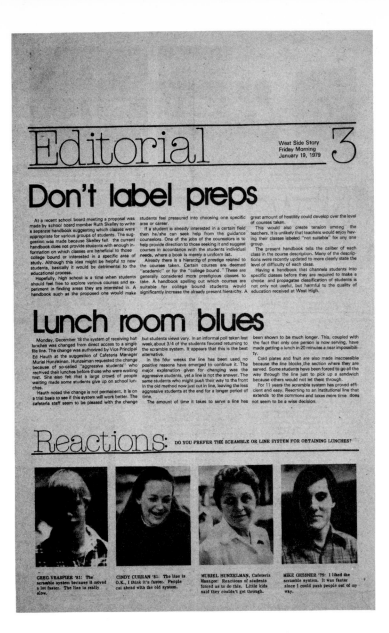

Figure 19.5 The editorial page for the paper at West High School, Iowa City, Iowa, with a feature at the bottom. Notice the deep sink (the wide band of white at the top), the large but lightface heading, and the large page number. Ben Van Zante is the advisor to the staff of this paper.

Among inside pages, none deserves more care than the editorial page. It is not a page that interests all readers, but good design can enhance its appeal. It is important that the editorial page be placed where its devotees can find it easily each day. That placement should be consistent. For most papers, the page becomes the third from the last page—a left-hand page—in the first section. The op-ed page (opposite-editorial, given over to columns and other commentary, usually) is at the right.

The Editorial Page

Many readers have never quite understood the distinction newspapers make between objective news coverage and editorial comment. So the editorial page and the op-ed page must look different. "Certainly a change in page format or typography will not solve the problem for us," observes Edmund C. Arnold. "But at least it might act as a mild flag to alert the reader that this page isn't quite like all the other pages."

Arnold suggests different column measures, different—or at least larger—body type, and different type styles for headlines, all of which have been made easier by the new technology. "Today changing line-length means simply turning a dial; so does changing point size of body type. And in cold type there is a wide selection of fine headletters that are relatively inexpensive and, incidentally, almost completely overlooked by publishers who choose headline faces," says Arnold.

Arnold sees the design of an editorial page as an exercise in salesmanship. The reader must be lured onto the page. One approach to designing an editorial page is to make it look pretty much the same each day. Another is to bring great variety to it, sometimes running photos, moving the editorial cartoon around, or putting the editorials in a column other than the first column. A newspaper should at least be willing to vary the length of the column of editorials. If events dictate only a couple of short editorials for the day, so be it. Another day may bring more and longer editorials.

The reader should be able to tell an editorial from a regular, bylined column on the same page. That the editorial is unsigned provides one hint. But its typography should be different, too. On most papers the editorials are wider. Being wider, they are set in larger type. To prevent any doubt, a heading such as "Editorials" or "Our Opinion" is used. Many papers run editorials as blocks of two columns, with headlines that are often centered, running over each block.

Some papers break up the grayness of the column of editorials with cartoon illustrations. It is important to pick strongly drawn, uncomplicated cartoons to be used in this way.

The main editorial cartoon, run apart from the column of editorials, turns out to be the focal point of the page for most readers. A guest editorial cartoon or two may bring additional vitality to the page or to the op-ed page. A little color can do wonders for the editorial cartoon. And you do not have to confine your color to a locally produced editorial cartoon. You can have your staff artist prepare a second-color overlay for the syndicated cartoon. *Time* and *Newsweek* do this with editorial cartoons they reprint from newspapers. The cartoons appeared originally in black and white.

One way to help the reader identify parts of the page is to organize the page in obvious sections and give them names. For instance, having established the fact with some kind of logo that the page is a page of opinion, you can call the editorials "Ours," the columns "Theirs," and the letters "Yours," as the *Oregon Daily Emerald* and probably other papers do.

The letters-to-the-editor column, probably the most-read feature on the page, often carries some instruction to would-be letter writers, telling them, for instance, how long their letters may be. That instruction, which is often boxed, becomes a design element. Because the column runs letters of various lengths, some editors are tempted to break it into two parts, one on the editorial page itself, the other on the op-ed page. But it is best to keep all the letters together in one place, unless a collection of them is meant to comment on a single topic. Minor errors in grammar and in spelling that occur in letters should be corrected. And to prevent confusion, references to previously published editorials as "columns," and to previously published letters and columns as "editorials" should also be changed. Readers are often shaky on such terminology.

Two or more letters that are run on a single topic should be grouped, either under one inclusive heading or special headings for each letter. Because the letters run under a "Letters" heading, it is not necessary to include salutations like "Dear Editor."

Once in a while a letter comes in that is so thoughtful and thorough it deserves special graphic treatment. It is boxed and illustrated, and it probably carries a special identification of the author.

The op-ed page should carry over the design principles of the editorial page. Perhaps all the letters should go there. Perhaps that is where the guest editorial cartoons should be. The *Los Angeles Times,* feeling that its own editorial cartoonist, Paul Conrad, was not always concurring with the staff-written editorials, moved his cartoons to the op-ed page.

Arnold suggests that the op-ed page need not be opposite the editorial page. It could go anywhere in the paper. Maybe two pages of heavy thinking in succession are too much for the reader.

Very few newspapers allow an advertisement on the editorial page, but the op-ed page is not quite so guarded. Because the op-ed page represents an expansion, a newspaper might settle for just half a page, for instance, giving over the rest to local advertisers, as the *New Haven* (Conn.) *Journal-Courier* does.

W. Sprague Holden, chairman of the journalism department of Wayne State University, has suggested the elimination of editorial pages and the scattering of editorials throughout the paper so that editorials appear next to the news stories they relate to. In the unlikely event you would do that, you would probably want to box the editorials and clearly label them as editorials.

Figure 19.6 For this "Living" page, the *Boston Sunday Globe* brings an illustration and both rectangular and silhouetted photographs together, and pushes all the art to the outside edges to help frame the columns of copy. To make the page interesting, the paper allows the art at the upper right to expand out of its box, and at the upper left it overlaps two pieces of art. At the bottom right, the paper butts two photographs together, not using the usual strip of white most papers use between related pictures. Most pictures at the edges of the page generally face inward. Like many other papers, the *Globe* surrounds its photographs with a thin black line. (Reprinted courtesy of the *Boston Globe.*)

Features and Special Sections

The trend in the late 1970s to fill newspapers with service features instead of hard news prompted a satirical column by Russell Baker on how to read a newspaper. "People are always asking me how I get the newspaper read and still find the time left over to catch a little sleep each week," Baker said. "The first thing I do is open to the obituary page to make sure I haven't died while reading yesterday's paper."

Laying Out Inside Pages

But to many readers, the features are what matter. In many cases, they draw younger readers to the newspaper. They are the answer to the city magazines that have sprung up to challenge newspapers' dominance as the local print media. These features tell how to survive in the city and how to make life more interesting. They call for a treatment different from the treatment of news stories and editorials.

The appearance of these features and of special sections that carry them is more a magazine than a newspaper look, even though the pages are mostly standard newspaper size. A fashion section, for instance, might look entirely different from anything else found in the newspaper. The fashion section's headlines might be in Helvetica or Baskerville type styles while the other headlines would be in, say, Bodoni or Cheltenham; more white space might be used; photos might be bigger and outlined with black lines; and horizontal lines or bars might separate the stories and features. And, of course, only fashion advertisers would have ads there.

Layout of feature pages or special sections moves away from grids and allows for more flexibility. Art usually appears in a larger size and white space becomes more important. The editor-designer approaches such pages as an art director approaches magazine spreads. In some cases the sections actually become magazines.

Conclusion

Although inside pages do not offer the clean slates for design that front pages offer, editors are no longer merely dumping news and features into the irregular holes left by the advertising. They are laying out these pages with the same care they use in laying out front pages. In some cases they are directing their advertising departments to arrange ads into rectangles rather than into half pyramids. This gives editors more leeway in design.

Editorial pages and special feature pages offer the best layout possibilities inside the paper. More white space and more flexibility in typography often give these pages a magazine look.

20 Newspaper Magazines

Newspapers at one time prided themselves on their difference from magazines and looked upon magazines as competitors, and inferior competitors at that. Today, however, the two media borrow from each other and even take on similar appearances. The "magazine look" is the look some newspaper designers seem to aim for.

Moreover, weekly or monthly magazines have become part of many newspapers. The newspaper-produced magazine is likely to be a little more crudely produced than a slick, general-circulation magazine found on the newsstands but it has most of the characteristics of the magazine format.

Most newspaper-produced magazines are tabloids. They are usually printed by offset lithography. Newspapers that cannot afford to produce their own magazines or want to supplement their magazines' local coverage with national coverage subscribe to syndicated magazines printed by rotogravure.

This chapter deals mainly with the problems of producing locally edited newspaper magazine sections.

The Magazine Format

Years ago rotogravure sections appeared in many major American newspapers. Printed in dark brown ink on slick paper, these full-size newspaper sections presented features illustrated with fine-screen photographs which were often cut in circles and other shapes and accompanied by decorative borders. In the pre-TV era, these locally edited sections offered plenty of diversion for lazy Sunday afternoons. Often they were printed out of town, for few papers had their own rotogravure presses.

Rotogravure sections were expensive to produce, and during the Depression, costs caught up with them. For the magazine touch, then, newspapers generally faced two choices; either they subscribed to a syndicated magazine section like *American Weekly* (defunct), *This Week* (defunct), *Parade* (still going), or *Family Weekly* (also still going), or they developed their own tabloid magazine sections. A few papers carried both syndicated and locally edited magazines as part of their Sunday or weekend editions.

In recent years some specialized syndicated magazines have emerged, including magazines dealing with sports, ethnic groups, and other groups and subjects. For instance, *Dawn Magazine,* a monthly syndicated supplement edited for blacks, goes to the Baltimore *Afro-American,* the *New York Amsterdam News,* the Chicago *Defender,* and a number of other papers.

Sometimes the locally produced magazine may be a full-size regular section in the paper, possibly on a tinted stock. The *Seattle Times* publishes a "Jr. Times" section as two pages of a regular section run sideways. A dotted line running up the side invites young readers to clip the sheet and then fold it into a tabloid-size unit.

The tabloid format used by most newspaper magazines differs from standard magazine format in that pages are not bound. One set of four fits loosely into another, and those two fit into another, and so on, just as regular newspaper pages do.

Unlike the newspaper, which strives to interest a broad audience, the magazine often concentrates on a group. The group may consist of younger, more affluent readers. The advertising would reflect this. If the magazine specializes, the design would reflect the specialization. It is possible through design to make a magazine look upbeat, homey, or cultural, for example, through choices of typefaces and styles of art.

For its Sunday edition, a big daily may run several locally produced magazines, including a book review section. A book review section is especially difficult to design. For one thing, what can you use for art? If you reproduce the book's jacket, it may look as though you are advertising rather than reviewing the book. Anyway, the advertising in the section is likely to reproduce jackets. You do not want to repeat the effect. You can use photographs of the author, of course, and sample art from the book. A number of book review sections use old-fashioned public-domain art more as decoration than anything else.

Many newspapers issue local TV guides, feeling that *TV Guide* cannot get down to the local level except for bare listings. Plenty of free publicity shots are available. The newspapers' staff artists can show off their talent with full-color cover art, something they may not be able to do elsewhere in the papers. The real design challenge here is to make the schedule easy to follow and the format appropriate for week-long reference.

Occasionally, a newspaper magazine puts out a theme issue, with all articles related. This calls for great design unity. The business side exploits the theme issue by going out after advertisers interested in the subject.

Any newspaper magazine tries to offer material different from the content of the rest of the paper. It leaves news to the regular section.

Figure 20.1 *Saturday Magazine,* part of the Scottsdale (Ariz.) *Daily Progress,* usually runs photographs or drawings, along with blurbs, on the cover. But for an issue *(right)* that carried an article on the *Tombstone Epitaph,* a historic newspaper now published by students at the University of Arizona, *Saturday Magazine* ran a reproduction of an early issue of the paper with "100 YEARS" in red running across it diagonally. The "In this issue/100 years at the Epitaph/Parents of gays/ Book reviews" blurb at the bottom ran in red in a mortise.

Newspaper magazines do not have room for fiction. They run mostly *articles.* How do articles differ from the *features* run in regular sections of the newspaper? Articles are usually longer, less frothy and more controversial. Each must appeal to a large percentage of the readers because so few articles can be included. The short features in the regular newspaper are more likely than articles to be considered mere filler.

The articles take as their subjects local personalities, personal experiences, and the arts, entertainment, and recreation nearby. Combined with the articles are reviews, home and garden hints, poems, and cartoons.

Some of the magazines use local columnists. A column is likely to appear in the same place in each issue and carry a standing, illustrated heading along with a special title. The designer makes the column look different from other features in the magazine.

To help readers find their way through the variety of features, the editor of a newspaper magazine puts a great deal of thought into the organization and design of a full table of contents that usually appears just inside the front cover.

Figure 20.2 The "100 years at the Tombstone Epitaph" article in "Saturday Magazine" started on a right-hand page and ran for six pages, interrupted by some advertising. The use of double-deck headlines and column rules gave the pages an old-fashioned feel.

100 years of the Tombstone Epitaph

Newspaper too tough to die isn't ready for obituary

Epitaph born May 1880 and still going strong

by Kurt Pfitzer

The Tombstone Epitaph in 1923 moved to this building which was constructed in 1881.

It was shortly after midnight on Dec. 15, 1881. A six-horse stagecoach had completed four miles of its journey from Tombstone across the desert to Tucson.

A command to "Halt!" suddenly greeted the vehicle and was followed quickly by a flurry of gunshots from a group of armed bandits. Despite injuries to its driver and lead horse, the coach managed to flee to safety. But the target of the attack — John P. Clum, mayor of Tombstone, founder and editor of the Tombstone Epitaph and a staunch advocate of law and order in the West's most lawless mining camp — disappeared.

Since printing the first edition of the Epitaph on May 1, 1880, Clum had earned the hatred of Tombstone's cattle rustlers and gunmen. He attacked them constantly with editorials and news stories that were colorful, sarcastic and frequently slanted. To Clum, Tombstone's violent elements were "cow-boys" who threatened the amazing prosperity silver mining had brought to the boom town.

Clum survived the ambush unharmed — he walked to a nearby mill and rode a horse to Benson. The Epitaph reacted to his near-murder with characteristic indignation.

"The assault upon the Benson stage by would-be assassins Wednesday night within four miles of town is the greatest outrage ever perpetrated upon the traveling public of Arizona, and is an event calculated to do more harm to the business interests of Tombstone than all other causes operating against us put together," said an editorial dated Dec. 16, 1881.

"That the damnable deed miscarried does not rob the event of one jot or tittle of its enormity," the editorial continued. "The killings and attempted killings heretofore recorded in Tombstone and the surrounding country have been the outgrowth of drunkenness, wrongs or fancied

Kurt Pfitzer was editor of the Tombstone Epitaph at the University of Arizona where he is studying for his master's degree in journalism.

wrongs, suffered at the hands of one or the other parties to the difficulties."

Clum already had established his place in American history before he started writing Tombstone's Epitaph. A native of New York, he attended Rutgers College before heading west and taking an appointment as Arizona's first civilian Indian agent in 1874. For three years, he governed 4,500 Apaches at the San Carlos Indian Reservation; and in 1877, after a 400-mile trek across Arizona and New Mexico, he became the first — and only — white man ever to capture Geronimo.

But it is the Tombstone Epitaph for which Clum is best remembered today. The newspaper he began printing in a canvas tent more than 99 years ago ranks today as Arizona's third oldest continuously published newspaper. In its 100th year of publication, the Epitaph serves as one of Arizona's leading tourist attractions, a town synonymous with Western legend, and a town which celebrated its own centennial this part March.

It hasn't been an easy 99 years. Like Tombstone, whose population dwindled from 6,500 in 1882, when $5 million in silver was mined, to a few hundred after water filled the mines and shut down operations, the Epitaph has come close to folding more than once.

Twice during its first decade, the Epitaph had to merge with competing newspapers, becoming at first a semiweekly, and then, for a time, the Sunday edition of the Tombstone Prospector.

In 1975, faced with insufficient advertising revenues and rising costs, the group which then owned the Epitaph sold the paper's publishing rights to the University of Arizona, where it is currently printed every two weeks by students in the Department of Journalism.

The Epitaph has never missed a publication date, nor has it ever passed up an opportunity to boast Tombstone. Largely because of the newspaper's leadership, Tombstone avoided the ghost-town fate that overtook so many other dying mining camps and instead became a mecca for America's vacationing travelers and Old West afficionados.

It was the Epitaph's editors who half a century ago first called upon the town to restore its old 1880s buildings and develop a tourist industry.

SLAUGHTERED.

Brutal Murder of an Upright Citizen at Charleston by a Desperado.

And it was the Epitaph which coined the phrase by which Tombstone is known today in hundreds of history books and travel agencies — "The Town Too Tough To Die."

Clum set the standards of inspiration, humor and loyalty to Tombstone which guided future Epitaph editors. In the paper's first editorial, titled "The First Trumpet," he wrote:

"Tombstone is a city set upon a hill, promising to vie with ancient Rome, upon her seven hills, in a fame different in character but no less in importance.

"No tombstone is complete without its epitaph," the editorial continued, "and so we have come to fill the void and make all happy in the consequent perfection."

Through the Epitaph, Clum attempted to motivate Tombstone's citizens to build a town worthy of pride. In an article in the Sept. 1, 1880, issue, the editor noted the lack of a single church in Tombstone and wrote:

"We presume there is not another town of the same size and age of Tombstone in the United States that does not contain at least one church ... It can't be that Tombstone differs so much from the ordinary mining camp in California, where a hat passed to raise money to build a church would almost have the bottom knocked out by the contributions of all classes of citizens."

Clum's accounts of the numerous shooting deaths that gave early Tombstone its rowdy reputation were colorful, long-winded and frequently libelous. In short, they resembled the style of sensational journalism that prevailed in the late 19th century.

One such example appeared in the Jan. 17, 1881, Epitaph, when Clum made a judgment of murder against a man who had yet to stand trial.

"About 7 o'clock last evening the pistol was again used with fatal effect on Allen Street, resulting in the death of T. J. Waters from gunshot wounds in the hands of E. L. Bradshaw."

In the same issue, Clum passed the guilty sentence on a character known as "Johnny-Behind-the-Deuce" in a

(Continued on Page 8)

Scottsdale Progress/Saturday Magazine   Aug. 11, 1979   7

The Magazine Editor at Work

The staff member with a flair for writing features and an interest in magazines is the person who usually draws the assignment to edit a newspaper magazine. Such a person probably has a greater interest in graphic design than the typical reporter or editor, although the design of the magazine often falls to a staff artist or, better, a graphics designer. On some magazines, the editor and art director share top billing on the masthead. More than the newspaper itself, the magazine recognizes the importance of good design. And the weekly deadline allows more careful design than a daily deadline does. The magazine may do its own copy editing rather than put copy into regular channels.

Material going into the magazines comes partly from staff members but mostly from freelancers. The editors spend much of

Figure 20.3 It was a tough decision, but when *Northwest,* the Sunday magazine of the *Oregonian,* ran an article on abortion, it decided to run a full-color cover shot of an actual abortion. The cover's shock value caused a number of reader complaints, but editor Joe Bianco felt the picture was not in bad taste, considering the nature of the article.

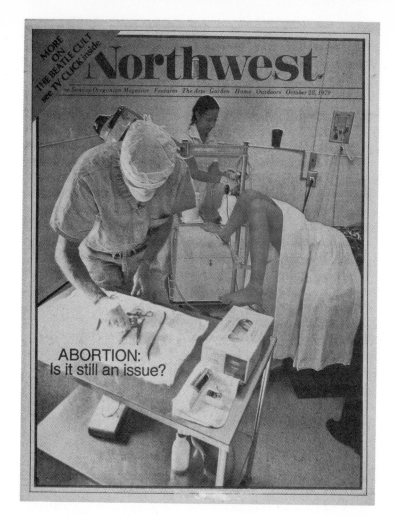

their time going over unsolicited manuscripts, looking for the occasional gem that merits publication. So wasteful does this activity become that many editors seek known freelancers and make assignments.

Unsolicited material is valuable, though, in that it suggests areas to be explored that editors do not think of. Sometimes the articles submitted are not good enough, but the ideas are worthy. With the writers' permission, the editors rewrite the material and pay the writers a lesser fee. In some cases editors pay writers small fees just for the ideas.

Working with freelancers, editors find it necessary to set up a records system so that they know at all times the status of contributed pieces. Prompt decisions on submissions are appreciated by freelancers. The better newsstand magazines pay authors upon acceptance, but newspaper magazines tend to pay after publication.

Coordinating accepted articles with art is one of the principal jobs of magazine editors. Fortunately, a lot of freelance material comes complete with captioned photographs. But in other cases editors have to dream up illustrative ideas and bring in staff artists or photographers or freelancers who specialize in art. Sometimes it is a matter of turning the manuscript over to a photographer or illustrator, who supplies the idea for the art as well as the art itself.

Magazine design differs from newspaper design in a number of ways.

1. Pages are smaller, so organization is more compact. You have fewer items to contend with.
2. In some cases, production facilities are better. You get better printing. You may use better paper. You have more access to color.

3. A standard grid of columns gives way to a more flexible grid, allowing for a greater variety of design approaches. Each article or feature in an issue may get its own design. Typefaces may change for each article.
4. The sequence of pages becomes more important. Even if each article is custom designed, a pattern emerges that tends to relate all the pages.
5. You no longer are designing single pages; instead you are designing spreads or units of two facing pages. The pages are small enough so that the reader can take in two of them together.

This means that a good part of your designing involves finding ways to bridge the gutter (the fold) between pages. You do what you can to tie the pages together. For instance, you run a photograph large enough so that part of it rests on one page, part on another. Because you strive mostly for informal balance (it is more lively than formal balance), you put most the photograph on either the left- or right-hand page. Of course you divide the photograph at a noncrucial point. An important figure in the photograph, for instance, would stay on one side of the gutter.

Another way to bridge the gutter is by running a title across it, which allows the gutter to intrude between words but not between letters of a word. (If the type is large enough, however, the separation could come between letters.)

Other ways to unite facing pages are to line up columns along a common horizontal axis, repeat an art style or color on the facing page, keep the same typefaces on the two pages, and arrange the art on the left-hand page to face the opposite page. Many pieces of art have a visual thrust, such as the direction in which a pictured person is facing, that may influence where a reader looks. Do not get the idea that each spread has to be informally balanced. Sometimes formal balance provides the best solution. It can be simple and forceful.

Not all the designing involves two-page spreads. If the spread carries a full-page ad, you are left with a single page design. The page may be a good place to try formal balance: a centered title and blurb, perhaps a horizontal line or bar, and a big centered photograph with copy in columns below.

The best display comes with article openings. The opening may involve two pages or, if the left-hand page carries an ad or the ending of an earlier article, a single page. If the article continues on the next page, you do not need a *continued* line.

In setting a style you must decide whether you want each article completed before a new one begins or whether you want to open several in quick succession and carry their conclusions to the back. Readers prefer not moving back and forth, but that probably

means you would have to keep your articles short. Articles in newspaper magazines tend to be shorter than articles in general-circulation magazines.

The "back of the book" (as magazine editors call the later pages) is always a problem. The small ads and the carryovers mixed together cause clutter. The area looks like a dumping ground. There is not much you can do back there except to organize the material logically. You can bring some graphic relief to back pages by running small gag cartoons.

Your job is easier if the advertising staff sells mostly large ads and discourages a lot of small one-column ones. If the ads could be confined to separate pages instead of being scattered through the editorial material, your job of designing would be even easier.

Sometimes you face the problem of putting two or more short articles on a two-page spread. If the articles are of equal size, you may devote the left-hand page to one article, the right-hand page to the other. Then you would use the gutter as a fence rather than as a bridge. Often the short articles are of unequal length, which creates a problem. One solution is to run both articles across the gutter, one over the other. That way you would have two horizontal thrusts of unequal depths. You can also box one article to separate it from the other.

White space becomes especially important in magazine design. A little of it can do a lot, because on small pages it becomes increasingly noticeable. The idea is to concentrate white space rather than scatter it. Wisely used, the white space can nicely display your titles and make giant-size letters unnecessary. Even so,

Figure 20.5 The locally edited *Boston Globe Magazine* goes for a strong, clean, readable look, as this two-page spread demonstrates. The across-the-gutter photograph is all the more dramatic because it moves in close on its subjects. As a result, the heads are life size. The photograph is cropped to form a diagonal thrust that runs from the baby along the mother's shoulder, up to her ear, and then into the start of the feature. (Reprinted courtesy of the *Boston Globe*.)

Figure 20.6 *Parade* often uses a single page for an article or an article opener that puts vertical art in the middle. Here are two variations. The "Sandy Duncan" article allows copy to break through a rule and wrap around the subject, taking part in the stretch that is pictured. The "Meet the Man Called Prophet" article is more subdued but still pleasing in design, with a drawing instead of a silhouetted photograph and with the title below rather than above the art. Both articles begin with an initial letter in the same face used for the title. These pages are different enough to bring variety to the magazine but similar enough to show design consistency.

a lot of newspaper magazines avoid white space, purposely going after a crowded look. A number of the slick newsstand magazines have shown that you can achieve a contemporary look without giving away a lot of space.

Much of your design activity centers on what you do with your titles. The choice of a typeface for each title becomes crucial. How you fit the letters and words together and align the title with the art is important, too.

The title is often preceded by or followed by a blurb—an elaboration in smaller type that goes on for a sentence or two. Other blurbs may occur inside the article when it carries over to other pages. A blurb inserted in the article is likely to be a quotation from the article. It is reproduced in larger-than-body-copy type. Its main purpose is to stop readers who did not stop at the title and get them to go back and try out the article. It also adds a little graphic relief to a page of gray type. Such blurbs are often referred to as "lift-outs."

Initial letters are useful in helping the reader jump from the title to the beginning of the article. And they are useful inside the article, too, for graphic relief. Many newspaper magazines find them more useful than subheads.

In recent years many designers have offered readers circus-like layouts, using lots of boxes, bursts of color, and pieces of art in silhouette as well as in rectangles and squares. Column rules and other lines are used where they might have been abandoned elsewhere in the paper. Such a look calls for a good understanding of design principles.

The Design Phase

With copyread manuscripts and art on hand the editor goes into the design phase or, in a larger operation, confers with the art director.

Perhaps some of the articles will have to be cut. The cutting could involve the copy or the art. Fewer photographs could be used, for instance, or some of them could be used in smaller sizes. Articles usually are assigned a set number of printed pages early, before the art is in. An easy way to make an article fit is to work it from the back, see how much space remains, and then decide on how splashy an opening you want, what photographs to use, and how big the type should be. But usually, the fitting of the article involves going back and forth, moving copy around, cutting and expanding where necessary, considering and reconsidering pictures, and cropping where that will help.

The design may be worked out ahead of time, with copy written to fit and art produced to order.

The Magazine Cover

The newsstand magazine needs a cover that will stop passers-by and get them to purchase the magazine on impulse. The cover also needs to stand out enough so that the frequent buyer will quickly spot the magazine. The cover becomes something of a poster, with colorful art and intriguing blurbs that promise fulfillment on the inside pages. The choice of cover art can seriously affect newsstand sales. That is why the circulation manager frequently has a say about what goes on the cover.

A newspaper magazine does not put quite so much stock in its cover; its audience is going to get the magazine without buying it separately. Still, the editor wants the reader to go inside, so the cover takes on some importance. The art—photograph, drawing, or painting—is almost always related to an article inside. A blurb repeats, or nearly repeats, the title of the article. Perhaps a couple of other blurbs refer to lesser articles and even give the articles' page numbers. In that respect, the cover acts as a sort of table of contents.

The nameplate (magazine editors call it a "logo") is an important part of the cover. It need not be of the same design as the newspaper's front-page nameplate. The logo should be readable and yet have character that sets it apart from ordinary type. Color, if available, almost surely will be incorporated into the logo.

The logo on magazines that depend on newsstand sales must appear in the same spot in each issue, usually at the upper left or at least across the top so that the magazine can be recognized when crowded next to its competitors. Other magazines can move the logo around, change its size, and even change its design from issue to issue. *Westways,* the handsome monthly of the Automobile Club

Figure 20.7 These rough sketches show typical approaches to design used by editors of newspaper magazines. Boxes within boxes organize and contain material. Horizontal lines, sometimes so thick they are really bars, do the same thing, and they help give the spreads a horizontal look. In some cases, magazine editors use vertical column rules to dress up pages, although regular news sections have discontinued the use of such rules. Initial letters are often helpful in breaking long columns of copy into shorter, easier-to-read sections.

Figure 20.7 *(continued)*

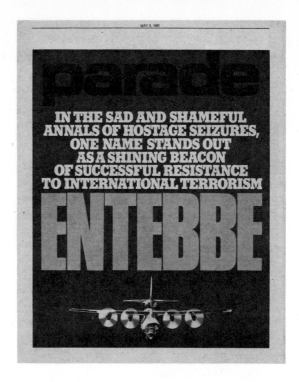

of Southern California, has gained considerable respect among designers for its covers, which incorporate fine arts paintings with logos newly designed and placed each time to fill the page.

A newsstand magazine or an association or company magazine can do all kinds of things with its cover. It can make a gatefold of the cover so that it opens out to an extra two pages. If the cover is on a heavier stock, as it often is, the newsstand magazine can take a cut out of it (one magazine was known as the publication with the hole in the cover) or emboss it. Some of the most exciting covers came with *Esquire* magazine in the 1960s, with George Lois in charge. You might want to look some of these up in the library for inspiration for your own covers.

But you do not have quite the chance for novelty on a newspaper magazine cover that you would have on a newsstand magazine cover. You work with poorer paper stock and your production facilities are inferior. Still, you are free to come up with intriguing ideas for staged photographs or unusual abstract paintings and drawings. Certainly you can go beyond realism. You can do remarkable things with gracefully displayed type alone, especially if you have some color to work with.

The figure shows a two-page magazine spread. The headline reads:

THE RESCUE, THE LEGEND, THE LESSON
ENTEBBE

BY HERBERT KUPFERBERG

The miracle of Entebbe has left a permanent imprint upon Israel and perhaps the world

Homecoming, July 4, 1976: At top, freed Israeli hostages pour out of rescue plane at Lod Airport after their flight back from captivity. At left, Gen. Dan Shomron with commandos, some still wearing white tourist hats they put on to recognize one another in the dark. At right, Lt. Col. Jonathan Netanyahu, leader of the assault force, who was killed in the raid.

Once in a while you may want to start an article on the cover in display type and continue it inside in body type. But your article had better be important to merit such treatment. Your cover is an advertisement. It offers you one of your best chances to innovate with design. But you should never promise your reader more than you are prepared to deliver inside.

Figure 20.9 This is the opening spread for the "Entebbe" story in *Parade*. The typeface urgency and the head-on view of the plane is the same here as on the cover. Ira Yoffe is director of design at *Parade*.

The principles of good editing and design discussed in this book apply to newspaper magazines as well as to newspapers themselves. But the magazines offer editors and art directors some special challenges. For instance, the magazines run their articles and features as two-page spreads, so in laying out the pages, you deal with two pages at a time. You not only worry about drawing readers on to the next two pages but you also worry about helping them across the gutters that separate facing pages. This chapter has shown you ways to do this.

Conclusion

Magazine design also gives you greater flexibility in choosing typefaces and kinds of art. The more relaxed deadlines give you more time to exercise your creativity. You are more likely to choose a title typeface to reflect the mood of an article. You are also more likely to plan your art rather than simply use what is available. On a magazine you would work largely with freelancers. Much of your magazine's content would be determined by ideas coming to you from outsiders. If your paper is small, you might rely on your own staffers. You might even do much of the writing yourself.

The cover of the newspaper magazine is important to you, though not as important as the cover of a newsstand magazine. In designing the cover, you would think of it more as a poster than a mere page of type and photographs.

Additional Readings

Allen, Wallace. *A Design for News*. Minneapolis: Minneapolis Tribune, 1981. An associate editor of the *Tribune* explains how layout and design work on that paper. The redesign introduced by Frank Ariss is emphasized.

American Heritage Dictionary, The. New York: American Heritage and Houghton-Mifflin, 1965. This desk-size dictionary gives more attention to disputed points of usage than any other general dictionary. Perhaps because of a less traditional approach than Webster's *New World, American Heritage* is not widely used as a primary authority in journalism. The book contains a wealth of pictorial illustrations, however, and includes in the lexicon much other useful information, such as literary, historical, and geographical references, and abbreviations, that have been excluded from some other dictionaries, including Webster's *Unabridged*.

Arnold, Edmund C. *Designing the Total Newspaper*. New York: Harper & Row, 1981. A well-known newspaper design consultant and professor (Virginia Commonwealth University) replaces his earlier books of practical advice, *Functional Newspaper Design* and *Modern Newspaper Design*, with this new one.

Copperud, Roy H. *American Usage and Style: The Consensus*. New York: Van Nostrand Reinhold Co., 1980. A dictionary of usage that gives the preferences of authorities. It covers disputed points in language, including those characteristic of journalism.

Craig, James. *Production for the Graphic Designer*. New York: Watson-Guptill Publications, 1974. Although not written for newspaper designers, this beautifully produced book (something of a classic) covers intelligently much of what newspaper designers need to know about production, including the preparation of mechanicals or camera-ready copy and the details of getting ready for color.

Evans, Harold. *Editing and Design*. New York: Holt, Rinehart & Winston, 1973. A five-volume manual dealing with English usage, typography, and layout put together by the editor of the *Sunday Times* of London. Useful for American as well as British editors. Volume 1: *Newsman's English;* Volume 2: *Handling Newspaper Text;* Volume 3: *News Headlines;* Volume 4: *Picture Editing;* Volume 5: *Newspaper Design*.

————*Pictures on a Page: Photojournalism and Picture Editing.* Belmont, Calif.: Wadsworth Publishing Co., 1978. An interesting book showing how photographs should be used in newspapers and how they can be edited to make them more effective. The book also covers caption writing and display. Nearly 500 excellent photographs are shown, including many famous ones. Edwin Taylor, design director of the *Sunday Times,* collaborated with Evans.

Garcia, Mario R. *Contemporary Newspaper Design.* Englewood Cliffs, N. J.: Prentice-Hall, Inc., 1981. Twenty chapters of practical advice, with examples of pages from many papers. The author, formerly of Syracuse University, is now at the University of South Florida.

Miller, Bobby Ray. *The UPI Stylebook.* New York: United Press International, 1977. Available from 220 E. 42nd St., New York, N.Y. 10017.

Mogdam, Dineh, ed. *Computers in Newspaper Publishing: User-oriented Systems.* New York: Marcel Dekker, Inc., 1978. A book that brings together information from various sources on computer equipment used in front-end operations of newspapers. Mogdam assumes that readers have no knowledge of computer technology.

Nelson, Roy Paul. *Publication Design,* 3d ed. Dubuque, Iowa: Wm. C. Brown Co. Publishers, 1983. While this book has mostly magazines in mind, much of what it says is applicable to newspapers, especially the chapters on typography and art. A chapter on newspaper design is included.

Perrin, Porter G., and Wilma R. Ebbitt. *Writer's Guide and Index to English,* 5th ed. Glenview, Ill.: Scott, Foresman & Co., 1972. A superb reference for problems of grammar and writing in general. It is easy to use because the "Index," constituting half the book, is really a dictionary of grammatical terms and concepts and words that present difficulties. More detailed discussions are to be found in the chapters constituting the first half of the book.

Powell, Eileen Alt, and Howard Angione, eds. *The Associated Press Stylebook and Libel Manual.* New York: Associated Press, 1977. Available from the wire service at 50 Rockefeller Plaza, New York, N.Y. 10020.

Riblet, Carl, Jr. *The Solid Gold Copy Editor.* Chicago: Aldine Publishing Co., 1972. This book, while intended for professionals, can be a useful reference for students. Its 600-odd pages are filled with reproduced news stories and headlines, followed by criticisms and improved versions suggested by the author.

Stone, Bernard, and Arthur Eckstein. *Preparing Art for Printing.* New York: Van Nostrand Reinhold Co., 1965. This book has been around for a while, but its content is still current. It covers the mechanics of readying art, including art for color reproduction.

Strunk, William, Jr., and E. B. White. *The Elements of Style,* 3d ed. New York: Macmillan, 1979. This slender volume, which can be read in an hour or so, is widely regarded as the best concise guide to good writing in existence. It has sold millions of copies.

Additional Readings

Synonym Finder, The. Emmaus, Pa.: Rodale Books, 1961. While there
are several books of synonyms, sometimes called thesauruses, on
the market, this one is recommended for its comprehensiveness and
ease of use. Students are warned, however, that such books seldom
solve the problems of headline composition; they are generally
more useful in writing and editing.

Turnbull, Arthur T., and Russell N. Baird. *The Graphics of
Communication,* 4th ed. New York: Holt, Rinehart & Winston,
1980. A solid textbook covering typography, layout, design and
production in the print media, with one chapter given over to
newspapers. This fourth edition goes deeply into technological
changes in printing and typesetting.

Webster's New World Dictionary, 2d College ed., New York: Collins-
World, 1970. The desk-size dictionary that has been designated the
primary authority of the wire services, the *New York Times* and
the *Los Angeles Times.* Because most newspapers use the wire
services' style books, Webster's *New World* may be regarded as the
primary authority for American journalism generally. This book is
not to be confused, despite the similarity in names, with Webster
dictionaries published by the G. & C. Merriam Co.

Webster's Third New International Dictionary. Springfield, Mass.: G.
& C. Merriam, Co., 1961. The most comprehensive unabridged
American dictionary, also available in updated desk or "collegiate"
editions. This book has been widely adopted as a secondary
authority for words not to be found in *Webster's New World,*
which, as an abridgment, has many omissions.

Words Into Type, 3d ed. Englewood Cliffs, N.J.: Prentice-Hall Inc.,
1974. A valuable reference for all aspects of converting typescript
into printed pages.

Glossary

This glossary is intended as a ready reference for terms peculiar to newspaper production. It does not contain those that are in common use, like ad *for* advertisement.

ABC   The letters stand for Audit Bureau of Circulations, an organization that collects and verifies newspaper circulation data.

add   Material added to a news story. Sometimes the term is applied to all pages following the first page of typescript (e.g., add 1, add 2, etc.), or it may apply to new material that covers later developments and that will be appended to a story written earlier.

advance   A news story written to announce a coming event.

agate   5½-or 6-point type, generally used for classified ads and tabular matter such as box scores.

agate line   Measurement of area used in billing display advertising. Area is 1/14 of an inch deep and 1 column wide.

air   White space on a page, whether between unruled columns, around pictures or special displays.

alive   The term is used to describe news copy that may still be used because it has not been overtaken by the event or otherwise gone out of date.

A-matter (*advance* matter)   Background or supplementary material that will form the lower part of a story for which the top, or lead, will be sent to composition when information on later developments is available.

anchor   To place strong display elements in the corners of the page.

angle   The approach taken with or the emphasis given to a news story. A development in a news story may be referred to as a new angle. A story so constructed as to emphasize a particular aspect is angled to that aspect.

anytime   Editorial matter that need not be used immediately. Synonymous terms in use in various places are "H- matter" (for *hold*) "time copy" and "use soon." Such material, usually feature stories, is set in type and held in reserve against the need to fill extra space.

AP   Associated Press, one of the two major American wire services.

art   All pictorial matter in a newspaper. It includes photographs and drawings of any kind. Also refers to any original copy for the platemaker.

ascender   That portion of a lowercase letter extending above the *x*-height (the height of the letter *x* and others of the same size). Also the letter itself: *h, b.*

attribution   Giving the source of information in a news story; the phrases "he said" and "she said" are probably the simplest and commonest forms of attribution. Such phrases are sometimes referred to as *speech tags.*

A-wire   The transmission system of a press association carrying the fullest report, as distinguished from systems that may transmit only the news of a given state, or concerning a particular subject, such as sports or finance.

bad break   An awkward or unattractive continuation of a story from one column to the next; an erroneous division of a word at the end of a line.

bank   See *deck*.

banner   A large headline that extends across the top of a page, usually the front page. Also known as a line, ribbon, or streamer.

billboard   Headline on the cover of a magazine referring to an article inside. Also called "blurb."

black letter (or text)   The technically correct names for the classification of type usually referred to as Old English.

blip   Colloquial for *cursor*. See *cursor*.

blotter   See *police blotter*.

blow up   To make a printing plate larger than the original picture. Noun form: blowup.

blurb   Short excerpt taken from an article and given extra display on a page. See also *billboard, liftout*.

body type   The type in which the text of news stories is set, as distinguished from headlines and other display faces.

boil   To make a news story shorter by small cuts here and there.

boiler plate   Syndicated material, such as columns or features, that is sent in a form ready to incorporate into a page.

boldface   A version of a typeface having bolder strokes than the basic design.

break   The point at which a story is interrupted by division into segments in different columns, or by continuation to another page.

breakover   See *jump,* the commoner term.

bright   A short, amusing news story, so called because it is regarded as offering relief from more serious news. Sometimes spelled *brite*.

broadsheet   Full-size newspaper. Compare with *tabloid*.

budget   A summary of the important stories to be transmitted in the day's report by a wire service. The day's report then follows, amplified by stories that developed during the time of transmission and could not be foreseen.

bullet   A large round dot used instead of numbers or letters to set off items in a list.

bulletin   A brief announcement, sent by a wire service, of a forthcoming news story of exceptional importance. See also *flash*.

buried   Placed in an inconspicuous position (in reference to a statement in a news story or a news story itself).

camera-ready copy   Material ready to be photographed in the process of making a printing place.

cap, caps   Clipped forms of *capital letter(s)*.

caption   Explanatory matter accompanying a picture. More commonly used concerning magazines; such matter in newspapers is generally referred to as *cutlines*. A caption may also be the headline for a picture.

catchline   The word or phrase used to identify a story in the process of publishing it; e.g., "storm," "coup." More commonly, *slug;* sometimes, *guideline*.

center spread   Two facing pages at the center of a section of a newspaper or magazine. See also *double truck*.

clean   Requiring little correction; said of typescript or proofs.

clipsheet   A printed sheet sent out by a syndicate, from which articles, columns and the like are intended to be selected and clipped for use in the subscribing newspaper.

cold type Composition produced by phototypesetting or by strike-on machines or from paste-on alphabets. Also, the process itself, as contrasted with hot type.

color Said of elements that contribute particular interest, humor, or drama to a story. A color story may run beside a straight news story to convey the atmosphere, as distinguished from the bald facts of an event. A *colored* story is one into which bias has been introduced, but more commonly such a story is said to be *slanted*. Also, printing other than black.

column inch An area 1 inch deep and 1 column wide used for measuring newspaper content, especially advertising.

composition The act of setting copy into type, either by assembling or casting type into metal molds (*hot type*), a process rapidly becoming obsolete, or by producing a photographic image that can be used in producing a printing plate.

computer Computers are employed by newspapers to justify lines of type being composed (i.e., make them the same length and decide where words shall be broken), to edit and store copy, to make up pages, and to perform bookkeeping, billing, and other functions.

condensed A version of a typeface narrower than the basic design.

continuous tone. Describes photographic or hand art such as oil painting or watercolor in which gradations of tone are present. Such art must be reproduced by halftones.

copy Material that the compositor sets into type or from which printing plates are made.

copy editing, copyreading Preparing typescript or copy flashed on a video screen for compositon by correcting and otherwise improving it. To be distinguished from *proofreading*.

credit line An indication of the source of a story, e.g., "By the Associated Press," "Compiled from Wire Services." Also, recognition of the creator of a photograph or drawing.

crop To eliminate an unwanted portion of a photograph by cutting it off or, more often, indicating by marginal marks that it should be omitted.

cropper's L's L-shaped pieces of cardboard or metal used to form rectangles and isolate the pertinent portion of a photograph for cropping.

CRT A cathode-ray tube, which forms the screen on which copy is displayed in electronic composition or editing of stories.

cursive A classification of type resembling handwriting but in which the letters are not joined, as contrasted with *script*.

cursor A rectangular spot of light on a video screen that indicates the point where electronic editing is to be done.

cut Originally, a printing plate used to reproduce a picture. Also, any picture reproduced in a newspaper. Verb form: to shorten a news story.

cutlines Explanatory matter accompanying pictures; the term *caption* is often used interchangeably; in magazines, usually called *caption*.

cutoff A thin rule that separates elements on a newspaper page, such as a picture and an unrelated story.

dateline An indication at the beginning of a story giving the point of origin; e.g., WASHINGTON, D.C.; almost invariably set in capitals. If the story comes from a press association, its logotype will be included (AP, UPI). The term *dateline* derives from the fact that in the past the date of transmission was included but now the date is seldom used.

dealer   A term sometimes used in the West for the supervisory copy editor. The new printing technology is rendering this term obsolete.

deck   A subordinate headline appearing beneath and supplementing the headline above; a bank. On some newspapers, the term *deck* refers to a single line of a headline.

descender   That portion of a lowercase letter (*p, q*) that extends below the baseline. Also, the letter itself.

dirty   Containing numerous errors; said of either typescript or proof.

display type   The large type used for headlines; any large type intended to attract attention.

double truck   A story or layout spanning two facing pages; a center spread.

down   Commonly used synonym for *lowercase.*

downstyle   In text, a style in which generic terms are lowercased, e.g., Mississippi river (rather than Mississippi River, which exemplifies up style). Down style refers also to a general tendency away from ceremonious capitalization, for example, capitalizing titles when they stand alone: "The Senator said. . . ." In reference to headlines, down style denotes a new practice in which headlines are capitalized in the same manner as sentences in text.

dummy   A small diagram of a page, indicating placement of news stories, pictures, and other elements.

ear   Box or unit of special information; located on either side of the nameplate.

editorial   An ambiguous term, though the context usually makes its application specific. As an adjective in reference to the content of a newspaper, it denotes everything that is not advertising—not only news stories, but also illustrations, columns and comic strips. As a noun, it refers to an article on the editorial page in which the newspaper expresses its own opinion.

editorializing   Unwarranted or objectionable expression of the writer's or the newspaper's opinion in a news story. News stories of all kinds are growing less impersonal and objective than they were formerly, and often, especially in expository or feature material, judgments are permitted that once would have been forbidden as editorializing. Articles in news magazines are often an inseparable blend of the objective and the editorial.

electronic formatting   Making up an entire newspaper page electronically.

em   Width of a capital *M* in any typeface.

en   Width of a capital *N* in any typeface.

engraving   A metal printing plate of a picture; also, the more formal term for *cut.*

extended   A version of a typeface having characters wider than the basic design.

extra bold   A version of a typeface having extremely bold strokes.

eyebrow   A synonym for *kicker.*

face   A particular style of type.

FAX   Facsimile. Refers to transmission of a page or picture by wire.

first-day story   The initial account of a news development, in contrast to sequels giving further developments. Compare *follow-up.*

flag   Nameplate. The name of a newspaper in display form on page one. Erroneously called *masthead.*

flash   A brief preliminary announcement by a wire service of a news story of transcendent importance; takes precedence over a bulletin.

flop   To reverse an illustration, particularly a photograph, in the process of reproduction so that right becomes left and vice versa.

flush left   The predominant pattern of headline in use today, which takes its name from the fact that all lines begin at the left-hand margin. The lines may be uneven in length, but not unduly so, so that some raggedness at the right end of the headline is permissible.

folio   The material beneath the nameplate of a newspaper giving the place and date of publication, the volume and serial number, and sometimes other general information, such as the subscription price or circulation. Also, the page and section number on inside pages.

folo   The newsroom version of *follow,* used to mark copy to be appended to something prepared earlier.

followup   In a running account of a story that develops from day to day, any story succeeding the first.

format   General design of a newspaper, especially page size and number of columns; physical form of a publication.

four-color process   The process by which color photographs are reproduced by separating their constituent tones and making plates from which each component color (red, yellow, blue, and black) will be printed.

galley proof   The first impression of type, on which errors are marked.

glossy (print)   A photograph with a shiny finish; these are preferred for reproduction in printing because they have sharper contrast.

graf   The newsroom version, for convenience, of *paragraph.*

gravure   Intaglio printing.

gray areas   Large areas of body type on a page, unbroken by headlines or pictures. They are to be avoided because they have an oppressive effect on the reader.

guideline   A word or phrase used to identify a story in editing and composition. Also (more commonly) *slug, catchline.*

halftone   Reproduction by patterns of dots or lines of continuous-tone art such as photographs. Also any picture so reproduced; a printing plate that reproduces such an image.

handout   A press release.

hanging indentation   A pattern of headline, used notably for decks in *The Wall Street Journal*, in which the first line is set the width of the column and succeeding lines (usually two) are indented.

hard copy   Readable copy on paper, as distinguished from punched tape or the illuminated image on a screen.

hard news   A story (as contrasted with a feature) whose primary purpose is to convey new information, rather than to entertain or explain.

head schedule   A catalog of all the headlines in use by a given newspaper, including their designations, counts, and samples of them.

head shot   Picture of a person's head and shoulders; also mug shot, face shot.

hold for release   The instruction on stories that have been embargoed, that is, made available in advance to newspapers for publication at a specified future time.

holdover   Composition that would not fit in the day's paper, but which is kept and checked the next day for possible inclusion in the succeeding issue.

hole   A story is said to have a hole when it raises a question in the reader's mind that is not answered. See also *news hole.*

horizontal display   A page layout in which shapes that are wider than they are high predominate.

hot metal, hot type   Composition with type cast from molten metal, especially in contrast to phototypesetting.

HTC, HTK   The notation (*head to come*) made on news stories that are sent for composition before the headlines have been written.

idiot tape   Raw punched tape carrying no instructions for justification.

insert   As a noun, an addition to a story to be placed at a designated point.

intaglio   A method of printing from plates carrying the image as incised lines or dots; gravure.

italic   A form of letter that slants to the right.

joints   Segments of a story placed side by side.

jump   To continue a story from one page to another. Also, the portion continued.

jump head   A headline that identifies the continuation of a story on another page.

justify   To set type so that the lines are of equal length. Also, to make all columns on a page the same length.

kicker   A small headline, usually underscored, that rides above and at the left of the main head.

kill   To withhold a story or part of one from publication.

label head   One that lacks a verb: "Terms of the agreement."

layout   The arrangement of elements (pictures, body type, headlines) on a page. Verb form: *lay out.*

leader   A row of periods or hyphens used in tabular matter to connect an entry with a figure, for example, that relates to it: "New Mexico .... 25."

legibility   The quality of type or handwriting that affects the ability to identify the characters. Often confused with *readability.*

letterpress   The printing process in which a raised image is inked and pressed against paper.

library   A newspaper's own reference center, including clippings filed by subject, files of previous issues and reference books. Traditionally referred to as the *morgue.*

liftout   A few lines taken from a story and set in larger type. Usually set off by rules and intended to break up the expanse of body type.

light pencil   A device that emits a beam of light and is used to move blocks of copy around in electronic layout.

linage   A measure of published advertising, consisting of totals of agate lines or the equivalent.

line art   Illustrations (such as cartoons) composed of lines, pattern and solid black with no gradations of tone.

linecasting   Setting type by means of machines such as the Linotype or Intertype that cast it in solid lines.

line conversion   Photograph reproduced as if it were line art.

Linotype   A machine that produces a line of type as a metal bar; the original linecaster, now a museum piece.

lithography   A planographic (flat-surface) printing process based on the mutual repulsion of oil and water. See *offset.*

localize   To rewrite or rearrange a wire story to emphasize its local aspects.

logo   Abbreviation of *logotype:* identification of a page or section in a newspaper. A newspaper nameplate; the signature on an advertisement.

lowercase   Small letters. The term comes from the fact that at one time small letters were stored in the lower of two trays used in hand composition of type.

make over   To rearrange the material on a page, usually to accommodate developments in the news or to change the emphasis or purpose of the page and to make a new printing plate. Noun form: *makeover,* a page that has been made over.

makeup   The arrangement of news stories and pictures on a page. Synonymous with *layout.* Verb forms: *make up, lay out.*

masthead   A collection of information including the name of the publisher, time and place of publication and the like, usually found on the editorial page. Erroneously used to refer to the nameplate.

matrix   A mold from which type characters, newspaper pages, illustrations and the like are cast. A brass matrix is used for casting type singly or in complete lines; stereotype molds of heavy laminated paper are used for casting whole pages. Usually referred to as a "mat."

meanline   An imaginary line along the top of letters such as *a, c, m, o, x* and others.

measure   The length of a line of type.

microfiche   A card carrying many negatives of newspaper pages or other items in microscopic size.

microfilm   A negative carrying images of newspaper pages or other items in greatly reduced size.

monitor   Typed copy accompanying punched tape; hard copy.

morgue   The colloquial term for a newspaper's *library*.

mortise   To cut out an area from an engraving to permit the insertion of type or another picture. Noun form: the cutout area itself.

mug shot   See *head shot*.

must, must go   An instruction on a piece of copy indicating that it must be published.

nameplate   The flag or logo, the name of the newspaper in display form as it appears on page one. Erroneously called masthead.

new lead   A substitute lead covering new developments in a story. New leads are frequently transmitted by the wire services, and a newspaper's own reporters write new leads for a story that develops during a day's editions.

news hole   The amount of space available for editorial content in a newspaper after allowance for advertisements. Generally figured in terms of columns.

OCR   Optical character recognition. Performed by machines that read letters (characters) and record the information on perforated or magnetic tape that will operate a computer or typesetting equipment.

offset   Clipped term for *offset lithography,* a printing process in which the image is transferred from the printing plate to a rubber blanket and then to paper. See *lithography.*

Old English   A variety of the text or black letter style of type.

opaque   To blot out flaws in a photographic negative by painting.

op-ed   Opposite-editorial. A page of comment and opinion, usually facing the editorial page.

overline   A headline over a picture; now generally considered poor positioning. A caption, in the strictly correct sense.

overset   Composition omitted from the paper for lack of space.

padding   Superfluous material in a story, or superfluous words in a headline.

paste-on, paste-down   Disposable cold-type characters printed on light cardboard that may be arranged and affixed to paper and from which a printing plate is made photographically.

pasteup   Master copy of a page prepared by pasting composed stories and headlines on a cardboard backing. This is then photographed to produce the plate from which printing will be done. Verb form: *paste up,* denoting the process of producing the master copy.

perfecting   The printer's term for printing on both sides of the paper.

perforating   Punching small holes, in code form, in paper tape used to actuate a computer or typesetting machines.

photocomposition   Process of composing by means of assembling photographic images mechanically and automatically (in place of using metal type). A high-speed system that is rapidly displacing older methods.

photolithography The full term for *lithography* as used in printing.

pica Twelve points (one-sixth inch). A unit of measurement used to designate length of a line. When used with a period, as 12.4 picas, the digit after the period designates printer's points.

pick up An instruction indicating where to add copy to a new lead or insert.

pix Journalistic and printers' jargon for picture(s).

plate The surface (metal, sometimes now plastic) which makes the impression on paper in printing.

point Basic American unit of printer's measurement, approximately 1/72 inch, actually .01384 of an inch.

police blotter The rough record kept by the police of arrests and other police activity. Why it is referred to as a blotter is one of the enduring mysteries of journalism.

precede A new lead or top intended, as the term indicates, to begin a previously transmitted story. Usually accompanied by instructions as to where the previous transmission shall be picked up or joined to the new material.

preferred position A position specified by an advertiser for an ad on the assumption it will give better selling power.

proof A preliminary impression of composition on which errors are marked.

proofreading Reading *proof* to correct mechanical errors introduced in composition. Sometimes confused with *copyreading* or *copy editing,* the process of correcting stories before composition.

quadrant A pattern of makeup in which the page is divided into quarters by imaginary lines bisecting it in both directions; each quarter has a strong element, such as a picture or a large headline.

railroad To rush copy through under pressure to meet a deadline, without careful editing.

raw tape Tape that carries no instructions for justification.

readability Ease of comprehension created by the quality or nature of the writing. Contrast *legibility.*

reefer A line or two of type set into a news story, referring the reader to related material elsewhere in the paper. The term derives from *refer.*

register Alignment of plates in color printing.

repro(duction) proof A careful proof intended to be photographed in the process of making a printing plate. A synonym for *pasteup.* Usually referred to as a *repro* or *repro proof.*

reverse To print by creating white (type, for instance) on a dark background, as for example over a halftone.

revise A proof made after errors on an initial proof have been corrected.

rivers Streaks of white running vertically through composition; caused by excessive spacing between words.

roll up To bring copy onto a video screen.

roman A classification of type having thick and thin strokes, swelling and diminution of curves, and serifs. Also, the perpendicular version of any typeface, as distinguished from italic.

rotary press A printing press in which an image on a curved plate prints on a continuous roll of paper known as a web.

rotogravure Gravure printing adapted to a rotary press as used by newspapers.

roundup A collection of small items on similar topics combined into a single story or running under one head.

run in An instruction on copy to set names or other material in paragraph form from a vertical list.

running story A story that has new developments from day to day.

sacred cow A person, subject, or institution singled out by the management of a newspaper for continuing favorable treatment.

sans serifs A classification of a relatively new type design in more or less block-letter form, and lacking serifs. A popular style for headlines.

scale To determine the size of a plate to be made from artwork of specific size.

scaling wheel A circular form of slide rule used to determine the final size of art.

scanning Mechanical inspection of images or tonal values and conversion of images and values into electrical impulses for use by typesetter, computer, or photographic processor.

screen A device used to convert continuous tone original art, usually photos, to a halftone plate by breaking it into dots of various sizes. Also, designation of fineness of halftone so produced; e.g., "85-line screen" indicates a plate with 85 lines of dots per linear inch. Also, to reduce the tone of black areas of art or type by superimposing a pattern of white dots on the printing surfaces; or to produce a printing plate.

script A style of type in which the characters are joined to resemble handwriting. Compare *cursive*.

see copy An instruction on a proof to compare it with the copy from which it was set.

serif A small finishing stroke at the end of the main strokes of the letters. The distinguishing feature of the roman style of type.

set To compose type for printing.

shirttail A short, related story appended to another.

shoot down To make a printing plate smaller than the original art; reduce.

sidebar A news story that amplifies a basic story and is run beside it.

skylining Running a headline, or headline and story, above the nameplate.

slant To give a news story an emphasis unwarranted by objective treatment; generally considered unethical. A story may be given a slant, or emphasis, for ethical reasons, however, reflecting an honest opinion as to the news value of a certain aspect.

slot The slot was the inner part of the now obsolete horseshoe-shaped copydesk; the supervisor who sat there was in charge of the copy editors, who inhabited the outer rim.

slug Sometimes *slug line*. A significant word or phrase that identifies a story throughout its processing. Also *catchline*.

software The intangible part of computer functioning; the program, as contrasted to hardware, the actual machinery.

solid Said of type set without additional spacing between lines.

square serif A style of type having serifs that are as heavy as the main strokes; sometimes called *Egyptian*. Typefaces in this style often have names derived from ancient Egypt, such as Karnak and Memphis.

standing heads Usually, headings on columns and the like, which are kept standing and used repeatedly in the same form.

step, or stepped, head A pattern of headline, now little used, in which the lines are of equal length and arranged to form a stepped pattern. Also, *dropline head*.

stet A mark (Latin for "let it stand") used in copy editing and proofreading to indicate that a previously marked change is to be disregarded.

streamer   See *banner*.

strike-on   Composition produced by a typewriter or similar machine.

stringer   A correspondent who is paid by the inch of published material; clippings of such material, constituting a "string," are pasted together and periodically sent in to the office for payment.

strip in   To combine line work, especially type, with halftone on a negative from which a printing plate will be made.

stylebook   A collection of rules governing arbitrary choices as to abbreviation, capitalization and the like, as used by a given newspaper or press association, and often containing other information about handling of copy.

sub   Substitute. An indication that copy so marked is to be substituted for something else.

subhead   A heading, usually centered and set in boldface of the body type, or sometimes in boldface capitals, that is inserted at intervals of three or four paragraphs to break up a column of type.

syndicate   An organization that sells feature material, usually of no particular timeliness, including columns and comic strips, to newspapers.

tabloid   A newspaper in half-size format, usually five columns wide and 16″ to 18″ deep.

take   A segment of a story sent to composition as it is written. This is done to speed production when time is short.

tape   Narrow roll of paper carrying perforations in code to actuate typesetting machines.

telegraph editor   An old-fashioned term for *news editor*.

teleprinter   Mechanical typing device over which copy is transmitted by news services; an automatically operated teletype machine. Often shortened to *printer*.

Teletype   A machine that actuates another, producing typewritten copy, at a distant point by electrical impulses transmitted by wire. Also a receiving unit in such a system.

teletypesetting   A system for operating linecasting machines automatically by means of perforated tape.

text   A style of type also called black letter or, inaccurately though very commonly, Old English.

thumbnail   A half-column cut; also, a small rough sketch for an ad.

time copy   Material of no special timeliness that may be kept standing in type as needed to fill space.

tint block   A colored or shaded area on a printed page.

tombstones   Two or more heads side by side. Objectionable tombstones are in the same size, pattern and style of type, and create the danger of being read across.

top   Press association lingo for the introductory part of a news story.

TTS   Abbreviation for teletypesetter, a typesetting machine that is driven by perforated tape.

type dress   The complete range of styles and sizes of type used by a newspaper. Compare *head schedule*.

typemetal   An alloy of lead, tin and antimony, used in hot-type composition and printing.

typo   A clipped form for *typographical error*.

typographer   An artist-craftsman concerned with design of type styles, or with the selection and use of type faces.

typography   The art of designing or selecting type; the appearance of a piece of printing as created by the selection of type faces.

undated   Said of a news story transmitted without a dateline by a wire service because the information in it had no single point of origin.

universal desk   A copydesk that handles both local and wire copy.

UPI   United Press International, one of the two major American wire services.

uppercase   Capitals

upstyle   The style of capitalization in which generic terms are capitalized (e.g., *Roosevelt School* vs. *Roosevelt school,* which is downstyle). Upstyle in headlines refers to the traditional practice, now being displaced by downstyle, of capitalizing principal words.

VDT   Video display terminal, a device for writing or editing copy electronically.

Velox   A photoprint with a halftone pattern instead of continuous tone.

web   A wide strip of paper, feeding off a roll, which is printed on a rotary press.

widow   A short line standing at the top of a column. Avoided in careful composition because it is unattractive. Also any short line at the end of a paragraph.

wild   Describes a picture that does not accompany a story; such a picture is said to "run wild."

wire editor   Another term for news editor or telegraph editor.

wirephoto   Another term for *telephoto.*

wooden   Said of a headline or a lead that is dull, prosy, or lifeless.

wrong font (wf)   A mark indicating type of a style different from that which is required, usually a random letter accidentally introduced.

xerography   Electrostatic printing, commonly used in modern office duplicating machines.

x-height   The distance between the baseline and the meanline of type. The height of letters that do not have ascenders or descenders, such as *m, o, a,* and *x* itself.

Index

variation, 74
verbs, 133
vertical design, 202, 211
video display terminals (VDT),
    7, 15, 16, 18, 152

Warren, Samuel, 146
Watch Your Language, 118
Watson, Billy, 156

Weaver, David, 211
*Webster's New International
    Dictionary*, 67
which, 108
while, 124
White, E. B., 11, 96
who, whom, 128
Winners & Sinners, 89, 101
wire services, 5

wit, 46
with, 129
wooden headlines, 26, 48
Write It Right, 78
*Writer's Guide and Index to
    English*, 82, 124

Zapf, Hermann, 164